P9-DDO-890

HANDBOOK FOR EFFECTIVE SUPERVISION OF INSTRUCTION

HANDBOOK FOR EFFECTIVE SUPERVISION OF INSTRUCTION

ROSS L. NEAGLEY

Director of the Department of Educational Administration, College of Education Temple University

N. DEAN EVANS

Regional Assistant County Superintendent Delaware County Schools Media, Pennsylvania

Prentice-Hall, Inc. *Englewood Cliffs, N. J.*

PRENTICE-HALL INTERNATIONAL, INC. *London*
PRENTICE-HALL OF AUSTRALIA, PTY., LTD. *Sydney*
PRENTICE-HALL OF CANADA, LTD. *Toronto*

PRENTICE-HALL OF INDIA PRIVATE LIMITED *New Delhi*
PRENTICE-HALL OF JAPAN, INC. *Tokyo*

Fifth printing .... September, 1965

Library of Congress Catalog Card No.: 63-18601

Printed in the United States of America
37265-C

To Isabel and Jacqueline

PREFACE

Many books have been written in recent years on the theory of modern school supervision. The tasks of definition and identification of the supervisory role have been reasonably well accomplished. However, in the thinking of many supervisors and administrators, few guidelines have been developed to help reconcile the theory of supervision with the practical teaching-learning situations which school officials and teachers meet each day.

It is the purpose of this handbook, therefore, to apply the emerging concepts and principles of modern school supervision to the practical situations in which administrators, supervisors, coordinators, and teachers are working.

In Chapter I a summary of the theory and function of supervision in the modern public school system is presented. Chapters II, III, and IV outline ways of organizing for effective supervision of instruction in small, intermediate, and larger school districts. Chapters V, VI, and VII discuss the roles of various persons usually involved in the supervisory process. In Chapter VIII certain factors that influence change in individuals are presented, since progress in the improvement of instruction often depends on the ability of persons to modify understandings, attitudes, appreciations, and practices. Ways of working with individuals and groups to improve instruction are detailed in Chapters IX and X. A step-by-step approach to curriculum study and development is presented in Chapter XI. Methods of evaluating supervisory programs are discussed in Chapter XII; and Chapter XIII takes a look at our changing society and the possible implications for school supervision in the future.

The authors hope that educators will find this handbook to be a helpful guide to the supervisory role in the following positions: superintendent or chief school administrator; assistant superintendent in charge of instruction; director or coordinator of instruction; elementary or secondary supervisor; director or coordinator of elementary or secondary education; elementary principal; secondary principal; assistant principal; team leader; department head; and special-area coordinator or supervisor. In addition, the handbook has been designed for use as a basic or supplementary text for graduate students in such fields as supervision, curriculum development, in-service education, and evaluation of the supervisory function.

R.L.N.

N.D.E.

TABLE OF CONTENTS

LIST OF ILLUSTRATIONS

chapter one

The Theory and Function of Supervision in the Modern Public School System

Effective supervision of instruction can improve the quality of teaching and learning in the classroom. Modern supervision at its finest is both dynamic and democratic, reflecting the vitality of enlightened and informed leadership. All human beings in the educative process—students, teachers, administrators, and supervisors—are individuals of worth, endowed with unique talents and capacities. The primary aim of supervision must be to recognize the inherent value of each person, to the end that the full potential of all will be realized.

Researchers in educational theory agree that supervision exists for the primary purpose of improving instruction. A few definitions should clarify the current thinking on the scope, purpose, and nature of modern supervision. According to Burton and Brueckner, it is:

> . . . an expert technical service primarily aimed at studying and improving co-operatively all factors which affect child growth and development. . . . Its characteristics may be summarized in outline form for brevity and clarity.
>
> 1. Modern supervision directs attention toward the fundamentals of education and orients learning and its improvement within the general aim of education.
> 2. The aim of supervision is the improvement of the total teaching-learning process, the total setting for learning, rather than the narrow and limited aim of improving teachers in service.
> 3. The focus is on the setting for learning, not on a person or group of persons. All persons are co-workers aiming at the improvement of a situation. One group is not superior to another, operating to "improve" the inferior group.
> 4. The teacher is removed from his embarrassing position as the focus of attention and the weak link in the educational process. He assumes his rightful position as a co-operating member of a group concerned with the improvement of learning.[1]

Supervision, according to Good, is:

> All efforts of designated school officials directed toward providing leadership to teachers and other educational workers in the improvement of instruction; involves the stimulation of professional growth and development of teachers, the selection and revision of educational objectives, materials of instruction, and methods of teaching; and the evaluation of instruction.[2]

Wiles defines modern supervision as "assistance in the development of a better teaching-learning situation."[3]

Moorer says, "In modern education the term 'supervision' is used to describe those activities which are primarily and directly concerned with studying and improving the conditions which surround the learning and growth of pupils and teachers."[4]

According to Melchior,

> . . . supervision is concerned with oversight of the instructional program. The term "instructional supervision" is used frequently to differentiate the latter aspect even more specifically . . . the words "supervisor,"

---

[1] William H. Burton and Leo J. Brueckner, *Supervision: A Social Process* (New York: Appleton-Century-Crofts, Inc., 1955), pp. 11-13. (Copyright © 1955, Appleton-Century-Crofts, Inc.)

[2] Carter V. Good, ed., *Dictionary of Education* (New York: McGraw-Hill Book Co., Inc., 1945), p. 400.

[3] Kimball Wiles, *Supervision For Better Schools: The Role of the Official Leader in Program Development* (Englewood Cliffs, N.J.: Prentice-Hall, Inc., 1955), p. 8.

[4] Sam H. Moorer, "Supervision: The Keystone to Educational Progress," *Bulletin*, State Department of Education, Tallahassee, Florida; April, 1956; p. 1.

"supervision," and "supervisory program" relate to the instructional phases of school plans and activities. . . .[5]

In summary, then, modern school supervision is positive, democratic action aimed at the improvement of classroom instruction through the continual growth of all concerned—the child, the teacher, the supervisor, the administrator, and the parent or other interested lay person.

THE NEED FOR SUPERVISION

American society in the 1960's is making fantastic, yet exciting demands upon the public schools. The continuing explosion of man's knowledge staggers the imagination and forces increasing intellectual and vocational specialization in a highly complex society. It is impossible for one even to be cognizant of the broad categories of man's knowledge in a lifetime, let alone master any significant amount of this accumulated knowledge of mankind. And yet man is a total being—an entity. He must be able to coordinate his various experiences into a meaningful whole if he is to lead a productive life and be reasonably adjusted physically, mentally, socially, and emotionally.

Since the school curriculum represents ideally the distillation of man's most important experiences, ideals, attitudes, and hopes, this heartland of the educational institution demands more careful study and decision today than ever before. There is a pressing need in every school system to decide what to teach and how to teach it. Accompanying the increase of possible contents is the tremendous growth in number and type of instructional media, such as programmed learning materials, instructional films, and educational television. To cope with these excessive demands that are pressing on the existing school structure, such organizational patterns as team teaching, ungraded units, and advanced placement classes have been advocated and tried experimentally. All of this means an increasing rate of obsolescence in content, methods, and materials of instruction.

Supervision, then, seems destined to play an essential role in deciding the nature and content of the curriculum, in selecting the school organizational patterns and learning materials to facilitate teaching, and in evaluating the entire educational process. Effective coordination of the total program, kindergarten through high school, has never been achieved in most school systems, although this is one of the most pressing needs in American public education today. And increasing numbers of districts

[5] William T. Melchior, *Instructional Supervision* (Boston: D. C. Heath and Co., 1950), pp. 3-4.

are adding grades 13 and 14. We can no longer afford the waste of human resources that is involved in overlapping courses, duplication of teaching effort, and lack of continuity from one school level to the next. A careful curriculum plan embracing the entire school experience from initial entry to graduation is imperative and long overdue. An effective supervisory program is needed in every school district—small, intermediate, or large—to launch or coordinate this effort.

THE CHARACTERISTICS OF MODERN SUPERVISION

The professional literature of the past decade is full of the theory of modern supervision. Terms such as "democratic," "team effort," and "group process" have been lavishly used in an attempt to show that present-day supervision is a far cry from the autocracy supposedly exhibited by the early twentieth-century administrator and supervisor. According to the theorists, all decisions of any importance in the modern school system should involve the entire staff, and each professional employee must feel that he is a part of the team. The age of group dynamics has left its imprint in that all staff members are expected to interact with considerable understanding of each other's problems and the needs of the total group. The image of democracy in action at the school and district level has been planted very firmly by the writers of almost every book in the field.

Brickell, in a recent study of the dynamics of instructional change in the schools of New York State, breaks the bubble of naïve acceptance of current theory.

> The language which has been developed to describe school administration, a language used almost universally by practicing administrators as well as by college professors in the field of administration, is not descriptive of the actual process. Phrases like "democratic administration," "the team approach," "shared decision-making," and "staff involvement" are commonplace. Behavior to match them is rare. The phrases themselves are often used with the intention of hiding the great strength of administrative action.
>
> The participation patterns in widespread use are very often little more than enabling arrangements, organized after an administrator has decided the general direction (and in some cases the actual details) of an instructional change. . . .
>
> His subtle leadership—or undercover direction—is thought by the practicing administrator to be most successful when he can say at the end: "They think they thought of it themselves." [6]

---

[6] Henry M. Brickell, *Organizing New York State For Educational Change* (Albany, N.Y.: State Education Department, 1961), pp. 23-24.

It is apparent from a review of the literature that some of the theorists have strayed rather far from a workable concept of school supervision. Equally, if the above-quoted conclusion is accurate and representative, many administrators and supervisors are verbalizing democracy and the other popular terms while practicing either authoritarian control or manipulation of staff to achieve their own goals, often in the name of democracy.

What, then, should be the major principles and characteristics of modern school supervision if the full potentialities of individuals and society are to be realized and are then to be translated into the most effective learning experiences for students?

1. The establishment and maintenance of satisfactory human relations among all staff members is primary. The Judaeo-Christian ethic of the ultimate worth of each individual must be basic in the philosophy of a school system and its administrators. Any supervisory program will succeed only to the extent that each person involved is considered as a human being with a unique contribution to make in the educative process. Relationships among all personnel must be friendly, open, and informal to a great extent. Mutual trust and respect are essential, and the person in the supervisory role must set the tone. It is increasingly apparent that the realities of today's world demand better human relationships if mankind is to survive. It is therefore imperative that the school staff, potentially one of the most influential groups of individuals in society, have the opportunity to develop and maintain a high level of personal interaction. According to Wiles, "A group's productiveness is affected by the quality of its human relations, and the supervisor must work constantly for the improvement of group cohesiveness." [7]

The selection of administrators and supervisors with a fundamental philosophy of positive human relationships is obviously essential to the implementation of this principle. And it must be admitted that research is inadequate in the area of candidate evaluation.

2. Modern supervision is democratic, in the most enlightened sense. "Democracy" does not mean "laissez-faire," with each staff member proceeding as he pleases. Rather, the term implies a dynamic, understanding, sensitive leadership role. Throughout the history of democratic institutions the importance of the leader is emphasized. On a school staff different individuals may assume the function at various times, but real, affirmative guidance is continually needed to focus attention on the improvement of instruction and to involve actively all concerned persons.

---

[7] Kimball Wiles, "Supervision," *Encyclopedia of Educational Research,* 3rd ed. (New York: The Macmillan Co., 1960), p. 1443.

A healthy rapport should exist among staff members in a give-and-take atmosphere which is conducive to objective consideration of the educational theories and problems of the day and of the school. A cooperative and creative approach to topics of joint concern is basic. Ideally, no personality, including the administrator or supervisor, dominates the group, but the considered judgments of all are felt to be valuable. At times the leader may have to exercise his rightful veto power or cast the deciding vote. However, most decisions should be made by consensus after thorough research and adequate discussion in the area under study. Too many voting situations may result in division of the staff, particularly if some persons find themselves in the minority on several successive occasions.

Individuals should be included in basic policy planning, in studies of the instructional program, and in all fundamental changes which affect them or their position directly. This does not mean that everyone must or should be involved in every decision. For example, if the assistant superintendent in charge of instruction needs to change the agenda of a curriculum workday because of a consultant's schedule, he should feel free to act without total staff approval. However, the same administrator would not usually purchase a set of filmstrips for use in the Language Arts program unless he had the advice of those who would be using these materials. The person in the supervisory position has the responsibility for deciding when individuals should be consulted. This is one of his most difficult tasks and points up the need for real stature in personnel leadership. When people are involved, then, there must be evidence that their creative participation is eagerly sought and that their contributions to the group decision are significant. There is absolutely no place in democratic supervision for "window-dressing" or autocratic administrative action based on token staff consultation.

In summary, democracy in supervision means active, cooperative involvement of all staff members in aspects of the instructional program which concern them, under the leadership of a well-informed, capable, and discerning administrator or supervisor who believes in the primacy of positive human relationships.

3. Modern supervision is comprehensive in scope. As indicated earlier, it embraces the total public school program, kindergarten through the twelfth or fourteenth years, depending on the organization of the school district. The curriculum is, or should be, a developing, ongoing process involving the child from kindergarten enrollment through high school or junior college graduation.

Almost all researchers are agreed that some district-wide coordination of the educational effort is essential. However, the means of effecting this desirable outcome and the degree of coordination necessary are areas of continuing debate, which are discussed later in this chapter.

Furthermore, modern supervision is comprehensive in its view of the teacher and the learner. Historically, the supervisory concept was narrow in scope, focusing mainly on criticism of the teacher in the classroom, followed sometimes by attempts to get him to improve his teaching skills. Today, supervision is directed at improving all factors involved in pupil learning. Gone are the days of attempting to improve the teacher without regard to the totality of the teaching-learning situation in the school. The modern supervisory role reaches far beyond the traditional "classroom visitation." In Chapters IX, X, and XI, various group and individual techniques in contemporary school supervision are discussed in considerable detail. Some examples will help to verify the broad scope of modern supervision in action.

Group Techniques

(1) Cooperative curriculum study and development is essential to the maintenance of up-to-date and worthwhile classroom experiences for students. Every staff member should be involved in this work. Among the positive outcomes will be: improved courses of study based on latest research findings; better staff understanding and relationships; improved articulation among the various school units, such as elementary and junior high; and a general awakening of interest in newer trends, materials of instruction, and methods of school organization.

(2) A carefully planned staff in-service program can contribute much to intellectual growth in the areas where research and experimentation are having an impact.

(3) The proper orientation of teachers to the school and community is a vital supervisory function. The instructional program is vastly improved through happy, well-adjusted teachers who feel secure in their assignments and in their new homes. An alert supervisor will solve many problems before they arise by initiating a comprehensive teacher-orientation program.

(4) Action research and experimentation at the district level are desperately needed in American public education. Too great a percentage of our already inadequate research dollar is being spent on isolated laboratory experiments. What better place could be found for meaningful, controlled studies with programmed learning materials, for example, than the public school classroom? Of course, proper safeguards need to be developed to make certain that students are not continually exposed to untested materials or methods. Recent research at Temple University

has revealed that the attitudes of parents and other lay persons toward research in the classroom are favorable.

(5) The coordination of special services and subjects such as art, music, physical education, speech correction, and developmental reading with the total program is a supervisory problem of the first magnitude. Too many schools have not even defined the role of the art specialist, for instance. Is this individual most effective as a resource person "on call," as a teacher regularly scheduled in classrooms, or as a supervisor of art activities in the district? Or should there be several specialists to fill these roles?

(6) The establishment and coordination of a program of student teaching in cooperation with neighboring colleges or universities can make a significant contribution to classroom instruction and to the individual college student as a prospective member of the teaching profession. Again, effective supervisory practice is needed if a student-teacher program is to be beneficial to all concerned.

Individual Techniques

(1) Classroom visitation is still an important part of a supervisory program. In fact, there can be no real understanding of the curriculum in action unless those responsible for supervision visit classrooms regularly. If satisfactory human relations exist, as discussed earlier in this chapter, supervisors will feel free to visit classes at will and most teachers will welcome them. The main purposes of this technique are: sensing the status of the curriculum and the experiences which students are having; discovering ideas that can be shared; establishing common bases for curriculum planning or in-service education; and, sometimes, helping to improve the teaching-learning situation.

(2) Individual teacher conferences should be prominent in any comprehensive supervisory plan. These are usually held after classroom visitations or at the request of the teacher or supervisor. They can be most valuable in providing for an exchange of ideas; in giving an opportunity for constructive suggestions about classroom techniques or materials of instruction; and in identifying possible areas for curriculum study or for professional growth of the teacher.

(3) The selection and assignment of well-qualified professional personnel is the basis on which a sound program of supervision must be built. This process can be quite time-consuming but will pay off when highly qualified and suitable teachers are found for the various openings. Many future teaching-learning problems can be avoided or mitigated by careful selection of classroom teachers. It is equally important that other personnel, such as principals and supervisors themselves, be chosen with regard

to the demands of the position and the personal and professional qualities required.

(4) The encouragement of professional writing by capable personnel who have something to report to the profession is a function of the supervisor. Local-district research or experimentation can be reported, as well as findings of research on a nationwide base. Too many educational writers have little or nothing to say. There is continuing need, however, for scholarly articles and books on current trends in the areas of the curriculum and in other professional fields.

Specific suggestions for initiating and carrying out these supervisory techniques and many others will be found in Chapters IX, X, and XI. From this brief summary, it should be apparent that modern supervision is indeed comprehensive in scope.

SELECTING AND ORGANIZING PERSONNEL FOR EFFECTIVE SUPERVISION OF INSTRUCTION

It is obvious that such a concept of supervision requires a high level of educational leadership for its implementation. The supervisor must be equipped personally and professionally to handle the position of responsibility to which he is called. Although research studies in selection of supervisors and administrators are quite limited, certain conclusions seem evident.

The modern school supervisor must have the personal attributes, first of all, that make a good teacher. He needs high native intelligence, a broad grasp of the educational process in society, a likable personality, and great skill in human relations. He must have a love for children and an abiding interest in them and their learning problems. His skill in the use of group processes is vital, and he needs to show a working understanding of the team concept in democratic supervision. He must be willing to subjugate his own personal ideas to the combined judgment of the team at times; yet he must possess the ability and fortitude to hold fast to his convictions unless additional evidence is presented. A good supervisor always should be guided by the findings of educational research and should have little time for pure opinion in group discussion and individual conference.

While the supervisor cannot possibly be expert in all of the fields which he coordinates, his knowledge should include the availability of resource leaders in all the areas of school supervision and improvement of instruction. He may be a specialist in certain disciplines, but he has to be a generalist in his approach to the total school program.

Tompkins and Beckley further define the necessary qualities of a supervisor: "His intuition, humility, friendliness, thoughtfulness, sense of humor—his effect on others—as well as his patience are essential characteristics, because supervision deals with relationships between people. His effectiveness depends on his understanding of human behavior. . . ."[8] According to Wiles,

> A supervisor is concerned with providing effective leadership within the staff. To do this, he should seek constantly to improve his sensitivity to the feelings of others, to increase the accuracy of his estimate of group opinion on important issues, to become more cooperative in his working relationships, to seek to establish higher goals for himself, and to interact more frequently with those in the group with which he works.[9]

In short, the modern supervisor must be capable, well trained in education and psychology, likable, and expert in the democratic group process. He recognizes his role as leader, and cooperatively involves his fellow administrators and teachers in all major decisions affecting them and the teaching-learning situation.

The personnel actually involved in supervision will vary according to the size of the district and the importance ascribed to supervisory activities.

The small school district, which is discussed fully in Chapter II, consists of one or two elementary schools and a small high school; or it may be a combination of small elementary or rural schools, with perhaps a common high school. The total pupil population is usually less than 1,000. In smaller organizations like this, administrative personnel usually will have the responsibility for supervisory activities as well. For example, the chief school administrator generally will be the supervisor of the total instructional program, elementary through high school. He might have a full- or part-time high school principal, but in many cases he will also assume that position himself. At the elementary level there may be a nonteaching principal or two, but often these schools will be administered by head teachers or teaching principals. These overworked professionals certainly have little or no time for supervisory activities. Even full-time principals must devote a significant portion of their workday to the administration of their buildings. Thus, it can be seen that no one person is fully assigned to the supervision of instruction in the typical small school district. Those involved to some extent in supervision would be

---

[8] Ellsworth Tompkins and Ralph Beckley, *Selected References to Secondary School Supervision* (Washington, D.C.: U.S. Department of Health, Education, and Welfare, Office of Education, Circular No. 389, February, 1954), p. 2.

[9] Wiles, "Supervision," *Encyclopedia of Educational Research*, p. 1442.

the chief administrator, the principals (if any), and, hopefully, the classroom teachers.

The intermediate-size school system, as defined by the authors in Chapter III, is made up of three or more elementary schools (or combinations of rural schools), one or more secondary schools, and a total pupil population of 1,000 to 6,000, generally. Personnel with supervisory roles would include the chief school administrator, the principals of the elementary and secondary schools, and possibly one or more of the following: special-area supervisors or coordinators (see Chapter VII), department heads, team leaders (if any), assistant superintendent in charge of instruction, coordinator of elementary education, and coordinator of secondary education. Any of the last three positions would be largely supervisory in nature and the personnel appointed to them would devote full time to the direct improvement of instruction and the coordination of the educational program at all levels throughout the district. Only a few intermediate-size systems would fill all three of these positions.

The larger school system is identified (Chapter IV) as having six or more elementary schools, three or more secondary schools, and a total pupil population of at least 6,000. The *very* large city is not discussed in detail because of the particular aspects of organization for supervision which apply primarily to densely populated urban centers with vast numbers of school buildings and subdivision of the system into city districts. Although suggestions made throughout this handbook may be helpful in implementing programs of supervision in the very large city, little attempt is made in Chapter IV or elsewhere to deal specifically with the unique patterns, problems, or supervisory needs of *these* city schools.

In the larger district, as defined above, there will usually be an assistant superintendent in charge of instruction, a coordinator of elementary education, and a coordinator of secondary education, with these coordinators responsible to the assistant superintendent. These three persons would work almost entirely in the areas of curriculum development and improvement of instruction. The coordinators would work directly and cooperatively with the building principals, who customarily would be full-time in the larger districts. The following personnel also would be involved, at least part-time, in supervisory activities: the superintendent (Chapter V), special-area supervisors or coordinators (Chapter VII), department heads, team leaders (if any), and possibly some curriculum personnel and subject-area consultants.

Role of the Principals and Teachers

In any size district, the principal should be recognized as the educational leader of his school and immediate community, responsible for the supervision of instruction as well as for the execution of administrative functions. On a district-wide level, the principal will cooperate with his colleagues in other schools and with all personnel who have supervisory functions. The philosophy of modern supervision which the authors advocate obviously dictates that classroom teachers in all districts should be an integral part of the supervisory program. They must have opportunities to participate in: evaluation of the district instructional program, curriculum development and revision, and analysis of their own teaching-learning situations. In other words, the professional integrity of the school principal and the classroom teacher are basic tenets of any effective program of supervision in the modern public school.

Persons who are likely to be involved in the supervisory process in various-size districts have been identified above. How best can these individuals be organized as a supervisory team? Are supervisors line officers or staff consultants? How much district-wide coordination is essential, and how much freedom of action should be left to principals and their staffs? Who coordinates the supervisory program? In the next six chapters these controversial questions and many others pertaining to the organization and function of personnel in supervision are discussed in detail. Opposing concepts are often presented, with reasons for each. Suggestions are intended to be practical, and honest differences in methods of organizing supervisory programs are explored fully. A brief discussion of some of the major issues follows.

Is District-Wide Coordination of the Educational Program Desirable?

Virtually all researchers and authorities reported in the current literature advocate some coordination of the program in a school district. The luxury of disjointed elementary and secondary curriculums can no longer be tolerated in a society where every hour spent in the classroom must be productive. It does not make sense for two junior high schools in a district to operate independently of each other. The important question to be decided is, "How much district-wide coordination is desirable?" If local building autonomy under a principal is important, how far should a staff go in merging its professional judgment with that of colleagues from other schools? There should be a cooperatively developed, flexible district policy so that each person with supervisory responsibilities will know the extent of his final authority and the areas in which he is to work cooperatively with others. The scope of a principal's independent action with his staff should be defined, for example, as well as those areas in which he would cooperate with other principals, supervisors, and chief administrators. A list of topics for district-wide coordination might include the following:

1. Curriculum study and development.
2. Evaluation of and selection of instructional materials.
3. Planning of in-service training programs.
4. Orientation of new teachers.
5. Action research and experimentation in newer organizational plans, teaching techniques, and materials of instruction, such as team teaching and programmed learning.
6. Function of special personnel in such fields as art, music, and physical education.
7. Student-teaching procedures in the district.
8. Selection of professional staff members.
9. Evaluation of professional personnel.

The chief administrator and his administrative-supervisory team must take the lead in establishing district-wide policies for coordination of the educational program, where they seem to be needed.

Should Supervisory Personnel Be Line or Staff?

By definition,

> . . . line organization is basically simple in that it involves a direct flow of authority upward and downward. A line officer has power and authority over subordinates. He is a generalist who executes administrative actions.
>
> Staff officers do not stand in the direct line of descending or ascending authority although they may, on occasion, exercise line authority. They can be divided into three types in relation to the functions which they perform: *service, coordinative,* and *advisory.*
>
> Although the line and staff concept of administration has been held in considerable disrepute, there is no way of abolishing line authority without making administration chaotic. The important point is that the operation of line authority should be consistent with reasonable goals of democratic administration. . . . (Also) the number of authority levels and line officers are kept at a minimum.[10]

The chief school administrator, assistant superintendent in charge of

---

[10] *Modern Practices and Concepts of Staffing Schools* (Albany, N.Y.: Cooperative Development of Public School Administration in New York State, 1956), pp. 8, 33, 35.

instruction (if any), and the full-time principals and assistant principals are generally line officials in the organization of a school district. A portion of their time and responsibilities would normally be devoted to supervisory activities, and in this work their line authority should be deemphasized to the end that effective democratic action may arise from sound human relationships and dynamic, sensitive leadership.

A real issue arises when the positions of coordinator of elementary education, coordinator of secondary education, and special-area supervisors are considered. Some researchers emphatically conclude that general supervisors or coordinators should be line personnel, while others find that these positions should be strictly staff. Some studies advocate both line and staff functions. The research offers conflicting evidence.

A study by the Cooperative Development of Public School Administration in New York State recommended that "the role of the building principal as an educational leader in his school unit should be enhanced. He should report directly to the chief school officer in all but the largest school situations, and should be responsible for the total education of the child in his school." [11] This and other studies suggest, for example, that the position of elementary supervisor or coordinator be a staff assignment, with the supervisor serving as a resource person on call of the building principals. Arguments in favor of this conclusion can be summarized briefly as follows:

1. A sound educational program demands strong building principals, reporting directly to the chief school administrator.
2. For most effective organization, the number of authority levels and line officers should be kept to a minimum.[12]
3. A principals' council, with rotating leadership, can coordinate the program, under the general direction of the chief school administrator or assistant superintendent.

On the other hand, Evans found that the position of elementary school supervisor (or coordinator) is necessary for the most effective coordination of the total elementary program.

> Coordination is important in the elementary schools of a district, and the elementary supervisor is in a position to see the broad approach to curriculum and instruction district-wide. The elementary supervisor is in a line-and-staff organization but the line relationship is not overemphasized. The supervisor is responsible to the superintendent in the areas of curriculum and instruction. The principals are responsible to the elementary supervisor for matters of curriculum and instruction, and are directly

---

[11] *Ibid.*, p. 35.
[12] *Ibid.*, p. 33.

responsible to the chief school official in administrative areas. The supervisor does not participate in building administration.[13]

The advantages of the general supervisor or coordinator as a line officer seem to be as follows:

1. The supervisor should have the time and the vision to offer leadership in coordinating the total program. He is in a position to see the broad approach to curriculum and instruction district-wide.
2. The principals necessarily have a limited view of one school and community, and do not generally have the perspective or the time to work together in effective coordination of the instructional program.
3. It is possible to have strong building principals and effective supervisors in line, if the district table of organization is democratically established and carried out. (However, it must be admitted that an autocratic supervisor coupled with poorly defined administrative staffing policy can result in weak building principals.)

Obviously, no one pattern of organization for supervision will serve all school districts. The personnel involved in administrative and supervisory roles determine to a significant extent the patterns that emerge. An autocratic and insecure elementary supervisor will often dominate young and inexperienced principals, refusing to let them develop the educational leadership needed in the modern elementary school. Conversely, an experienced, well-balanced principal, with a thorough background in positive human relationships and democratic supervision, can become a most effective elementary or secondary coordinator. Each school district must decide its own pattern of organization.

It is hoped that suggested guidelines in the following six chapters will assist administrators and supervisors in establishing or reorganizing a plan for efficient supervision of instruction. It is important that lines of responsibility be carefully, yet sensibly, established. Sound organization avoids many basic conflicts, duplication of effort, confusion, and lack of coordinated effort.

CAN WE DIFFERENTIATE BETWEEN ADMINISTRATION AND SUPERVISION?

Since this is a handbook for the effective supervision of instruction, the question must be answered. Many authorities say that it is impossible to

---

[13] N. Dean Evans, "The Status and Function of the Public Elementary School Supervisor in the Third and Fourth Class Districts of the Pennsylvania Counties of Chester, Delaware, and Montgomery" (Doctoral dissertation, Temple University, 1958), pp. 235-236.

separate administration and supervision because almost every administrative activity contributes in some way to the educational program. The two fields certainly overlap, as indicated by Otto.

> In the operation of schools today it is difficult, if not impossible, to draw fine distinctions between administrative, supervisory, and leadership functions. Although there are some activities which fall clearly in one or another of these categories, there are endless numbers of activities which overlap two or more of the rubrics.[14]

Burton and Brueckner further sharpen the problem by stating,

> The two can be separated arbitrarily only for the sake of analysis. A separation in function is impossible . . . mere inspection of the typical division between administrative and supervisory duties would indicate that the division can be only an arbitrary one for purposes of discussion. Intimate interrelationship and overlap are inherent and inevitable.[15]

Perhaps an answer to the apparent impasse may be found in analyzing the purpose for which various activities are performed. If the *primary* aim is the improvement of classroom instruction, then the act may well be designated supervisory in nature. For example, a supervisor or coordinator might visit a teacher's class for the purpose of making observations that could possibly lead to improvements in the teaching-learning situation. This would be a supervisory function. On the other hand, the same teacher's principal might visit him the next day for the purpose of rating in the merit salary program. This might well be an administrative function. In general, the acts of administrators and supervisors that are mainly associated with the efficient operation of the school would be designated administration. These would include transportation of pupils, direction of custodians, financial operation of the cafeteria, reports, and record-keeping. Of course, the keeping of achievement-test records could be supervision if the main aim were evaluation of the teaching-learning situation with a view toward improving instruction.

In summary, administration or administrative function, for the purposes of this handbook, will refer to aspects of school organization and direction that are not primarily concerned with or directly related to supervision as previously defined. While it is recognized that there will always be some overlapping and some disagreement as to the nature of a particular act, any leadership function which is primarily concerned with the im-

---

[14] Henry J. Otto, *Elementary School Organization and Administration* (New York: Appleton-Century-Crofts, Inc., 1944), p. 296.

[15] Burton and Brueckner, *Supervision: A Social Process, op. cit.*, pp. 96-98. (Copyright © 1955, Appleton-Century-Crofts, Inc.)

provement of classroom instruction or curriculum development will be considered supervision.

SUMMARY

Modern supervision is positive, dynamic, democratic action designed to improve classroom instruction through the continual growth of all concerned individuals—the child, the teacher, the supervisor, the administrator, and the parent or other lay person.

There is a pressing need for improved supervision in modern school systems which must develop and evaluate instructional programs in an ever-changing society.

The major principles and characteristics of modern school supervision can be summarized as follows:

1. The establishment and maintenance of positive human relationships is essential.
2. Modern supervision is democratic, with active, cooperative involvement of all staff members under the leadership of capable, understanding, and discerning administrators. Each person must be willing to assume some responsibility in the supervisory program.
3. Modern supervision is comprehensive in scope, embracing all school experiences from kindergarten through high school or junior college. All factors involved in pupil learning are important. The totality of the teaching-learning situations is considered. The supervisory role reaches far beyond the traditional "classroom visitation" and encompasses a variety of individual and group techniques.

Effective supervision requires a high level of leadership. The successful supervisor is intelligent, well-trained in education and psychology, likable, experienced, and expert in the democratic group process.

The size of a school district and the importance it assigns to supervisory activities will determine the number and function of personnel actually involved in supervision.

Some cooperative, district-wide coordination of the educational program is thought essential by most researchers. Principals are the educational leaders of their schools, but they must work together with the other administrators and supervisors to assure an integrated program from kindergarten through high school.

With regard to line or staff organization of supervisory personnel, the research evidence is conflicting. Each district must decide its own patterns after considering the various conclusions. It is essential that areas of responsibility be carefully, yet sensibly and flexibly, established. Sound organization for supervision avoids many basic conflicts, unnecessary overlapping, and confusion of effort.

For the purpose of this handbook, *administration* will refer to the phases of school organization and operation that are not mainly concerned with classroom instruction. Any leadership function which is primarily related to the improvement of instruction or curriculum development will be considered *supervision.*

The instructional program represents the impact of the school on children and youth. Constant evaluation and improvement of that program must be the major task of all educators.

ORGANIZATION OF HANDBOOK

1. Chapters II through VII detail the specific functions of the various supervisory personnel, all within the organizational framework of school districts of various sizes. The interrelationships of superintendents, principals, coordinators, and special supervisors or coordinators are discussed; job analyses and areas of responsibility and authority are suggested.
2. Chapter VIII is a discussion of the various factors that impede or encourage change as staff members work together to improve the instructional process.
3. Chapters IX and X give specific suggestions for practicing individual and group techniques in modern supervison.
4. Chapter XI presents a detailed plan for organizing and carrying out a program of curriculum study and development in any district.
5. Chapter XII discusses methods for evaluating the effectiveness of a supervisory program.
6. Chapter XIII attempts to predict what the supervisory program of the future might be like in view of the fantastic explosion of knowledge and constant societal change.

DEFINITION OF TERMS

Throughout this handbook the term *supervisor* is used in reference to all personnel who render supervisory services. This includes, for example, the chief school official, assistant superintendent in charge of instruction, the coordinators of elementary and secondary education, building principals, and special supervisors or coordinators.

The terms *superintendent, chief school administrator,* and *chief school official* are synonymous and are used interchangeably.

To express more accurately the authors' concept of democratic supervision, the word *coordinator* will often be used instead of *supervisor* or *director* in discussing such positions as elementary supervisor and director of elementary or secondary education.

SUGGESTED ACTIVITIES AND PROBLEMS

1. Develop a comprehensive definition of *supervision.*
2. What is the need for supervision in the modern public school system?
3. Prepare an outline of the major characteristics of modern supervision.
4. List and differentiate between group and individual supervisory techniques.
5. Write a paragraph summarizing the desirable professional and personal characteristics of a supervisor.
6. Is district-wide coordination of the educational program desirable? Defend your answer.
7. Prove or refute this statement: "An intermediate-size school district with four elementary schools should have an elementary school supervisor or coordinator."
8. Do you believe it is possible to separate by definition the terms *supervision* and *administration?* Why or why not?

SELECTED READINGS

Brickell, Henry M., *Organizing New York State for Educational Change.* Albany, N. Y.: State Education Department, 1961.

Burton, William H., and Leo J. Brueckner, *Supervision: A Social Process,* Chaps. 1-7. New York: Appleton-Century-Crofts, Inc., 1955.

Lucio, William H., and John D. McNeil, *Supervision—A Synthesis of Thought and Action,* Chaps. 1-3. New York: McGraw-Hill Book Company, Inc., 1962.

Modern Practices and Concepts of Staffing Schools. Albany, N.Y.: Cooperative Development of Public School Administration in New York State, 1956.

Wiles, Kimball, *Supervision for Better Schools: The Role of the Official Leader in Program Development,* Chaps. 1-2. Englewood Cliffs, N.J.: Prentice-Hall, Inc., 1955.

chapter two

Organization and Function of Supervision in the Small District

Despite the nationwide trend toward larger and more efficient administrative units, vast numbers of children are being educated in small school systems today. For example, in 1961 there were 16,551 districts in the United States employing nine teachers or fewer. In the same year, there were still 15,018 one-teacher schools in operation. In 18,480 districts only elementary schools were operated in 1961, and in 1,179 districts only secondary schools were being operated.[1]

It is the purpose of this chapter to suggest methods of improving the supervisory program of the small district, taking full advantage of all

---

[1] American Association of School Administrators and Department of Rural Education, *School District Organization, Journey That Must Not End* (Washington, D.C.: National Education Association. 1962), pp. 10-12.

resources that are available or that can be mobilized. It is possible for a small school system to improve instruction today, instead of merely waiting for the inevitable larger district of tomorrow to do it. All children deserve the best possible instructional program now as well as in the future.

CHARACTERISTICS OF THE SMALL SCHOOL DISTRICT

The small district is usually found in rural areas, or in suburban communities whose total geographic area provides no room for additional growth. The K-12 pupil population of the entire district is generally less than 1,000. In some cases, the people live close together within the boundaries of a small town. In others, the inhabitants may be spread throughout an entire rural county of several hundred square miles. Schools might be organized into one county unit or into several tiny districts.

Although small school systems do vary widely in many respects, the typical small district can be defined in terms of usual plant and staff resources.

School-Plant Facilities

At the elementary level, there are one or two complete unit schools, with one or two sections of each grade, kindergarten (or first) through sixth. In more sparsely settled areas, there may be a number of one- to four-teacher rural schools, or a combination of one complete elementary school and several of the rural buildings.

A small junior-senior high school, serving pupils in grades seven through twelve, is usually the only secondary facility in the small district, if any is provided at all. Many school systems of this size operate elementary schools only and have no high schools of their own. Pupils must be sent on a tuition basis to other secondary schools that have space and are willing to receive them. In some instances, several of these small elementary districts join together at the secondary level to provide a common high school.

Staff Requirements

Twenty-five or fewer teachers make up the total elementary staff and sufficient secondary personnel are employed to staff the junior-senior high school, if one is maintained. In addition, there might be several special teachers, generally in art, music, and physical education, who serve both elementary and secondary pupils.

Administrative and supervisory personnel. To be functioning at optimum efficiency on the administrative level, a small district employs a full-time superintendent or supervising principal as chief administrator. In very small districts, the chief administrator may be principal of the high school and/or one of the elementary schools, in addition to his general administrative responsibilities.[2]

There is or should be a full-time principal of the junior-senior high school. (However, some small secondary schools operate with part-time principals who teach several periods per day.) If the enrollment is larger than 600 because of tuition pupils from other districts, the principal undoubtedly needs a full-time assistant administrator.

Each elementary school should have a full-time, non-teaching principal. Ideally, no elementary school ought to exist if it is not large enough to support a full-time principal. The lowest ratio that usually can be supported is one principal to twelve classroom teachers, or to approximately two sections of each grade.[3] If the elementary grades are scattered in smaller buildings and cannot be consolidated in one school, they should be arranged in administrative units of approximately 12 to 20 teachers, with a full-time principal in charge of each unit. It is almost impossible to have a comprehensive program of supervision and curriculum development in a district where the individual elementary schools have no administrative head, or at best employ a teaching principal or head teacher. In such situations, at least one area is bound to suffer: the principal's classroom teaching, building administration, or the supervision of instruction. Therefore, the first step toward effective supervision at the elementary level is the organization of schools geographically into units that can be directed by full-time, non-teaching principals.

In the small school district, no one person has full-time responsibility for supervision. All administrators must be responsible for improvement of instruction and the administration of their schools. They are generalists and not specialists in curriculum development, school finance, or in-service training, for example. Or, at least, they cannot function as specialists in the small district. Because of the comprehensive nature of their positions, each administrator should be fully qualified and certified for the position he holds. Of course, this is not the existing situation in many smaller systems, but it is the key to effective supervision of instruction. An

---

[2] *Modern Practices and Concepts of Staffing Schools* (Albany, N.Y.: Cooperative Development of Public School Administration in New York State, 1956), pp. 20-23.

[3] Educational Service Bureau, Temple University, *A Report of Findings, Conclusions and Recommendations of a Survey of the Solanco Area Schools* (Philadelphia: The Bureau, 1957) (Mimeographed), p. 23.

administrator must be well-trained, experienced, and personable. Most important of all, he must have the ability to work cooperatively and positively with his fellow administrators, teachers, pupils, and parents. Then he will have a reasonable chance of developing an adequate program of supervision for the small school district he serves.

ORGANIZING FOR SUPERVISION

Lack of effective coordination of the elementary and secondary curriculums in many of the nation's school systems was cited in Chapter I as a major supervisory problem. According to Evans, this is particularly true in small districts. "There is apparently little concerted effort made to coordinate the total program of many districts from kindergarten through twelfth grade." [4]

How can a small school district organize for good supervision? Although he wears many hats, the chief school administrator must assume leadership as the coordinator of instruction and curriculum. It certainly is true that budgets, bus schedules, board meetings, custodial direction, endless reports to the state, and other primarily administrative functions seem to dominate the daily calendar. Yet research has shown that the chief administrator, by his initiative, sets the tone for instructional improvement.[5] If he devotes time and effort to the organization and operation of the supervisory program, it has a good chance of success. If he does not assume this responsibility in the small district, effective supervision will be nonexistent or limited to individual schools with first-rate principals.

Specifically, the chief administrator should assume leadership in the following areas:

1. Whenever there is more than one school unit in a district, it is essential that all administrators be called to meet on a top-level, executive basis. Here is the opportunity to share ideas, to plan joint curriculum evaluation and development, and to work out common district policy on problems and issues that require thinking beyond the confines of one principal's building and staff. The chief school official would normally chair this administrative council, although the chairmanship could rotate. Agenda items should be supervisory as well as administrative.

2. Constructive classroom visitation is one of the basic supervisory techniques. The chief administrator should schedule observations so that

---

[4] Evans, "The Status and Function of the Public Elementary School Supervisor in the Third and Fourth Class Districts of the Pennsylvania Counties of Chester, Delaware, and Montgomery," *op. cit.*, p. 238.

[5] Brickell, *Organizing New York State For Educational Change, op. cit.*, p. 24.

he can visit each teacher at least once or twice a year. If he also is a building principal, he should be in each classroom for an extended period three or four times per year. A comprehensive plan of teacher visitation, detailing the responsibilities of all district administrators, should be developed by the administrative council.

3. The recruitment, selection, orientation, and assignment of teachers is an important function, requiring definition of policy and procedures.

4. The chief administrator must be concerned with his own professional growth through continuing graduate work, participation in conventions and conferences, and occasional college teaching if he has the opportunity.

5. The professional growth of the administrative and teaching staffs through in-service programs, graduate work, and conferences is largely influenced by the interest of the chief administrator.

6. Through the administrative council, or independently, if there is only one district administrator, policies on special services to pupils, promotion and grouping, evaluation of pupil progress, and public relations must be developed and carried out with the teaching staff.

(See Chapters IX, X, and XI for further ideas on various supervisory techniques.)

Many chief school administrators of small districts are aware of their supervisory roles but are often short of time and assistance to accomplish the various tasks. In the matter of time, one must make a basic decision. Is curriculum development as important as the cafeteria account? Shouldn't classroom visitation to observe the present instructional program take precedence over a lengthy conference with a salesman who has no appointment? In other words, can't time be found for supervision if it is really considered important? Occasionally it is a good idea for a chief administrator to run an analysis of the time he spends on various activities during a week. In the small district, such a survey will usually show a deficiency in time devoted to the direct improvement of instruction through supervision.

There is considerable resource help available to the chief school official who wants to move ahead in his supervisory program. Curriculum consultants, in-service ideas, research services, and valuable publications may be obtained, often without charge, from the following organizations and offices.

(More detailed information may be found in Chapter XI and in Appendix One, pp. 241-244.)

1. The United States Office of Education.
2. The National Education Association and its affiliated state associations.

3. State departments of education and county superintendents' offices.
4. Nearby colleges and universities with good schools of education.
5. Study councils, although these must be evaluated carefully. Some are very good; others are not worth the time and money spent for affiliation. In any event, they never take the place of a district program of curriculum development. Their studies can be helpful if applied to local needs and problems in supervision.
6. Courses of study and curriculum materials from nearby districts of comparable size and effort. Some guides from big-city school districts with full-time curriculum staffs are valuable, too. For example, the physical education courses of study developed by the Los Angeles City Schools would be quite useful to any chief administrator who plans to evaluate the physical education program of his district.
7. Special projects and studies, such as the small-high school study conducted in New York State.[6]

The chief administrator, of course, must expect and receive strong support from the building principals who make up the administrative council in the small district. If some of these principals are part-time or head teachers, every effort should be made to establish school units large enough to support full-time principals. Failing in this, the chief administrator should involve his part-time administrators in supervisory activities to the maximum extent possible. This would include, for example, the hiring of substitute teachers so that teaching principals could attend administrative council meetings and otherwise work as supervisors.

To be a leader in supervision, the chief school administrator of the small district needs vision, courage, and resourcefulness. However, the job can be done, and it must be done.

The supervisory role of the principals in the small district is of vital importance to the success or failure of the program to improve instruction. The individual principal, as the educational leader of his school, is directly responsible to the chief school administrator for the instructional program in his building. He serves on the administrative council and cooperates with other district administrators in determining policy matters that concern all schools.

Primarily the principal leads his own faculty in the improvement of instruction. He is largely responsible for the morale of his staff members and their general attitudes toward the school program and its enrichment. To be effective, he must be vitally interested in his teachers and be able

[6] *Catskill Area Project in Small School Design* (Oneonta, N.Y.: Catskill Area Project in Small School Design, 1959).

to assess their strengths, needs, and individual abilities to function as members of a professional staff. Not all will be (or will want to become) master teachers. The good principal maintains close working relationships with all his colleagues, however, and does not permit the poorest or laziest to set the tone for the instructional program.

The principal, too, needs to find a balance between supervision and administration. At least half of his time should be planned for such supervisory activities as the following:

1. Individual teacher conferences, mostly informal.
2. Regular classroom visitations.
3. Action research in the classroom.
4. Coordination of special subjects (art, music, and physical education) with the academic curriculum (see Chapter VII).
5. Demonstration and substitute teaching on occasion.
6. Participation in principals' organizations and conferences.
7. An active role in district-wide curriculum development.
8. Planning and presenting in-service programs.

(Principals should find Chapters VI, IX, X, and XI to be helpful in planning their supervisory activities.)

The chief school administrator who also is building principal in the small district must divide his time between the general supervisory functions described earlier in this chapter and the more intimate role of the principal working with his staff. Such a position is most certainly demanding, but often challenging and satisfying.

Can a building principal in a small district do anything to improve instruction if his chief administrator pays little attention to the instructional program? Usually the answer is "yes." Often a superintendent will encourage a principal who desires to take some initiative in district-wide supervision. At the very least, a building principal can work extensively with his own staff to improve their own teaching-learning situations, within the framework of district policy, if any. In the absence of positive direction from the chief administrator, an alert principal can do much to stimulate good teaching and learning within his own school. The limitations of such an effort are, of course, recognized, and every attempt should be made to involve the superintendent in supervision of instruction. Indeed, it is the responsibility of a conscientious principal to try regularly and persistently to interest his chief administrator in supervisory activities. Some of the following techniques may help:

1. Send pertinent research findings, pamphlets, and summaries of curriculum studies to his desk.

2. Arrange for many informal and formal conferences to discuss various phases of the instructional program.
3. Take advantage of every contact with the chief administrator to talk supervision and its importance. Tell him what neighboring districts and leaders in other areas are doing.

The teaching principal faces a particularly difficult task in trying to provide leadership in the improvement of instruction. First of all, he has a full- or part-time job as a classroom teacher. At the elementary level, he may teach a self-contained classroom all day. As a secondary principal, he may teach several periods per day. Before and after school he must administer his building. Often it is almost impossible to find time for supervisory activities. The following suggestions may help:

1. Try to handle routine administrative matters by bulletin or note, and use staff-meeting time before or after school for discussion of curriculum and other instructional matters.
2. Request a substitute teacher for the principal's class or classes on a regular basis (a minimum of one day per week), to permit time for classroom visitation, teacher conferences, professional meetings outside the school system, and administrative council meetings in the district.
3. Teach pupils to handle certain responsibilities, such as counting lunch money, answering the phone, and communicating with the custodian. (The elementary teaching principal should always have a sixth-grade class whenever possible.)

As indicated earlier, the most effective supervision of instruction demands the elimination of the head teacher or teaching principal. Persons in this position should do everything possible to convince their superiors of the hopelessness of the job. This may be done by keeping a list of important tasks that cannot be accomplished from day to day because of the pressure of the total load.

How Two or More Small Districts May Organize for Supervision

Chief school administrators should try to work cooperatively with their counterparts in neighboring small districts in the joint improvement of instruction.

In some cases, several elementary school systems send their pupils to a common high school. The superintendent or supervising principal of the district maintaining the secondary program is often considered the chief administrator of the area, and would therefore direct the over-all program of supervision, kindergarten through the twelfth or fourteenth grade. If no chief school official in a group of contiguous districts is so designated, then one of the number should be elected as chairman of an administrative council, to consist of all administrators in the group. Certainly every effort should be made to include all sending and receiving districts.

For example, since District A (Figure 1) does not operate a secondary program but sends its pupils on a tuition or joint-district arrangement to neighboring District B's high school, it is the responsibility of the two chief school officials involved to work together in establishing a K-12 curriculum. This they have done by organizing an administrative council with the chief administrator of District B as chairman and all of the principals of both districts and the chief school official of District A as members. This team can function in the coordination and improvement of instruction throughout the two districts. The following could be possible administrative council activities:

1. Determination of basic educational philosophy and resulting curricular needs.

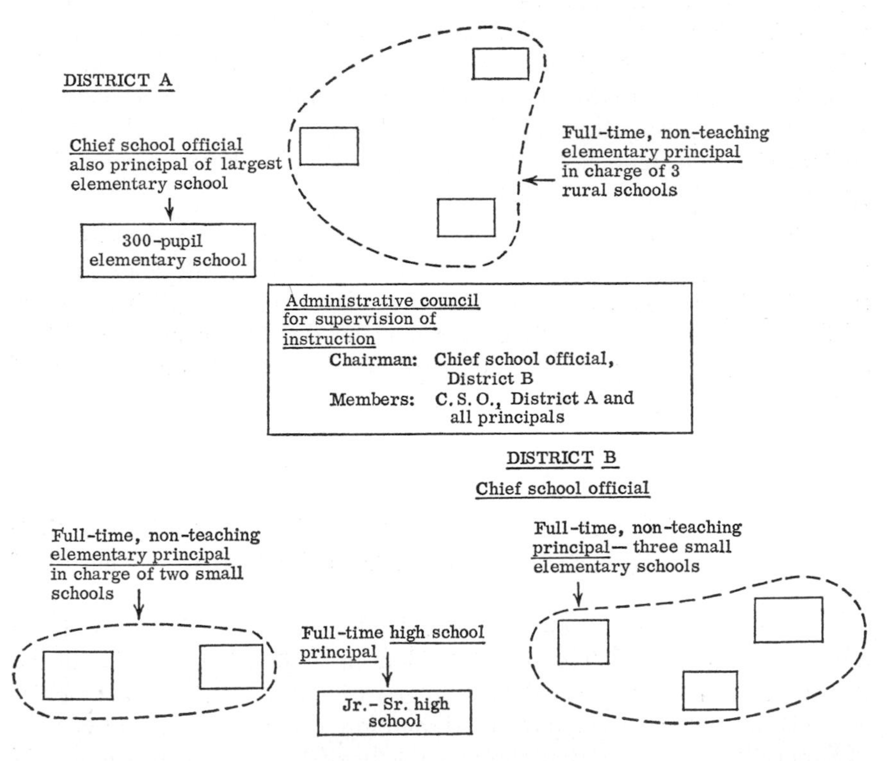

Fig. 1. Organization of Two Small Districts for Supervision of Instruction. (Note: All pupils from both districts attend District B's Jr.-Sr. high school.)

2. A K-12 program of curriculum development, using consultants and resources that neither district alone could afford. (This activity is essential, since all nine elementary schools feed the same high school. See Chapter XI for suggestions.)
3. Identification of areas in which over-all joint policy should be developed and those which should be the prerogative of each district and principal.
4. Development of joint program for special areas, such as art, music, physical education, speech, and reading (see Chapter VII).

(Many of the individual and group supervisory techniques described in Chapters IX and X could be profitably discussed by the administrative council.)

Failure of chief administrators to provide for such coordination as is shown in Figure 1 and described above results in elementary units of teaching that are duplicated in the high school; widely varying curriculums at the same level in different elementary schools; and many other evidences of poor supervision. It should be emphasized, however, that within this broad framework of coordination of instruction, there should be considerable latitude for each administrator to work with his own staff, pupils, and parents in evolving a curriculum that is particularly appropriate for his school and community. Effective supervision involves both district-wide planning and coordination and local school autonomy.

SUPERVISION IN THE BETHEL TOWNSHIP SCHOOL DISTRICT, BOOTHWYN, PENNSYLVANIA

Bethel Township is a rural community of 2,000 people, with no shopping centers, industries, or commercial activities. Practically all wage earners work outside the township in nearby metropolitan Wilmington, Delaware, or Chester, Pennsylvania. The population is gradually growing as the area becomes more suburban, but the present taxable wealth is quite limited.

There is one school in Bethel Township, the Francis Harvey Green Elementary School, with eight classrooms and a multipurpose room. The professional staff is comprised of nine classroom teachers, two part-time special teachers in art and music, and one full-time principal. The total pupil population averages 215, and there are one or two sections each of grades one through six. At the secondary level, pupils attend a joint high school operated with two other communities.

Until he answered the call of a larger district, Daniel E. Fitzpatrick was chief administrator in Bethel Township and principal of the school. In providing real instructional leadership, he directed a team of enthusiastic teachers who proved that progress in a small school need not await reorganization into larger units.

Operating in an atmosphere of positive human relations, Dan Fitzpatrick encouraged informality and personal interaction among his staff which led to joint interest in the learning problems of boys and girls. The first curriculum area they identified for study was physical education. Teachers expressed concern over the lack of organized activity on the playground. This quickly led to an evaluation of the school's entire physical education program. The principal secured one of the elementary evaluative criteria for this purpose. The entire staff met once a week after school for formal curriculum work, and each person spent many hours of his own time on the study. In addition, two full workshop days were made available. Two committees evolved, one at the primary level and the other at the intermediate. After the evaluation was completed, the principal secured research materials and courses of study in physical education from various school districts. The county superintendent's office provided some assistance in this phase. By the end of the school year, an outline of a course of study was emerging and all staff members were becoming experts in self-testing activities, rhythms, and games. During the summer the principal collated the work that had been done, duplicated it, and sent copies to the teachers for further study. In the fall the new physical education program began. Equipment to implement the new activities was purchased. Evaluation during the year revealed that instruction in physical education was improving markedly as the teachers eagerly taught the program they had developed. And, incidentally, the children had no further trouble organizing their own games at recess and during lunch hour.

An equally successful curriculum-development project in science was carried out. The staff first selected the area for study and then outlined the science units that were currently taught. The principal then asked the board of education for funds to hire two teachers for a short period during the summer. The request was granted and materials for the study were obtained. A regional science consultant from a nearby county superintendent's office assisted in planning the project. The two teachers (from first and fourth grades) met with the principal several times to organize the curriculum study. In the summer the new course of study for science, grades one through six, was developed and sent to the other teachers for review. In September final revisions were made, new materials of instruction were obtained, and the program was launched in each classroom. Later in the fall, a full in-service day was planned to give teachers an opportunity to share science experiences. Three teams of two teachers each were organized to demonstrate the use of different science materials.

In addition to curriculum development, Dan Fitzpatrick helped to improve instruction in many other ways. He observed his teachers in the classrooms every two weeks and held follow-up conferences with them. He encouraged graduate work at nearby colleges and universities. The board of education was asked to budget funds for professional conferences and study council activities. Teachers attended curriculum meetings and other worthwhile programs in the state and county.

Orientation of new teachers was no problem in this school. Newcomers became a part of the team immediately and were involved in the social and professional life of the staff.

Weekly bulletins to parents and frequent press releases kept the community informed of school activities and projects. Public relations were well handled.

Thus, it is apparent that the average small school district can make progress in the improvement of instruction if the dynamics of leadership and the science of human relations are present.

SUMMARY

Despite considerable progress in the reorganization of school districts, there are many small systems today in rural and suburban areas with pupil populations of less than 1,000.

The typical small district has one or two elementary schools or a number of one- to four-teacher rural buildings. The staff probably numbers 25 or less at the elementary level. A junior-senior high school is usually the only secondary facility, if any is provided at all.

No person has full-time responsibility for supervision in the small district. The chief administrator sometimes serves as elementary or secondary principal. Some small high schools operate with part-time principals who teach several periods per day. Although administrators should not be part-time teachers if they are to provide maximum instructional leadership, many elementary schools also employ teaching principals. If the elementary grades are scattered in smaller buildings and cannot be consolidated in one school, they should be arranged in administrative units of approximately 12 to 20 teachers, with a full-time principal in charge of each unit.

If the small district is to organize effectively for supervision, the chief administrator must assume leadership in organizing an administrative council; in visiting teachers; in selecting and orienting new staff members; in providing in-service growth experiences for teachers; and in cooperatively developing policies on special pupil services, promotion and grouping, evaluation of pupil progress, and public relations. Considerable resource help is available to the chief school official who wants to improve instruction.

The supervisory role of the principals in the small district is very important. As the educational leader of his school, the individual building principal is directly responsible to the chief administrator in administration and supervision. At least half of the principal's time should be planned for teacher conferences, classroom visitations, action research, curriculum development, and other supervisory activities.

Neighboring small school districts should work cooperatively in the improvement of instruction. If they send elementary pupils to the same high school, for example, a joint administrative council should be established to coordinate the programs kindergarten through high school.

The small district can make progress in the improvement of instruction if the principles and practices of modern, democratic supervision are evident.

SUGGESTED ACTIVITIES AND PROBLEMS

1. Define the typical small school district in terms of size, school plant facilities, and professional staff.

2. Select a small district and describe the organization for supervision, identifying all persons with supervisory roles.

3. Interview a teaching principal with the purpose of evaluating his effectiveness in improving the instructional program in his school.

4. How can the chief administrator provide leadership to organize and carry out the supervisory program?

5. Prepare a resource list for the small district administrator who wants to improve instruction. Be specific.

6. Define the supervisory role of the principal in the small school system.

7. How can an administrator in a small district find time for supervisory activities?

8. Locate several neighboring small school districts and develop a master plan for the coordination of supervision from kindergarten through high school.

9. You are the superintendent of a district with elementary teaching

principals in five small schools and one full-time principal of a small high school. How would you proceed to improve the instructional program?

SELECTED READINGS

Burnham, Reba M., and Martha L. King, *Supervision in Action.* Washington, D.C.: Association for Supervision and Curriculum Development, National Education Association, 1961.

Catskill Area Project in Small School Design. Oneonta, N.Y.: Catskill Area Project in Small School Design, 1959.

Current Practice in Administrative Staffing in New York State. Albany, N.Y.: Cooperative Development of Public School Administration in New York State, 1955.

Department of Rural Education, *The Rural Supervisor at Work,* 1949 Yearbook. Washington, D.C.: National Education Association, 1949.

Ford, Edmund A., *Rural Renaissance, Revitalizing Small High Schools.* Washington, D.C.: U.S. Department of Health, Education, and Welfare, Office of Education, Bulletin 1961, No. 11, 1961.

Franseth, Jane, *Supervision in Rural Schools.* Washington, D.C.: U.S. Department of Health, Education, and Welfare, Office of Education, Bulletin 1955, No. 11, 1955.

Nimnicht, Glendon P., and Arthur R. Partridge, *Designs for Small High Schools.* Greeley, Colo.: Educational Planning Service, Colorado State College, 1961.

Schmidt, Ralph L. W., "Supervisory Responsibilities of the Superintendent in Elementary Grades of Small, Twelve-Grade Systems," *Educational Administration and Supervision,* XXXIX, No. 1 (January, 1953), 27-35.

chapter three

Organization and Function of Supervision in the Intermediate-Size District

The intermediate-size district is found most commonly in the fast-growing suburban areas surrounding large cities and in rural regions where reorganization of school districts into larger units is underway. Usually there are mounting problems of mushrooming population, rapid expansion of all municipal services, and the direct concern of increased enrollments which complicate the task of effective instructional leadership. In these districts it is important that planning for supervision keep pace with the growth patterns.

CHARACTERISTICS OF THE INTERMEDIATE-SIZE SCHOOL DISTRICT

An *intermediate-size system* is defined as enrolling 1,000 to 6,000 pupils from kindergarten through secondary school. It is recognized that some districts of 7,000 pupils or more might better be described as intermediate rather than large, owing to such factors as density of population, ability of the budget to support full supervisory services, and the evolving organization for supervision. Administrators and supervisors from these borderline units might find some workable ideas in both Chapters III and IV.

At the other end of the pupil population scale, some districts with 1,000 to 1,500 pupils might be described more accurately as small school systems. In such instances, the organizational patterns in Chapter II could be more helpful.

Some intermediate-size districts operate only elementary schools and others are unified high school districts, serving secondary pupils only and receiving students from a number of elementary districts.

School-Plant Facilities

There are three or more complete-unit elementary schools, usually with one or two sections of each grade, kindergarten (or first) through sixth. Or there may be combinations of smaller rural schools into administrative units under full-time principals. Thus, some of the elementary buildings might be quite small while others are consolidated or neighborhood schools with 400 or more pupils. In rapidly expanding suburban communities, most of the elementary plants are new buildings housing at least two sections of each grade.

At the secondary level, the intermediate-size district will usually have at least one junior high school and one senior high school plant. Smaller intermediate systems may house all secondary pupils in one comprehensive junior-senior high school.

Staff Requirements

Personnel needs in the intermediate district may be summarized as follows.

Regular and special teachers. Depending on such variables as actual pupil population and class size, the elementary teaching staff would number approximately 25 to 125. Special teachers or coordinators in such subject areas as art, music, physical education, and possibly science and foreign languages would serve the elementary schools. Under certain plans of elementary-school organization, specialists would be required in other areas of the curriculum. In addition, guidance services might be available.

The teaching staff at the secondary level might number up to 115, with considerable variation possible owing to the size of the secondary student body, the organization of the curriculum, and the special services provided. The intermediate-size district will usually supply adequate guidance and psychological specialists to complement the instructional staff.

Administrative and supervisory personnel. There are at least two major points of view regarding the selection and organization of persons for optimum supervision of instruction in the intermediate district. Both philosophies are presented, with advantages and disadvantages of each.

Under *Plan 1* the following personnel would be directly involved in the supervisory program:

1. Chief school official.
2. Full-time elementary-school principals. (If some small buildings still exist and cannot be consolidated, they should be arranged in administrative units of approximately 12 to 20 teachers, with a full-time principal in charge of each unit.)
3. Full-time secondary-school principals.
4. Full-time assistant principals in schools with more than 600 pupils.
5. Special-area coordinators (if any).

It is recognized that flat charts are an imperfect and incomplete way of expressing organizational patterns and human relationships in supervision. At some risk of rigidity and oversimplification, then, the accompanying diagram (Figure 2, p. 37) shows the personnel in *Plan 1* and their line responsibilities. This plan provides for the coordination and supervision of instruction by the superintendent and the principals working with their staff members. A flat chart tends to appear inflexible in its delineation of line authority. Furthermore, it is impossible to indicate the flow of staff relationships that are an integral part of effective supervision. Therefore, the characteristics and principles of modern supervision outlined in Chapter I should be considered in the implementation of the organizational plans that follow.

Under *Plan 1*, the chief school official and the principals are both administrators and supervisors. The superintendent assumes the responsibility for district-wide coordination of instructional supervision and curriculum development. He can fill this role effectively if he has the training and experience and the time for the job. Some assistance is needed in the areas of business and personnel administration if the chief school official plans to coordinate the instructional program.

As indicated in the *Plan 1* chart (Figure 2), the principals are, in the total sense, educational leaders of their respective schools. They are responsible directly to the superintendent in all administrative and supervisory matters. This does not mean that the principals will have no

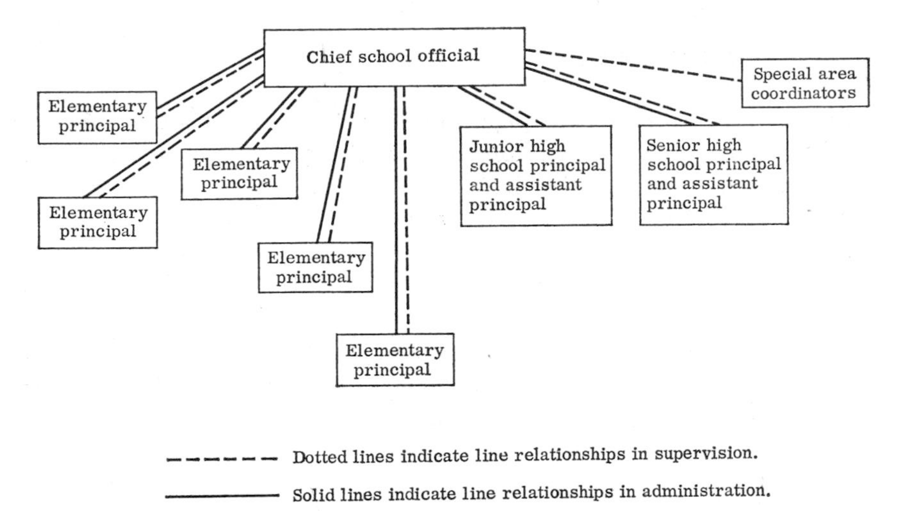

Fig. 2. Organization for Supervision—Plan 1. (All administrators are members of district administrative council.)

contact with other administrators. If the chief school official has administrative assistants, they will work closely with the building principals in such areas as attendance, selection and direction of custodians, and scheduling of buses. However, in this plan the primary line responsibility devolves from the superintendent to the principals.

Special-area coordinators in art, music, and physical education, for example, are directly responsible to the superintendent, and to the principal when working in a building. The chief school official coordinates their district-wide activities, and the principals work cooperatively with the specialists in scheduling and carrying out their programs in the various schools.

The district administrative council provides the key to the strong role of the school principals in the supervision and improvement of instruction. The chief school official usually chairs this group, which consists of all principals. On occasion assistant principals, secondary-school department heads (if any), special subject-area teachers or coordinators, and curriculum committee chairmen take part in administrative council meetings. All major issues affecting the instructional program are discussed by the council. The various principals assume group-delegated responsibilities on a district-wide level, such as organizing staff committees for curriculum study, conducting experimental research, and planning other in-service education programs. All of these activities are coordinated by the chief school official and the administrative council.

ADVANTAGES OF PLAN 1

1. The principals, who are closest to their staffs, pupils, and communities, have the main responsibilities in supervision of instruction. There is no intermediate line position between the chief school official and the principals. They have direct authority and responsibility.

2. The superintendent has the opportunity to coordinate directly the instructional program, and many experts say that this is, or should be, his main function.

3. Teachers work with a minimum of supervisory personnel, and thus should not be confused by a number of classroom visitors and coordinators. Furthermore, the table of organization is simple and should be easy to understand.

DISADVANTAGES OF PLAN 1

1. In a district of this size, the chief school official usually will not have the time necessary to be coordinator of instruction.

2. It is most difficult or impossible for a principal to have the perspective to understand district-wide problems, since his view is of necessity limited to one school and one portion of the total community.

3. Full-time building principals do not have time to be district curriculum coordinators, committee chairmen, and experimental research leaders. Furthermore, their background and experience often are not extensive enough to enable them to offer district-wide leadership in these areas.

4. The varied supervisory activities of an intermediate-size district need full-time coordination and leadership. Under *Plan 1,* no one has full-time responsibility for supervision of instruction.

Plan 2, as charted in the accompanying illustrations (Figures 3, 4, and 5), provides the following personnel for supervision.

1. Chief school official.
2. Assistant superintendent in charge of instruction

AND/OR

3. Coordinator of elementary education.
4. Coordinator of secondary education. (This position is occasionally found in larger intermediate districts.)
5. Full-time elementary-school principals.
6. Full-time secondary-school principals.
7. Full-time assistant principals in schools with more than 600 pupils.
8. Special-area coordinators (if any).

The three accompanying charts (Figures 3, 4, and 5) indicate possible organizational patterns for supervision of instruction in typical intermediate-size districts employing the personnel listed above. It can be seen that *Plan 2,* with its suggested variations, usually involves at least one line administrator or coordinator between the chief school official and the principals in the performance of the supervisory function.

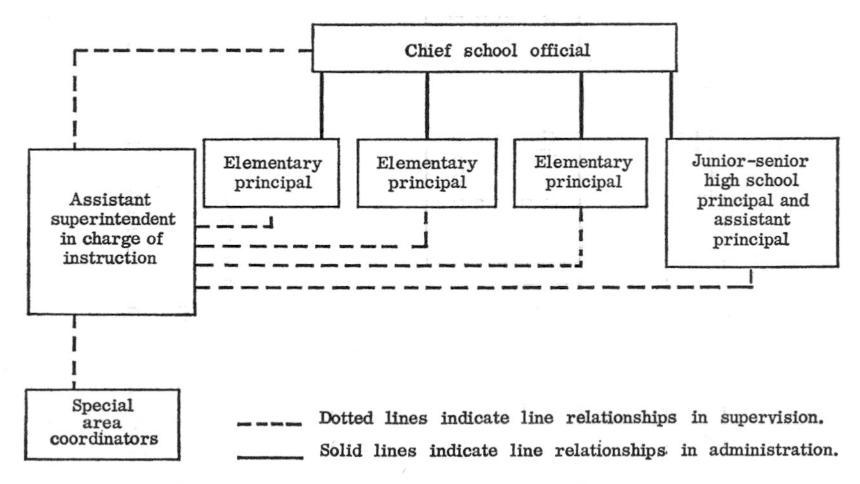

Fig. 3. Organization for Supervision—Plan 2. District with assistant superintendent in charge of instruction. (All administrators and coordinators are members of district administrative council.)

In *Plan 2,* the chief school official delegates considerable authority and responsibility to the assistant superintendent in charge of instruction, or to the coordinator of elementary education if there is no assistant superintendent. (In this instance, the chief school official continues to serve as the coordinator of the secondary-school program.) Curriculum coordination and development and the general improvement of classroom instruction are the areas usually assigned to these persons by the superintendent. In larger intermediate districts, there is a corresponding delegation of authority and responsibility from the assistant superintendent to the coordinator of elementary education and the coordinator of secondary education for their respective fields.

Although supervisory relationships are discussed in detail in Chapters V and VI, a brief summary of the function of the assistant superintendent in charge of instruction and the coordinators of elementary and secondary education follows.

1. They are both line and staff officers, but the line relationship is not overemphasized. They are responsible to their superior in the areas of

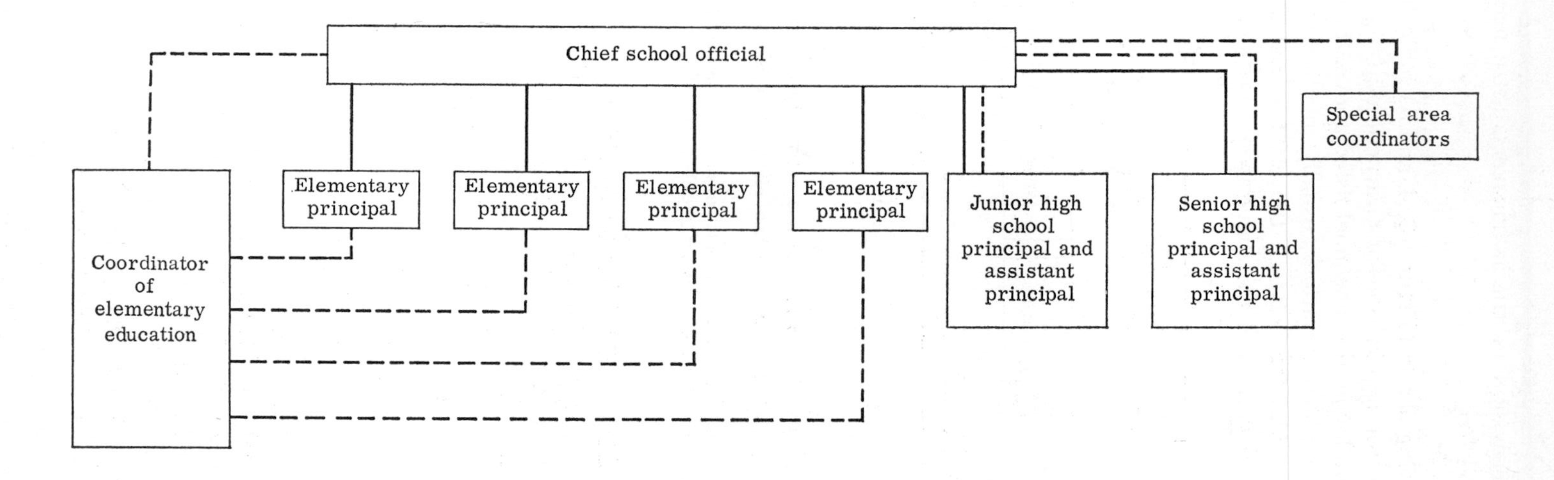

Fig. 4. Organization for Supervision—Plan 2. District with coordinator of elementary education. (All administrators and coordinators are members of district administrative council.)

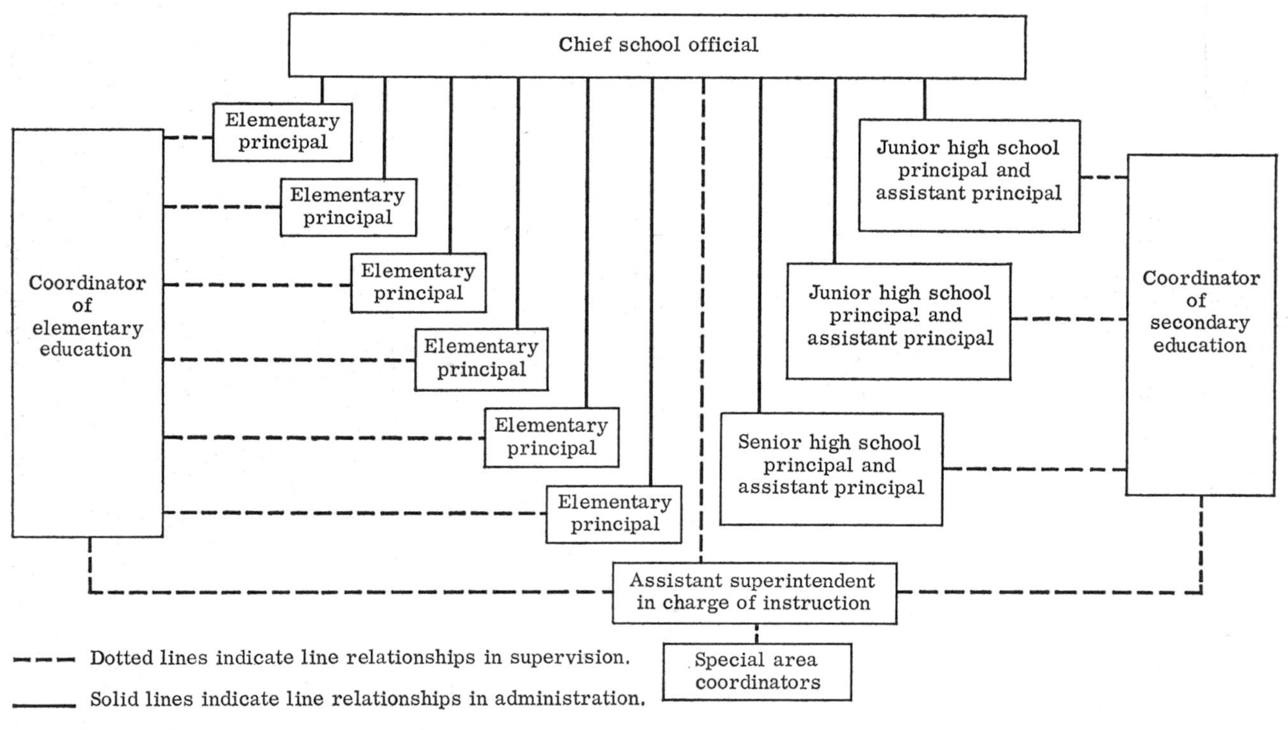

Fig. 5. Organization for Supervision—Plan 2. District with assistant superintendent in charge of instruction, coordinator of elementary education, and coordinator of secondary education. (All administrators and coordinators are members of district administrative council.)

curriculum and instruction. The principals are responsible to the coordinator or assistant superintendent (if any) in matters of curriculum and instruction but are directly responsible to the chief school official in administration.

2. The supervisory function is cooperative and democratic, and is shared under the over-all coordination of the assistant superintendent in charge of instruction or the coordinator of elementary education. In districts with no assistant superintendent or coordinator of secondary education, the chief school official himself will coordinate instruction with the principals at the secondary level. (See the organization charts above.) In such cases, the junior and senior high school principals are directly responsible to the superintendent in the areas of supervision *and* administration.

Regardless of the personnel available, all administrators and supervisors work together cooperatively in classroom visitation, curriculum development, other in-service program planning, workshops, and all other facets of the supervisory function.

3. The building principals are the educational leaders of their schools, exercising supervisory and administrative responsibility with their staffs. The assistant superintendent in charge of instruction and the coordinators (if any) work through and with the principals. They do not, however, participate in building administration, which is the province of the principal.

4. The assistant superintendent and the coordinators of elementary and secondary education serve also as resource persons who are on call to assist principals and classroom teachers in the improvement of instruction.

In *Plan 2*, then, at least one administrator or coordinator is assigned full-time responsibility for the instructional program. All supervisory functions are coordinated by the assistant superintendent in charge of instruction and/or the coordinators of elementary and secondary education, if these positions are filled.

The district administrative council is comprised of the chief school official, the assistant superintendent in charge of instruction, the coordinators of elementary and secondary education, and the elementary and secondary principals. At certain times the assistant principals, special-area coordinators, high school department heads (if any), curriculum committee chairmen, team leaders (if any) and other personnel play an active role in administrative council meetings. This group discusses and develops over-all district policy and guidelines for the supervision of the instructional program.

Under *Plan 2*, special-area coordinators (if any) are directly responsible to the chief school official or to the assistant superintendent in charge of instruction. Their function is primarily to provide coordination in the special areas they represent, and they are not line officers. When working in a school, they report directly to the principal and work as resource persons for teachers and administrators. (The role and function of the special supervisory personnel are detailed in Chapter VII.)

ADVANTAGES OF PLAN 2

1. The positions of assistant superintendent in charge of instruction and coordinators of elementary and secondary education are necessary for the most effective coordination of the total supervisory program, because these persons have district-wide perspective, kindergarten through twelfth grade. One of the most serious problems in American education today is the failure of elementary and junior and senior high schools to provide a unified, integrated K-12 program in a school district.
2. With the tremendous explosion of knowledge in our society, curriculum development and revision demand full-time attention. Superintendents and principals do not have enough time to devote to the instructional program, which is the heart of the school system. This plan provides experienced and well-educated leaders with the time needed for regular and efficient review of the district curriculum.
3. Curriculum research and resource materials can be obtained and utilized more effectively through a district office.

DISADVANTAGES OF PLAN 2

1. The building principal's authority must be shared in the areas of curriculum and improvement of instruction.
2. Problems may occur between principals and the assistant superintendent or the coordinators regarding areas of responsibility and authority. It is often difficult, for example, to separate administrative and supervisory functions, as noted in Chapter I.
3. The classroom teacher may not understand his relationship to all those who visit his classroom and who direct the in-service and curriculum-development programs.

In selecting a plan of organization for supervision, a district must consider its objectives, its personnel, and its aspirations for improvement of instruction in the future. The qualifications and personalities of present and prospective administrators and coordinators will help determine, to a large extent, the nature of the evolving supervisory organization.

ORGANIZING FOR SUPERVISION

In any intermediate-size district, the administrative council plays an important role in the coordinated K-12 program of instruction. Here is provided the opportunity for the chief school official or the assistant superintendent in charge of instruction to lead the executive team in policy decisions, in the development of district philosophy, and in the planning of various supervisory activities. The superintendent is involved at least to this extent in supervision, and he is therefore aware of any contemplated major changes or improvements in the school program.

The council includes the personnel previously listed plus the administrators of any elementary or secondary feeder districts who send pupils on a tuition or contract basis.

The administrative council functions are as follows:

1. The areas of district-wide responsibility and concern in the instructional program, and the corresponding limits of the individual building principals' authority must be determined. The district framework should be flexible enough to permit considerable latitude in principal-teacher interaction at the building level. Each professional employee needs to have a certain independence in his classroom or building, but each must also feel himself to be an integral part of the total district effort in the improvement of instruction.

For example, a fifth-grade teacher may want to initiate individualized reading in his classroom. May he do this independently; in consultation with his principal; or only after discussion with the coordinator of elementary education (if any) or the administrative council?

To take another case, are field-study trips planned by the classroom teacher; the building principal and his staff; or by these persons and others in the district?

2. General limits of authority and responsibility must be established so that all members of the supervisory staff are enabled to function effectively as team members. Job descriptions should be written, although it is recognized that these are only guides. Again, it is important to have broad-minded, competent personnel who share modern democratic concepts of supervision.

3. The administrative council approves all plans for in-service work, including curriculum development, to insure coordination of district activities.

4. All matters pertaining to supervision of instruction clear through the council. Agenda items are suggested by teachers, the chief school

official, or any member of the council. There is constant communication between the individual school faculties and their principals regarding agenda topics. All professional staff members have ample opportunity to react to proposals before these are finally accepted by the administrative council.

To illustrate the organization and function of supervision in the intermediate-size district, we have selected the Chatham Borough Schools, Chatham, New Jersey, and the Ridley Township School District, located in fast-growing Delaware County, Pennsylvania, immediately adjacent to Philadelphia.

THE CHATHAM BOROUGH SCHOOLS, CHATHAM, NEW JERSEY, ORGANIZE FOR SUPERVISION [1]

Chatham Borough is a residential suburban community composed of homes, whose occupants work mainly in New York City, Newark, New Jersey, and surrounding communities. The Borough has an area of approximately two square miles. The present general population of 10,000 has increased from 7300 during the last 10 years. The school enrollment of 2300 in grades 1 through 12 includes 360 nonresident children accepted on a tuition basis from a neighboring system. The majority of Chatham's tax revenue is secured from medium-sized homes, for there is practically no industry in the Borough. The average income of the community is estimated to be $14,000 per family.

In terms of school-plant facilities, there are three elementary schools housing kindergarten and two sections each of grades 1 through 6. One building was built in 1910, the second in 1949, and the most recent one in 1953. One junior high school serves the needs of the entire community, housing grades 7 through 9. This school was constructed in 1922, and an addition was built in 1936. The one senior high school was constructed in 1956 and houses grades 10 through 12.

There are 149 professional employees, including the superintendent, three elementary-school principals, one junior high school principal, one senior high school principal, and an assistant senior high school principal. Other staff members include the equivalent of seven guidance counselors, a director of physical education and health, and two remedial teachers. This provides a ratio of one professional person for each 15.4 pupils in grades K-12.

---

[1] Written by Jason F. Dreibelbis, Elementary Principal, Chatham Borough Schools, Chatham, New Jersey.

In a select community like Chatham Borough, the superintendent and board of education are in the fortunate situation of being able to truly *choose* professional employees who ultimately serve the community through the schools. Every teacher and principal is carefully selected for professional competence and leadership qualities which will contribute to the philosophy of meeting individual differences of the children attending the schools. Superintendent Noble C. Hiebert believes that there is need for considerable staff interaction. Therefore, a district such as Chatham Borough must select those people who display sound educational philosophy and the ability to work together for the common good of the entire school system. "Carefully selected personnel" is the credo of the district.

Superintendent Hiebert and Elementary Principal Jason F. Dreibelbis describe the system's approach to supervision as a direct, close working relationship between the chief school administrator and the principals. Superintendent Hiebert maintains a personal, face-to-face relationship with the principals of the system and encourages the discussion of items concerning curriculum and supervision.

As one reads the board of education policy manual containing the written job descriptions for the three types of principals, the supervisory philosophy is brought out by two statements. The first is: "The principal is the educational leader of the school to which he is assigned." The second statement is: "The principal is responsible to the superintendent for the educational program of the individual school." This, in capsule form, is the plan of supervision of the Chatham Borough Schools.

When one has a small, closely knit administrative organization such as that found in Chatham Borough, all members of the team, the superintendent and the various principals, become involved in the total supervisory program. In a true team concept, the principal handles the direct supervision, working out a program to meet the educational needs of the boys and girls of his school. The superintendent has an expressed desire to be kept informed on the supervisory program and frequently requests the principals to discuss with him the details concerning the program's status. These conferences particularly concern those staff members who are new to the system and philosophy of Chatham Borough or experienced members who present various problems which need close supervision.

The two remedial teachers, one primary and the other intermediate, were selected because of a superior job they had done as classroom teachers and because they had additional training in elementary-school guidance, remedial reading, and psychological techniques. They are directly responsible to the principals and do not supervise teachers. The assignment of the remedial teachers involves work in the three elementary schools to insure that individual differences in children are being met by the classroom teachers. These remedial teachers analyze the individual difficulties and make specific recommendations to the regular teachers for classroom use. Furthermore, background is developed for their own remedial work with the child. They also work with small groups of children, giving remedial help. During the summer, the remedial teachers are employed to perform statistical studies and analyses of the achievement and intellectual testing programs. These studies are used by the superintendent and the principals to plan for and implement the over-all program for the elementary schools.

The superintendent's administrative council meets at least once each month—more often, if necessary—upon the call of the superintendent. The members of this group are the five principals and the superintendent. Problems which involve other school personnel require individual meetings with the principals concerned, and applicable facts are presented to the administrative council for combined action. The superintendent prepares an agenda several days in advance and distributes it through the intra-district mail to each principal. This gives each person an opportunity to collect data and information concerning the topics to be discussed. Issues are debated and discussed in these meetings, but group decisions prevail and are always made on the basis of what is best for the children of the Chatham Borough Schools.

The superintendent is closely involved in the supervisory program of the schools. It is through individual conferences with the principals that he is kept informed concerning the status of the supervisory program. Advice, based on his over-all concept of the program, is freely given, and, through the common philosophy expressed above, the superintendent is able to build a system which is consistent throughout. It is through these conferences and the administrative council that coordination of the program, kindergarten through grade 12, is maintained. The leadership of the superintendent is expressed through the program which the principals conduct in the individual schools. The principal is the leader of the educational program; the superintendent is the coordinator and the chief adviser. The Chatham Borough superintendent considers this his first duty: building a strong school system through the improvement of instruction and the supervision of a select instructional staff.

Chatham Borough School District, with a board of education of nine college graduates, has for a long period of time demonstrated its concern for a good instructional program, and is providing the necessary leadership for effective supervision.

THE RIDLEY TOWNSHIP SCHOOLS, FOLSOM, PENNSYLVANIA, ORGANIZE FOR SUPERVISION

Ridley Township, a residential suburban community of homes and light industry, has experienced very rapid growth since World War II. The present general population is over 36,000 and the school enrollment of 5,000 pupils (grades 1-12) has doubled in the last ten years. There are no unusual sources of wealth in the community. In fact, many of the tax-producing units are small or medium-sized homes with modest assessments.

In terms of school-plant facilities, three of the eight existing elementary schools were built since 1951. There is one new junior high school serving grades 7 through 9, and one senior high school, the capacity of which has been doubled in recent years. Also, three of the elementary plants have been expanded to handle increasing enrollments.

There are over 250 professional employees, including the superintendent, assistant superintendent, elementary supervisor, five full-time elementary principals, junior high school principal, senior high school principal, and an assistant principal for each of the secondary schools. Other staff members include a reading consultant, a director of vocational education, and a supervisor of guidance who also serves as school psychologist.

Superintendent Robert V. Donato and Assistant Superintendent John W. O'Brien describe their approach to supervision as a three-dimensional team effort, involving all professional staff members. Furthermore, they believe it is impossible to express in flat chart form the nature of their staff relationships. Every teacher, supervisor, and administrator is recognized as possessing certain leadership qualities that contribute in one way or another to the improvement of instruction.

Superintendent Donato believes that it is essential to have the right person in each job; therefore, careful selection of administrative, supervisory, and classroom personnel is a key tenet of district policy. This is most important when people are expected to work in the type of relationship that defies graphic expression on a line-and-staff chart.

The following statement from the written district policy, *Administrative Organization and Operation,* typifies Ridley Township's philosophy: "The superintendent and assistant superintendent attempt to function as a team. It is their belief that it is difficult to determine a dichotomy between any two functions related to administrative responsibility. All are related, in a sense, like the warp and woof of cloth. Even though the team concept is evident in most administrative functions, the assistant superintendent takes a more active part in curriculum coordination, in in-service training, and in procurement of educational supplies, equipment, and apparatus related to the curriculum program. He also serves in an advisory capacity in searching for the solution of problems relating to school planning, school construction, school maintenance and operation, and personnel problems."

The assistant superintendent works very closely with the elementary supervisor and the two secondary principals to insure a coordinated approach to curriculum and other aspects of the improvement of instruction.

"The building principal occupies the key role in the whole educational program," according to Ridley Township's policy statement. "His principal function is to provide a continuing effort to strengthen, enrich and improve the whole instructional program. He discharges this responsibility as he stimulates, organizes and works with his own staff to discern, attack and seek solutions to problems relating to the whole educational program."

The elementary supervisor, working directly with the elementary principals, the reading consultant, and the supervisor of guidance, is responsible for the coordination of the elementary-school program. They meet twice monthly, with the supervisor as chairman, to plan curriculum studies and in-service training of teachers, to consider possible policy changes, and to "plumb the feelings of teachers as reflected by their principals." These meetings also serve as in-service training sessions for all elementary principals. The assistant superintendent often attends—for example, when the agenda calls for decisions on changes in the curriculum.

The elementary supervisor works with individual teachers in a staff relationship on problems relating to method and classroom practice. He assumes this function via the building principals.

The superintendent's cooperative planning committee meets every other week and "serves as a clearing house for all activities related to the instructional program." (This corresponds to the district administrative council suggested in this chapter.) The standing members are: the superintendent, assistant superintendent, elementary supervisor, high school principal, assistant high school principal, junior high school principal, assistant junior high school principal, supervisor of guidance services, guidance counselors, and the reading consultant. Usually one or two elementary principals attend, and they all are there when needed for agenda items concerning them or their program. "Subjects to be discussed or reviewed largely determine the number or selection of representatives to be invited to any particular meeting." The full committee on occasion may include teachers from any level, the school doctor, dental hygienist, or school nurse. In other words, if certain staff members are to be involved in a planning-committee decision or discussion, they or their representatives have an opportunity to attend. Minutes of each meeting are distributed to all professional employees, who may then react to proposals or contemplated policy changes before the next meeting. Final decisions are rarely made at any meeting on items presented for the first time. Regular and invited members of the planning committee gain perspective through the many discussons of learning activities and problems.

All members of the supervisory team at Ridley Township have a clear understanding of their roles in the process of improving instruction, and they all work diligently and cooperatively to fulfill them. The possible merits and deficiencies of new trends in classroom teaching are debated with vigor, and yet each person respects the professional integrity of the others. Principals are identified as *the* key individuals in the supervisory process, working closely with their teaching staffs in all phases of instruction. Behind the strong school lies the fundamental concept of a coordinated district-wide program for students in grades 1 through 12. To this end Assistant Superintendent John O'Brien and Elementary Supervisor George Noel devote their full-time energies. A vital, contemporary, and challenging curriculum is the result.

The Ridley Township community, by electing a dedicated board of school directors, has consistently demonstrated its interest in good education. With an average tax base and normal fiscal problems, this school district is providing the personnel and resources necessary for a well-balanced, sound program of instruction. Superintendent Robert Donato is proud of his professional staff and the job they do with their students. And Ridley Township is indeed fortunate to have a chief school administrator who knows how to organize and direct his team for effective instructional leadership.

SUMMARY

The intermediate-size district is usually found in fast-growing suburban areas and in rural regions where reorganization of school systems is under way. A total enrollment of approximately 1,000 to 6,000 pupils from kindergarten through high school identifies this size district. In terms of plant facilities, there are generally three or more complete-unit elementary schools and at least one junior high and one senior high school.

The elementary teaching staff will number approximately 25 to 125. At the secondary level, there might be as many as 115 teachers, with considerable variation possible owing to the size of the student body, the organization of the curriculum, and any special services provided.

There are at least two major points of view regarding the selection and organization of administrative and supervisory personnel in the intermediate-size district. Under *Plan 1,* the superintendent assumes the responsibility for district-wide coordination of instructional supervision and curriculum development. The principals are, in the total sense, educational leaders of their respective schools, reporting directly to the chief school official in all administrative and supervisory matters.

Plan 2 usually involves at least one line administrator or coordinator between the superintendent and the principals in the performance of the supervisory function. Under this plan, the chief school official delegates considerable authority and responsibility to an assistant superintendent in charge of instruction or to a coordinator of elementary education, for example. The principals are then responsible to the coordinator or assistant superintendent in the areas of curriculum and instruction but are directly responsible to the chief school official in administration. The supervisory function is cooperative and democratic, and is shared. The building principals are the educational leaders of their schools, exercising supervisory and administrative responsibility with their staffs. However, in *Plan 2,* it is recognized that at least one administrator or coordinator is assigned full-time responsibility for the coordination of instruction on a district-wide basis.

The administrative council plays an important role in coordinating the K-12 program. All supervisors and administrators are members, and other persons are invited to participate on occasion. Council functions include the determination of areas of district-wide concern in the instructional program and the corresponding limits of the authority of building principals. The framework should be flexible enough to permit considerable latitude in principal-teacher interaction. Each professional employee needs to have a certain independence in his classroom or building, but each must also feel himself to be an integral part of the total district effort in the improvement of instruction. Also, general limits of authority and responsibility should be established and job descriptions written as guides to action. The administrative council approves all plans for in-service work, including curriculum development, to insure coordination of district activities. In fact, all matters pertaining to the supervision of instruction clear through the council. Agenda items may be suggested by teachers, the chief school official, or any member of the council. Everyone has ample opportunity to react to proposals before final action is taken.

The intermediate-size district has the potential to organize effectively for supervision. The results will be determined primarily by the quality of the educational leadership at the building and district level.

SUGGESTED ACTIVITIES AND PROBLEMS

1. Locate an intermediate-size school district in your area and carry out the following projects:
   - A. Describe the characteristics of the district in a short summary.
   - B. Interview the superintendent or assistant superintendent in charge of instruction and explore in depth the district philosophy of supervision and the organization for improvement of instruction. Be sure to identify the roles of all personnel who have any supervisory responsibilities. Write up your findings.

2. In a short paper, prove the superiority of either *Plan 1* or *Plan 2* as a method of organizing for supervision. Document your conclusions from:
   - A. Interviews with supervisory personnel.
   - B. Supplementary reading.
   - C. Your own experience, if pertinent.

3. Outline the main functions of a district administrative council. Who should belong to this group? What is the role of the superintendent? Name some typical agenda items and show why they are appropriate for council consideration.

SELECTED READINGS

Burnham, Reba M., and Martha L. King, *Supervision in Action.* Washington, D.C.: Association for Supervision and Curriculum Development, National Education Association, 1961.

Current Practice in Administrative Staffing in New York State. Albany, N.Y.: Cooperative Development of Public School Administration in New York State, 1955.

Department of Elementary School Principals, "The Principal and Supervision," *Elementary School Principalship,* Thirty-Seventh Yearbook, Part 1, pp. 13-31. Washington, D.C.: Research Division, National Education Association, 1958.

Liebman, Malvina W., "The Principal as Instructional Supervisor," *Elementary School Principalship,* Thirty-Seventh Yearbook, Part 2, pp. 32-36. Washington, D.C.: Department of Elementary School Principals, National Education Association, 1958.

Modern Practices and Concepts of Staffing Schools. Albany, N.Y.: Cooperative Development of Public School Administration in New York State, 1956.

chapter four

Organization and Function of Supervision in Larger Districts

As more and more states pass and implement school district reorganization laws, the size of school districts in the United States will increase, with an accompanying reduction in the number of separate entities. These larger school districts of the nation are at present found in cities and in suburban communities with a large geographic area and a rapid growth pattern. The authors recognize that the largest city school systems in the country require more detailed organizational patterns for supervision than will be presented in this chapter. Nevertheless, the discussion here will be applicable to them to a large degree. This section, then, will be mainly concerned with supervision in large districts that are smaller than the ten or more very populous city school systems in the nation.

CHARACTERISTICS OF LARGER DISTRICTS

The school districts included in this category are those in the nation which enroll approximately 6,000 or more pupils on all levels, kindergarten through grade 12. This obviously covers a lot of territory. As suggested in Chapter III, some school districts with enrollments of 6,000 or more should, because of other characteristics, be considered as intermediate rather than large districts. Administrators and supervisors from these borderline units also should consult Chapter III.

School-Plant Facilities

The districts under discussion would have six or more elementary-school buildings and three or more secondary-school plants. When population growth results in the need for more than 15 elementary schools and six or more secondary-school plants, the feasibility of sub-districting for administrative and supervisory purposes should be studied.

Staff Requirements

Staff requirements for school districts of the same pupil population vary tremendously, depending upon extent of offerings, class size, and quantity and quality of administrative, supervisory, and special services.[1]

> The basic beliefs of the citizenry as interpreted by its board of education are the most important determiners of what services are considered essential. There is ample evidence that the citizens of a school district can and will have those educational services they feel are essential. The scope of a school system's offerings reflects the citizens' concepts of how essential services are.[2]

Regular and special teachers. The total elementary teaching staff would include 125 or more regular classroom teachers, and usually the number would fall within the range of 200 to 300 teachers. Special teachers or coordinators in art, music, physical education, and possibly other areas, such as science, foreign languages, and guidance, might serve each school or be shared by several buildings. Certain plans of elementary-school organization which are becoming popular in some school districts might require specialists in each area of the curriculum.

---

[1] For suggestions on staffing, see Howard Morris, Jr., *Staffing Schools for Essential Services* (Philadelphia: Temple University, Philadelphia Area School Study Council, Campus Division, 1957).

[2] *Ibid.*, p. ii.

The secondary-school staff in this size district would be adequate to provide a comprehensive program in all curricula, including guidance and other special services. The total teaching staff at the secondary level would include over 115 individuals, and usually the number would fall between 150 and 250 teachers. In the most populous areas, the secondary-school teaching staff would, of course, be much larger.

Administrative and supervisory personnel. Because of the wide range included in this category of school districts, the number of administrative and supervisory personnel also will vary greatly. However, the positions will be similar regardless of the number of buildings in the district. The following personnel would be essential for effective supervision of instruction in a larger school district:

1. Superintendent of schools.
2. Assistant superintendent in charge of instruction (sometimes designated as curriculum coordinator K-12).
3. Coordinator of elementary education.
4. Coordinator of secondary education.
5. Full-time, non-teaching principals for each elementary school of 12 or more teachers. If the staff exceeds 25, a full-time assistant principal should be provided.
6. One full-time principal for each secondary school. As previously stated, when the enrollment of any secondary school exceeds 600, a full-time assistant principal should be provided for each additional 600 pupils or 25 teachers, or major fraction thereof.
7. One part-time department head for each department or a team coordinator or leader if team teaching is employed. Some districts would prefer subject-area consultants to serve in this capacity.

The assistant superintendent in charge of instruction and the coordinators of elementary education and secondary education would work almost exclusively in the area of curriculum development and the coordination and improvement of instruction. They would not normally be involved in administrative matters.

In this size school district, the superintendent of schools would be kept fully informed on supervisory matters, but he would have little time to participate actively in supervisory activities. However, he plays a very important behind-the-scenes role.

The principals and assistant principals would be responsible for both the administration of their buildings and participation in the various phases of the supervisory programs. They would be considered in all respects the educational leaders of their respective schools. It is important to emphasize here that under no circumstances should they be bypassed by any of the general supervisory personnel in the development and execution of the supervisory program.

The qualifications for and the analysis of these positions are found in Chapters V and VI.

ORGANIZING FOR SUPERVISION

Although the superintendent has the final responsibility to the board of education for the instructional program, he will delegate to the assistant superintendent in charge of instruction the major responsibility and authority for the district-wide improvement and coordination of the instructional program. The coordinators of elementary and secondary education will assist in this role.

The principals, as educational leaders at the building level, will with their teaching staffs assume responsibility for the improvement of instruction in their buildings and see that the district-wide curriculum plan is implemented. This requires that all principals operate within a cooperatively developed framework of district-wide policy. The formulation of district-wide policy will involve the assistant superintendent, the two coordinators, and the building principals in cooperative planning. In all areas involving curriculum change and the improvement of instruction on a district-wide basis, the principals and the two coordinators work under the democratic leadership of the assistant superintendent.

At the elementary level, additional district-wide policy is determined by the principals working under the leadership of the coordinator of elementary education. District-wide policy on the secondary level would likewise be formulated by the secondary principals under the direction of the coordinator on this level.

It is very important that all line-and-staff relationships be carefully defined in an organization of this scope (see Chapters V and VI). Although the line organization is not to be overstressed, it must exist to provide the framework for over-all district-wide policy, which is essential to insure a highly organized and well-coordinated program of instruction. The larger the organization, the more difficult it is to make it operate as planned.

The following controls have been suggested to insure smooth functioning of the line-and-staff type of organization:

1. The *first* and simplest control is that of the coöperatively formulated general framework within which all are working.
2. The *second* is the coöperatively determined policy and distribution of shared duties set up especially for any given project. . . .

3. The *third* control is the recognition by any honest and sensible person that he loses the respect and confidence of his co-workers and actually destroys his own effectiveness if he ignores all controls.
4. The *fourth* control is (based on the theory that all) individuals will need to possess firm and lasting belief in the democratic process and be determined to uphold it by working within its self-assumed obligations.[3]

These relationships are developed in greater detail in subsequent chapters. It will suffice here to describe the organizational pattern of one rather large school district to illustrate the concepts expressed in this chapter. The reader should note that several of the titles are different from those which the writers have suggested. Nevertheless, they serve similar functions.

SCHOOL CITY OF GARY ORGANIZES FOR SUPERVISION AND CURRICULUM IMPROVEMENT

Gary, Indiana is an industrial city with a general population of approximately 180,000 and a public school enrollment of 45,824 pupils in grades K-12. This represents an increase of 19,889 pupils in the last ten years. The average income of the community is estimated to be $6,507 per family.

During the same ten years, 22 new elementary schools and two new junior high schools have been constructed, and one elementary school has been converted into a junior high.[4] At present there are 31 elementary schools, three junior high schools (6-8, 7-8, 7-9), and eight buildings with senior high school grades. However, only two of them have grades 9-12 exclusively. One building houses grades K-12 and five buildings each enroll grades 7-12.

There are approximately 1,864 professional employees, including the superintendent, three assistant superintendents, a general secondary supervisor, a general elementary supervisor, four elementary supervisors, one secondary supervisor, 56 elementary- and secondary-school principals, seven subject-area consultants, and six special-area supervisors.

For many years the Gary Schools were organized on the platoon system, and secondary-school buildings housed grades K-12. Beginning in 1956, under the leadership of Superintendent A. H. Blankenship, the

[3] A. S. Barr, William H. Burton, and Leo J. Brueckner, *Supervision, Democratic Leadership in the Improvement of Learning* (New York: Appleton-Century-Crofts, Inc., 1947), p. 103. (Copyright, 1938, 1947, D. Appleton-Century Company, Inc.)

[4] Twenty-five additions were also built to existing schools in the past ten years.

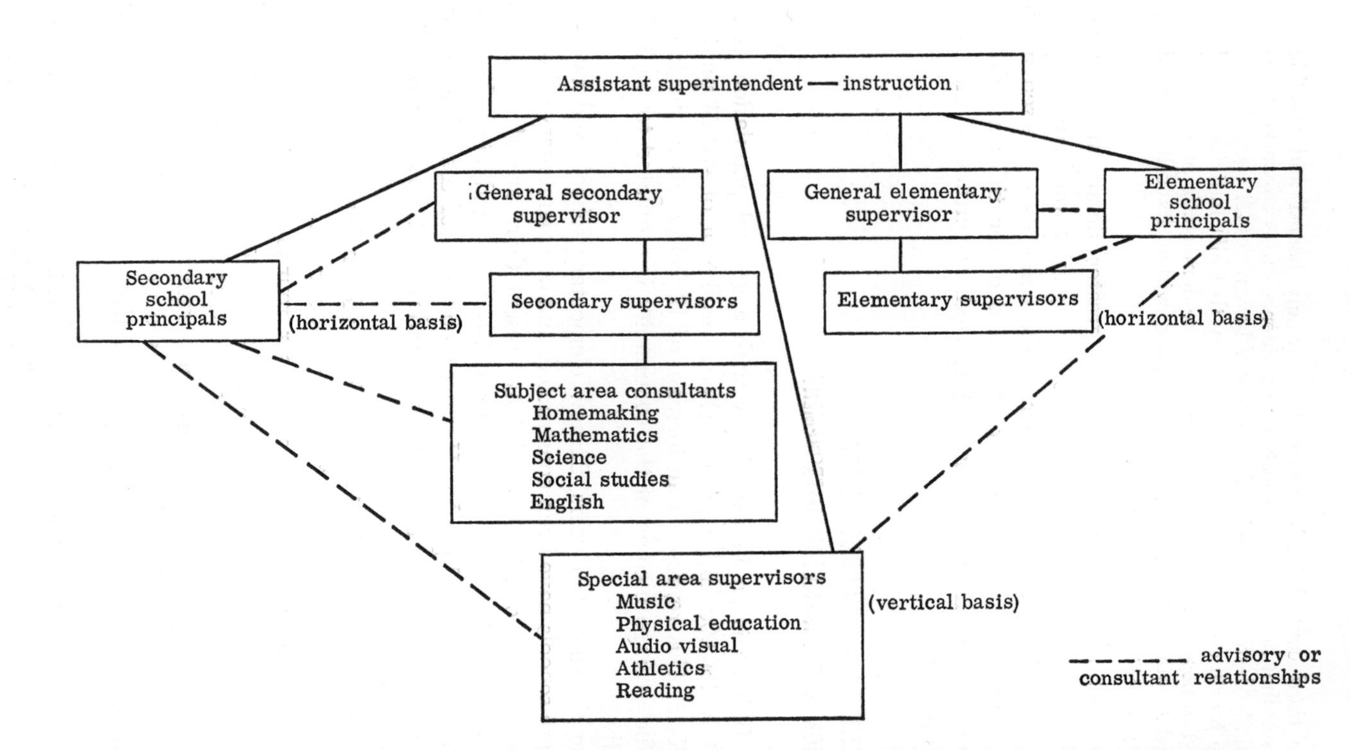

Fig. 6. Supervisory Organization for Gary (Indiana) City Schools. (Reproduced by permission of the Gary (Indiana) City Schools.)

schools were reorganized and the platoon system discontinued as rapidly as new buildings could be constructed.

By means of a careful plan of recruitment and selection, a supervisory staff of dedicated individuals has been assembled. Figure 6 displays Gary's plan of staff organization for the improvement of the curriculum and instruction. The next section of this chapter will be devoted to job descriptions of the assistant superintendent, general elementary supervisor, general secondary supervisor, elementary supervisors, and secondary supervisor as found in the School City of Gary.

Position: Assistant Superintendent in Charge of Instruction
Directly Responsible to: Superintendent of Schools
Responsible for: Secondary Supervision, Secondary Schools, Elementary Supervision, Elementary Schools, Special Area Supervision (athletics and recreation, physical education and health, music, homemaking, audio-visual, and secretarial service)

Outline of Functions

I. To provide leadership to the instructional program by:
   A. Maintaining educational policies and practices in accord with the policies of the Board of School Trustees, the State of Indiana, and educational accrediting agencies.
   B. Guiding the process of curriculum development.
   C. Guiding the selection, preparation and allocation of instructional materials.
   D. Guiding the processes for evaluating and improving instruction.
   E. Guiding the professional staff development program.
   F. Guiding the program for interpretation of the instructional program to the community.

II. To administer the instructional program by:
   A. Assigning the duties of the elementary and secondary supervisors.
   B. Recommending assignments for certificated personnel to the Superintendent in accordance with established policies and procedures.
   C. Reviewing requests for transfers of personnel from one school to another and recommending appropriate action to the Superintendent.
   D. Recommending the promotion of personnel to the Superintendent.
   E. Directing the placement of substitute teachers.
   F. Participating in the preparation of the annual budget with specific responsibility for the portion related to the instructional program.
   G. Directing the orientation of new teachers.
   H. Reviewing grievances and problems of staff relationships.
   I. Preparing current supply catalogs in cooperation with the Purchasing Department and such other staff members as may be involved.

III. To coordinate the instructional program by:
  A. Determining the apportionment of the instructional budget to assure suitable services, materials, and supplies for each school.
  B. Allocating instructional personnel to the schools.
  C. Directing the work of the instructional supervisors.
  D. Reviewing the recommendations of curriculum committees.
  E. Providing for regular meetings of the principals for review of instructional matters.
  F. Providing lists of approved instructional materials for use in the schools.
  G. Relating the needs of the instructional program to all other needs of the school system.
  H. Coordinating the Student Teaching program.
  I. Supervising the administration of policies affecting the coordination and control of student personnel.

IV. To assume other general responsibilities including:
  A. To act for the Superintendent in his absence.
  B. Maintaining adequate pupil and staff library services.
  C. Serving as military property custodian.
  D. Coordinating the work of committees appointed for special purposes.

V. To perform such other related duties as may be assigned by the Superintendent.

Position: General Elementary Supervisor
Directly Responsible to: Assistant Superintendent in Charge of Instruction
Responsible for: Elementary Education K-6 except Music and Physical Education

Outline of Functions

I. To provide leadership in the elementary instructional program of the School City of Gary.
  A. By supervising the total program for grades K-6, e.g.:
    1. Demonstrating teaching techniques.
    2. Assisting principals and teachers with individual problems.
    3. Sharing in the orientation of new teachers.
    4. Assisting principals and teachers in assessing and meeting needs.
    5. Visiting all the elementary schools at regular intervals and on request of the principals, teachers, Assistant Superintendent, and Superintendent.
    6. Working with principals and teachers in the improvement of the instructional program, e.g.:
      a. Conducting meetings building-wide, division-wide, and city-wide.
      b. Working with special committees in such areas as instructional materials, in testing, in language arts, in social studies, in science, in arithmetic, and in art.
      c. Sponsoring the work of Association for Childhood Education, Gary Council of the International Reading Association, and Kindergarten-Elementary Council.

d. Providing consultant services to principals and teachers.
e. Evaluating and improving a comprehensive language arts program, e.g.:
(1) Helping teachers and principals organize a developmental skill program in reading.
(2) Helping teachers and principals organize their reading programs on a co-basal plan of instruction.
(3) Helping teachers plan, develop, and evaluate their total Language Arts programs.
(a) Demonstrating the use of formal and informal tests as related to listening, speaking, reading readiness, reading, and writing.
(b) Helping teachers plan their instructional programs.
(c) Demonstrating good reading lessons and language lessons, as well as classroom management of class groups and small groups.

7. Conferring with teachers regarding special reading problems.
8. Providing services for professional improvement.

B. By assuming sole responsibility as listed above for:
1. The specific elementary schools as assigned by the Assistant Superintendent and the Superintendent.
2. The Helping Art Teachers.
3. The Individual Developmental Reading Teachers.
4. The Instructional Materials Coordinators.

II. To administer the elementary instructional program of the School City of Gary by such activities as:
A. Interpreting instructional problems arising in the elementary schools to the administrative staff, the supervisory staff, and the community.
B. Providing consultant services on organizational instructional problems of the elementary school.
C. Assigning and coordinating the work of student teachers.
D. Assisting the Assistant Superintendent in the selection of new members of the teaching staff.
1. Assist in recruiting and interviewing new staff members.
E. Developing the annual budget as related to the elementary educational program.
F. Preparing such reports and bulletins and keeping the necessary records requested by the Assistant Superintendent and the Superintendent.
1. Weekly reports for the Assistant Superintendent and the Superintendent.
2. An annual report.
3. Reports of results of pre-kindergarten tests.
4. Bulletins necessary to the improvement of the elementary instructional program.

III. To coordinate the activities of the elementary instructional program.
A. Coordinating the work of the elementary supervisors.
B. Coordinating the work of the following special committees: (1)

Language Arts, (2) Arithmetic, (3) Social Studies, (4) Science, (5) Art, (6) Instructional Materials, and (7) Individual Developmental Reading.

C. Coordinating the selection of the best available materials in all curriculum areas.

D. Coordinating the preparation, the writing, and the revision of all elementary instructional guides.

E. Coordinating the writing and revision of all elementary informal tests.

F. Coordinating the organization and work of the Instructional Materials Coordinators, Helping Art Teachers, and Individual Developmental Reading Teachers.

G. Working with principals and other staff members in making recommendations with respect to building and equipment needs.

H. Coordinating the pre-kindergarten testing program.

I. Identifying the needs and planning with teachers, principals, other supervisors, Assistant Superintendent, and the Superintendent for a professional in-service development program for elementary teachers.

1. Activities of the Elementary Council (composed of teachers, principals, supervisors, the Assistant Superintendent, and the Superintendent), such as:

a. Improvement activities for the elementary school, such as revision of report cards, preparation of the cumulative classroom record card, and studying "the gifted."

b. Methods of interpreting improvement to the elementary staff and community.

2. Problems in individual schools.

IV. To assume other general related responsibilities.

A. Conferring with representatives of book companies.

B. Attending professional meetings.

C. Participating in professional meetings at the local, state, and national level.

Position: General Supervisor of Secondary Education
Directly Responsible to: Assistant Superintendent in Charge of Instruction
Responsible for: Academic, Industrial Arts, Business Education, Art, and Library areas of the secondary program

Outline of Functions

I. To provide leadership for improving the instructional program through:

A. Development of the curriculum by:

1. Being responsible for the coordination of the supervisory activities of secondary education.

2. Working with individual teachers.

a. Observing classroom instruction.

b. Discussing improved methods and techniques.

c. Exploring teacher problems.

d. Sharing ideas based on the experience and study of other professional people.

3. Working with principals.
   a. Discussing the scheduling of new subject offerings in individual buildings.
   b. Reviewing problems of teachers and giving suggestions for help.
   c. Participating in principals' meetings in curriculum development.
4. Working with teacher coordinators.
   a. Developing courses of study.
   b. Reviewing individual teacher problems.
   c. Identifying problem situations which require additional help.

B. Development of instructional materials and facilities by:
1. Advising teachers and principals on selection of materials such as textbooks, audio-visual aids, brochures, practice materials for drill work, etc.
2. Developing textbook guides.
3. Developing a collection of professional books.
4. Identifying standards for equipment and facility needs.
5. Arranging for demonstration of new equipment, such as language laboratories, new developments in science equipment, etc.
6. Assisting in the selection of audio-visual equipment, such as new films, records, maps for specific subject areas, etc.
7. Preparing applications for federal or state aid, such as projects under Titles III and V, Public Law 85-864.
8. Assisting principals, teachers, and architects in the planning of specialized areas, such as shops, science rooms, counseling centers, libraries, foreign language laboratories, business education rooms, etc.
9. Preparing such orientation materials as sample four-year plan sheets, course description brochures, etc.
10. Reviewing budget requests in assigned areas through participation in budget committees.
11. Arranging for exhibits from business and community groups, such as Bell Telephone display, Remington Rand business machines exhibit, etc.

C. Development of professional staff by:
1. Visiting individual teachers in the classroom.
2. Conferring with teachers in regard to their instructional problems as needed.
3. Arranging for conferences with specialists in the field as consultants.
4. Interviewing teacher applicants.
5. Informing teachers about available scholarships, fellowships, institutes, etc.
6. Helping teachers become better acquainted with community resources through visits to industry, developing lists of resources, etc.
7. Helping teachers plan to meet the needs of individual students.

8. Helping teachers evaluate and improve instructional techniques and methods.

II. To facilitate the administration of the instructional program through:
   A. Being responsible for the professional duties of the supervisors of secondary education.
   B. Reviewing and approving textbook requisitions.
   C. Organizing and coordinating a student teacher training program in cooperation with various colleges.
   D. Organizing the orientation program for teachers new to the system.
   E. Being responsible for the professional duties of the teacher coordinators.
   F. Preparing and distributing materials for student orientation programs.
   G. Keeping the Assistant Superintendent of Schools informed as to progress of the instructional program.

III. To provide coordination for improving the instructional program through:
   A. Reviewing and revising the Curriculum Guide.
   B. Evaluating the present program of studies.
   C. Working with teacher committees in adopting textbooks.
   D. Working with teacher coordinators and teacher committees in developing courses of study.
   E. Utilizing the resources of research in evaluating student progress and determining curriculum needs.
   F. Working with teacher committees in developing differentiated programs for students with different levels of ability, such as accelerated programs in mathematics and science, special grouping in English, etc.

IV. To provide leadership in other related activities through:
   A. Organizing and coordinating system-wide programs, such as the Berg Science Seminars for gifted pupils conducted each week.
   B. Cooperating with community groups in the organization of city-wide activities, such as the student study tour to the United Nations in New York and foreign embassies in Washington, D. C., art contests conducted by local business groups, etc.
   C. Organizing other city-wide activities, such as career conferences, teen-age summer employment project, etc.
   D. Serving on committees for planning city-wide activities, such as convocation program, administrative workshop, summer school, etc.

V. To assume other general responsibilities as may be assigned.

Position: Elementary Supervisor
Directly Responsible to: General Elementary Supervisor
Responsible for: Elementary education K-6, except Music and Physical Education

Outline of Functions

I. To provide leadership in the elementary instructional program of the School City of Gary by:

A. Supervising instruction for grades K-6, in the schools assigned by:
   1. Demonstrating teaching techniques.
2. Assisting teachers in the schools assigned.
   a. Work with new teachers.
      (1) Plan and organize, with the General Elementary Supervisor, an orientation program consisting of:
         (a) General meeting of all new teachers.
         (b) Grade-level meetings with teachers relative to planning in general (long-range) and planning specifically good lessons in each area.
      (2) Provide informal conferences and demonstrations with principals and teachers individually and in small groups as a means of follow-up.
   b. Work with experienced teachers.
      (1) Programs related to specific goals are planned at the request of teachers and principals, with the supervisor helping in the assessment of needs.
   c. Help all teachers.
      (1) Plan informal group or individual conferences.
      (2) Demonstrate techniques of teaching related to a(1)(b) above.
      (3) Demonstrate techniques of teaching in all areas with individual teachers and small groups of teachers in a classroom situation.
      (4) Execute a follow-up program in all schools.
      (5) Develop cooperative procedures in the classroom.
      (6) Develop the use of the unit method of instruction.
      (7) Develop good guidance procedures.
      (8) Help teachers select, requisition, and use materials indicated in the recommended list.
      (9) Conduct city-wide workshops.
   d. Help student teachers.
      (1) Assist in assigning and coordinating the work of student teachers.
3. Visiting the elementary schools assigned at regular intervals and on the request of the principals, teachers, General Elementary Supervisor, Assistant Superintendent, and Superintendent.
4. Working with principals and teachers in the improvement of the instructional program, e.g.:
   a. Conducting meetings building-wide, division-wide, and city-wide.
   b. Working with special committees in such areas as instructional materials, in testing, in language arts, in social studies, in science, in arithmetic, and in art.
   c. Co-sponsoring the work of the Association for Childhood Education.
   d. Working with the Gary Council of the International Reading Association and the Kindergarten-Elementary Council.
   e. Providing consultant services to principals and teachers.

f. Evaluating and improving a comprehensive language arts program, e.g.:
   (1) Helping teachers and principals organize a developmental skill program in reading.
   (2) Helping teachers and principals organize their reading programs on a co-basal plan of instruction.
   (3) Helping teachers plan, develop, and evaluate their total language arts programs.
      (a) Demonstrating the use of formal and informal tests as related to listening, speaking, reading readiness, reading, and writing.
      (b) Helping teachers plan their instructional programs.
      (c) Demonstrating good reading lessons and language lessons as well as classroom management of class groups and small groups.

5. Conferring with teachers regarding special reading problems.
6. Providing services for professional improvement.
7. Interpreting instructional problems arising in the elementary schools to the administrative staff and to the community.
8. Providing consultant services on organizational instructional problems of the elementary school.
9. Assisting with the assignments and the work of the student teachers.
10. Assisting the Assistant Superintendent in the selection of new members of the teaching staff.
    a. Assist in recruiting and interviewing new staff members.
11. Preparing such reports and bulletins and keeping the necessary records requested by the General Elementary Supervisor, the Assistant Superintendent, and the Superintendent.
    a. Weekly reports for the General Elementary Supervisor, the Assistant Superintendent, and the Superintendent.
    b. An annual report.
    c. Reports of results of pre-kindergarten tests.
    d. Bulletins necessary to the improvement of the elementary instructional program with the approval of the General Elementary Supervisor.

II. To coordinate the activities of the elementary instructional program.
   A. Coordinating the work of special committees as assigned by the General Elementary Supervisor.
   B. Coordinating the selection of the best available materials in specific curriculum areas as assigned by the General Elementary Supervisor.
   C. Coordinating the preparation, writing, and revision of all elementary informal tests as directed by the General Elementary Supervisor.
   D. Working with principals and other staff members in making recommendations with respect to building and equipment needs.
   E. Assisting in the identification of the needs and planning with teachers, principals, General Elementary Supervisor, Assistant

Superintendent, and the Superintendent for a professional in-service development program for elementary teachers.
1. Activities of the Elementary Council.
2. Problems in individual schools.

III. To assume other general related responsibilities.
   A. Conferring with representatives of book companies.
   B. Attending professional meetings.
   C. Participating in professional meetings at local, state, and national level.
   D. Administering, scoring, and interpreting the pre-kindergarten test.
   E. Assisting principals and teachers in the interpretation of standardized test results.

Position: Supervisor of Secondary Education
Directly Responsible to: General Supervisor of Secondary Education
Responsible for: Assigned Subject Areas

Outline of Functions

I. To provide leadership for improving the instructional program through:
   A. Development of the curriculum by:
      1. Working with individual teachers.
         a. Observing classroom instruction.
         b. Discussing improved methods and techniques.
         c. Exploring teacher problems.
         d. Sharing ideas based on the experience and study of other professional people.
      2. Working with principals.
         a. Discussing the scheduling of new subject offerings in individual buildings.
         b. Reviewing problems of teachers and giving suggestions for help.
         c. Participating in principals' meetings in curriculum development.
      3. Working with teacher coordinators.
         a. Developing courses of study.
         b. Reviewing individual teacher problems.
         c. Identifying problem situations which require additional help.
   B. Development of instructional materials and facilities by:
      1. Advising teachers and principals on selection of materials such as textbooks, audio-visual aids, brochures, practice materials for drill work, etc.
      2. Developing textbook guides.
      3. Developing a collection of professional books.
      4. Identifying standards for equipment and facility needs.
      5. Arranging for demonstration of new equipment, such as language laboratories, new developments in science equipment, etc.
      6. Assisting in the selection of audio-visual equipment, such as new films, records, maps for specific subject areas, etc.

7. Preparing applications for federal or state aid, such as projects under Titles III and V, Public Law 85-864.
8. Assisting principals, teachers, and architects in the planning of specialized areas, such as shops, science rooms, counseling centers, libraries, foreign language laboratories, business education rooms, etc.
9. Preparing such orientation materials as sample four-year plan sheets, course description brochures, etc.
10. Reviewing budget requests in assigned areas through participation in budget committees.
11. Arranging for exhibits from business and community groups, such as Bell Telephone display, Remington Rand business machines exhibit, etc.

C. Development of professional staff by:
1. Visiting individual teachers in the classroom.
2. Conferring with teachers in regard to their instructional problems as needed.
3. Arranging for conferences with specialists in the field as consultants.
4. Interviewing teacher applicants.
5. Informing teachers about available scholarships, fellowships, institutes, etc.
6. Helping teachers become better acquainted with community resources through visits to industry, developing lists of resources, etc.
7. Helping teachers plan to meet the needs of individual students.
8. Helping teachers evaluate and improve instructional techniques and methods.

II. To facilitate the administration of the instructional program through:
A. Reviewing and approving textbook requisitions.
B. Organizing and coordinating a student teacher training program in cooperation with various colleges.
C. Organizing the orientation program for teachers new to the system.
D. Being responsible for the professional duties of the teacher coordinators.
E. Preparing and distributing materials for student orientation programs.
F. Keeping the General Supervisor of Secondary Education informed as to progress of the instructional program.

III. To provide coordination for improving the instructional program through:
A. Reviewing and revising the Curriculum Guide.
B. Evaluating the present program of studies in assigned areas.
C. Working with teacher committees in adopting textbooks.
D. Working with teacher coordinators and teacher committees in developing courses of study.
E. Utilizing the resources of research in evaluating student progress and determining curriculum needs.

F. Working with teacher committees in developing differentiated programs for students with different levels of ability, such as accelerated programs in mathematics and science, special grouping in English, etc.

IV. To provide leadership in other related activities through:
A. Organizing and coordinating system-wide programs, such as the Berg Science Seminars for gifted pupils conducted each week.
B. Cooperating with community groups in the organization of city-wide activities, such as the student study tour to the United Nations in New York and foreign embassies in Washington, D. C., art contests conducted by local business groups, etc.
C. Organizing other city-wide activities, such as career conferences, teen-age summer employment project, etc.
D. Serving on committees for planning city-wide activities, such as convocation program, administrative workshop, summer school, etc.

V. To assume other general responsibilities as may be assigned.[5]

SUMMARY

In small and intermediate-size school districts, it is possible for the superintendent of schools to take an active part in the supervisory program of the district. In large-size school systems, he plays a very important behind-the-scenes role but the more active role is assigned to the assistant superintendent in charge of instruction. This official is usually assisted by a coordinator of elementary education and a coordinator of secondary education. In addition, some districts employ elementary supervisors, secondary supervisors, and subject-area consultants. A variety of titles are used for these positions.

Regardless of the size of the school district, principals and assistant principals would, in addition to their administrative duties, be responsible for the supervisory programs in their respective buildings. They also would be expected to participate in various phases of the district-wide program. As members of the administrative council, principals would work on matters of policy concerned with all levels of the elementary and secondary schools. As members of the coordinators' teams, they would at times be concerned only with the elementary- or secondary-school program, depending upon the level on which they serve.

The largest school systems will be likely to form sub-districts for administrative and supervisory purposes. This plan of organization would provide district superintendents for each of the sub-districts. These offi-

---

[5] *Administrative Organization and Major Functions* (Gary, Ind.: School City of Gary, rev. ed., June, 1959).

cials would function in a line relationship to the assistant superintendent in charge of instruction in respect to all matters pertaining to instruction.

Chapters II and III, as well as this chapter, have emphasized the point that organizational patterns in themselves mean little. It is the individuals within the organization that make it work.

SUGGESTED ACTIVITIES AND PROBLEMS

1. Write to five large school systems and ask for a job description of the duties and responsibilities of the assistant superintendent in charge of instruction. Make a chart showing the similarities and differences in the roles played by this official in the systems surveyed.
2. Interview five teachers in a large school system to ascertain how they perceive the respective roles of three different officials in the improvement of the instructional program.
3. Write to five large school systems and ask for organizational charts. Analyze them in terms of personnel and line-and-staff relationships with respect to the improvement of instruction.
4. Draw up a plan for involving all staff members of a large school district in the improvement of some aspect of the instructional program.
5. Make an intensive study of the organization, procedures used, and accomplishments in the area of supervision *or* curriculum improvement of one large school district. On the basis of authoritative opinion, make suggestions for improving the services and procedures.

SELECTED READINGS

Burton, William H., and Leo J. Brueckner, *Supervision: A Social Process,* 3rd ed., Chap. 5. New York: Appleton-Century-Crofts, Inc., 1955.

Crosby, Muriel, *Supervision as Co-operative Action.* New York: Appleton-Century-Crofts, Inc., 1957.

Morris, Howard (Jr.), *Staffing Schools for Essential Services.* Philadelphia: Temple University, Philadelphia Area School Study Council, Campus Division, 1957.

U. S. Office of Education, *Fourth Conference for Supervision of Elementary Education in Large Cities.* Washington, D. C.: U. S. Department of Health, Education, and Welfare, March 24-27, 1959.

chapter five

The Superintendent, Assistant Superintendent, and Curriculum Coordinator at Work in Supervision

As is true of the administrative aspects of an educational enterprise, curriculum development and the improvement of instruction can be successfully accomplished only if a staff adequate to do the job is assembled. However, adequacy of numbers is not easy to determine. Students of educational administration have been struggling over the years to determine the optimum number of administrative and supervisory personnel required to get the job done effectively. Unfortunately, up to the present time no one has come up with a magic formula that works equally well in all organizations. This may be due to the fact that situations differ greatly and individuals vary tremendously in their energy output and effectiveness.

In previous chapters the authors have discussed the organization and function of supervision in small, intermediate, and large school districts. In this chapter the positions, job analysis, qualifications, and supervisory interrelationships of personnel above the rank of principal will be discussed.

THE SUPERINTENDENT OF SCHOOLS

Throughout this handbook the terms "superintendent of schools," "chief school administrator," and "chief school official" are used interchangeably to designate the executive officer of the board of education. This official is considered to be a key figure in the improvement of instruction and the curriculum, as the authors have stated in earlier chapters.

Job Analysis

Although the job of the superintendent has been defined in various ways, the functions of this position have been categorized more recently in the following four areas:

1. Maintaining effective interrelationships with the community.
2. Improving the scope and quality of educational opportunity.
3. Obtaining and developing personnel.
4. Providing and maintaining funds and facilities.[1]

Instructional leadership and curriculum improvement. Although everything the chief school official does affects the curriculum and the instructional program, functions related to items 2 and 3 above are most closely associated with them and, consequently, are the ones that will be discussed here.

"The superintendent is the key person in the cooperative problem-solving process. He is the player manager on the team."[2] Unless he enthusiastically supports educational change, it will not take place. In fact, he does much more than support change—he initiates it. According to the following statement from a recent study, innovations in instructional programs are introduced by administrators:

> Instructional changes which call for significant new ways of using professional talent, drawing upon instructional resources, allocating physical

[1] *A Developing Concept of the Superintendency of Education, Resource Manual 1* (rev. ed.) (Albany, N.Y.: Cooperative Development of Public School Administration in New York State, January, 1955), p. 8.

[2] American Association of School Administrators, *The Superintendent as Instructional Leader,* Thirty-fifth Yearbook (Washington, D.C.: National Education Association, 1957), p. 27.

facilities, scheduling instructional time or altering physical space—*rearrangements* of the *structural elements of the institution*—depend almost exclusively upon administrative initiative.[3]

If the superintendent is to be effective in his role as an instructional leader, there must be a similarity between the role which staff members believe the superintendent *should* assume and the one which they think he *is* carrying out. This apparently is more important than what he actually does.[4]

The roles of the chief school official in the improvement of instruction and in curriculum development may be quite different in the small district from the roles engaged in by this official in the other two categories of districts. In small school districts, the superintendent must either personally perform all the appropriate district-wide duties carried on in intermediate- and larger-size districts by the assistant superintendent in charge of instruction and the coordinators, or he must assign them to the principals. Although all of the superintendent's duties related to curriculum development and the improvement of instruction are not shown, Becker lists the following duties as performed by superintendents when there are no assistants or coordinators:

1. To conduct studies of need, determine policies and manageable projects.
2. To make the work of teachers more effective through such things as improved working conditions, better materials of instruction, improved methods of teaching, and in the preparation of courses of study.
3. To coordinate the efforts of principals, supervisors, helping teachers, and special service personnel.
4. To recognize individual group potential for continued growth and improvement.
5. To organize workshops and study groups that benefit all teachers in all grades either directly or indirectly.
6. To utilize consultants in the implementation of the in-service education program.
7. To supervise instruction through direct contact with the classroom teacher.
8. To evaluate the effectiveness of the instructional program in terms of what it does to the pupil.[5]

---

[3] Henry M. Brickell, *Organizing New York State For Educational Change* (Albany, N.Y.: State Education Department, 1961), p. 23.

[4] Andrew W. Halpin, *The Leadership Behavior of School Superintendents,* The School Community Development Study, Monograph No. 4 (Columbus: College of Education, The Ohio State University, 1956), pp. 74-78.

[5] James W. Becker, "Processes Used by Superintendents for the Improvement of Education in Selected School Districts" (Doctoral dissertation, Temple University, 1958), p. 120.

The same author depicts how the role of the superintendent changes when he assigns these duties to the principals or the assistant superintendent in charge of instruction. Under this arrangement, the superintendent:

1. Assigns the function to the principals or assistant superintendent.
2. Utilizes the board of education and the administrative staff in defining the duties for this function.
3. Holds each principal responsible for the educational program in his building or the assistant superintendent responsible for it from kindergarten through grade twelve.[6]

In addition to the above list of specific duties of the superintendent in the areas of curriculum improvement and instructional leadership, it seems desirable to suggest some additional responsibilities related to this phase of his job. Because of his key position, the superintendent is the one individual who can insure the development of a district-wide climate that is most favorable to the improvement of the curriculum and the instructional program. Therefore, he should use all the resources at his disposal to make certain that the following conditions and practices prevail in the school district for which he is responsible:

1. A carefully selected staff of competent teachers is secured and retained.

2. A sufficient number of supervisory personnel to get the job done adequately has been engaged.

3. Improved procedures for the orientation of new professional personnel have been formulated.

4. Ample instructional materials on a variety of levels of difficulty are available.

5. Good working conditions, including released time for curriculum work, exist.

6. Belief in and practice of democratic school administration by the superintendent is assured.

7. Regular delegation of authority with responsibility is practiced.

8. An honest desire on the part of the superintendent to see the instructional program improved is present.

9. Enthusiastic encouragement and support of curriculum projects by the superintendent is guaranteed.

10. An atmosphere in which teachers feel free to experiment is present.

11. Belief on the part of the superintendent that research has much to contribute to the solution of curricular and instructional problems is assured.

---

[6] *Ibid.*, pp. 117-118.

12. Caution and good common sense are exercised in the evaluation and study of "band wagon" practices before deciding to adopt or reject them.

13. Outside consultant help is provided when necessary.

14. The superintendent practices continuous self-improvement.

Qualifications

Numerous suggestions have been made concerning the qualifications necessary for success as a chief school official. The position varies so much from school district to school district that the qualifications needed for success in one situation might not be identical to those required in another school system. However, the personal characteristics and recommended professional preparation which are considered essential for dynamic leadership in the improvement of the curriculum and the instructional program will be listed.

Personal characteristics. More individuals fail because of deficiencies in the personal characteristics needed for the job than because of insufficient skills. The following personal characteristics are among those considered essential for the job:

1. ". . . intelligent and decisive, penetrating, yet flexible, a sophisticated analyst and a vigorous actor." [7]

2. ". . . the ability to see the whole picture . . . each problem in its broader context." [8]

3. Excellent physical and mental health with good emotional stability and self-control.

4. A sensitivity to and understanding of people and skill in human relations that enable him to work successfully with individuals and with groups.

5. A high degree of curiosity and infectious enthusiasm for education and what it can do for individuals and society.

6. A high degree of organizational skill.

7. Creative in his approach, with broad vision, abundant courage, and great integrity.

8. Open-minded and always exercises suspended judgment, but never vacillates in making decisions.

---

[7] Roald Campbell, *et al.*, *Improving Preparatory Programs for Educational Administrators in the United States: Some Action Guides* (Columbus: Universtiy Council for Educational Administration, 1962), p. 11.

[8] American Association of School Administrators, *Professional Administrators for America's Schools,* Thirty-eighth Yearbook (Washington, D.C.: National Education Association, 1960), p. 45.

9. Enjoys responsibility and recognizes the magnitude of his job—he is concerned but seldom worries.

10. Personal magnetism that attracts a corps of like-minded assistants who complement each other to form a superior administrative team.

Professional background. In the past decade great strides have been made in the upgrading of the programs for the preparation of chief school officials. State departments have made themselves felt in this endeavor by raising the certification requirements for this key position. The following are the new requirements in one forward-looking state:

1. Pennsylvania Provisional College Certificate.
2. Six (6) years of successful teaching experience, not less than three (3) of which shall have been in a supervisory or administrative capacity.
3. Doctor's Degree or seventy (70) hours of graduate study including a Master's Degree.
4. Included in the Doctor's Degree or the seventy (70) semester hours of approved graduate work, there must be a minimum of twenty-four (24) semester hours in educational administration and related courses such as Secondary School Administration, Elementary School Administration, School Finance, School Management, School Plant, Supervision of Personnel and Group Procedures, School Laws, Curriculum Development, Research, Measurement and Evaluation. In addition, a minimum of eighteen (18) semester hours of graduate work in at least three of the following areas shall be required: Public Finance, Economics, Sociology, Political Science and Public Administration.[9]

THE ASSISTANT SUPERINTENDENT IN CHARGE OF INSTRUCTION

The assistant superintendent in charge of instruction should be made responsible to the chief school official for the character and quality of the total instructional program in the school district. It should be his responsibility to provide the quality of leadership for a team of teachers, principals, supervisors, and other special resource persons that will result in a superior instructional program. To accomplish this, he must be adept at discovering, developing, and coordinating the various abilities, competencies, energies, and efforts of the members of his team.

Job Analysis

The responsibilities and duties of the assistant superintendent in charge of instruction are many and varied. No attempt will be made here to

[9] *Teacher Certification Regulations* (Harrisburg: Comonwealth of Pennsylvania, Department of Public Instruction, State Council of Education, February 1961), p. 95.

enumerate all of them, but the most important areas will be pointed out. These responsibilities and duties may be grouped as follows:

1. Those relative to the instructional program.
2. Those connected with staff leadership and professional growth.
3. Those relative to the obtaining of instructional materials, resources, and special services.

Under each of these areas may be listed a number of specific items which point up the role of the assistant superintendent in charge of instruction.

Instructional program. The development, coordination, and improvement of the instructional program is one of the most important tasks of the assistant superintendent. However, it is assumed that he will work democratically with a large number of persons in fulfilling his role. Some of these responsibilities and duties are:

1. To assist the superintendent as he works with the staff to formulate an adequate philosophy of education that is acceptable to the board of education, the professional staff, and the community.
2. To assume leadership for providing a continuous program of curriculum improvement.
3. To work with the staff in the development of instructional goals for the various levels and curriculum areas—kindergarten through grade twelve.
4. To work with the staff in the development of a system-wide program of evaluation and appraisal.
5. To be responsible for the development and supervision of programs for atypical children.
6. To work with the staff in the formulation of policies relative to pupil classification, marking, reporting, and promoting, and to execute the policies which are finally adopted.
7. To assume responsibility for determining the need for instructional-staff specialists and other resource personnel, and to direct, coordinate, and supervise their work so that they function as a smooth-working team.
8. To assume responsibility for the development, direction, and supervision of adult education programs in the district.

Staff leadership. The assistant superintendent in charge of instruction must be concerned with all district-wide matters pertaining to the instructional staff. However, he does not work alone. In carrying out all of the following responsibilities, he works with the superintendent, coordinators, and building principals:

1. To jointly assume responsibility for the recruitment, selection, and assignment of instructional personnel.

2. To assume responsibility for developing a comprehensive policy and program of in-service education for all professional staff members.

3. To jointly assume responsibility for the establishment and application of policies relative to promotion, transfer, and dismissal of instructional personnel.

4. To jointly assume responsibility for the promotion and supervision of experimentation with curriculum organization, instructional techniques, and instructional materials.

5. To assume responsibility for the development and operation of a comprehensive district-wide orientation program for new instructional personnel.

6. To jointly assume responsibility for the evaluation of all instructional personnel.

7. To serve by request as a consultant to principals, their staff, and individual teachers, but always with the approval of the building principal.

8. To assume responsibility to keep up to date professionally by reading widely, attending professional meetings, visiting other school systems, and any other means that will contribute to professional growth.

Instructional materials. The third and final area in which the assistant superintendent in charge of instruction operates is concerned with instructional materials, resources, and special services. The following responsibilities are included under this category:

1. To assume responsibility for the selection, procurement, and distribution of textbooks, library books, and all categories of instructional supplies and equipment. This responsibility must be carried out in close cooperation with the business manager, if there is one.

2. To assume responsibility for advising the superintendent on all budget items related to the instructional program.

3. To assume responsibility for the establishment and operation of a district-wide curriculum materials, audio-visual, and professional library center.

4. To assume responsibility for editing and publishing curriculum bulletins, guides, courses of study, pamphlets, and so forth, for use by the instructional staff.

5. To assume responsibility for the preparation of adequate reports and materials to provide the superintendent and board of education with summary information relative to the instructional personnel and program.

6. To assume responsibility for the preparation, with the approval of the superintendent, of bulletins, brochures, and reports on the instructional program for distribution to lay groups, P.T.A. committees, and the general public.

7. To assume responsibility for the identification and use of community, county, state, and national agencies and resources for the improvement of the instructional program.[10]

Qualifications

The assistant superintendent in charge of instruction needs to possess many of the personal characteristics listed for the superintendent. The scope of this position also demands a broad background of training and experience.

Personal characteristics. Dynamic leadership in the improvement of the instructional program and the curriculum requires, in addition to intelligence, a high degree of creativity. In a recent research report, the creative administrator was characterized as follows: He is an individual of curiosity and discontent, with unlimited enthusiasm for his work. He is a restless, intense, and strongly motivated person. He has the ability to create an atmosphere of excitement and urgency among his associates. He is open-minded and willing to listen to new ideas. He is unorthodox in his thinking, and he questions conventional ideas; he is goal-oriented rather than method-oriented.[11]

In addition, the following characteristics and competencies are highly desirable:

1. A sane, workable, consistent philosophy of education and the ability to translate it in terms of instructional purposes, programs, and procedures.
2. A person who receives a high degree of satisfaction in assisting others to develop their potential, possesses great skill in motivating others to action, and has the ability to be an astute observer of human personality.
3. Ability to establish rapport quickly with his peers, and a personality that encourages others to respect his professional competence and utilize his services.
4. Demonstrated ability in democratic leadership and effective decision-making.
5. Ability to supervise subordinates and to serve as an advisor to other line officers.

---

[10] The job analysis was adapted from: Educational Service Bureau, Temple University, *A Survey of The Cornwall-Lebanon Schools* (Philadelphia: The Bureau, 1962) (Mimeographed), pp. 111-115.

[11] Adapted from: E. Paul Torrance, "The Teacher as a Team Member: Team Leadership Through Creative Administration," in *Professional Growth for Administrators,* April 1961 (Arthur C. Croft Publications), and used by permission.

6. Competence in research methodology and the ability to interpret research.

7. Ability to write and speak effectively and to communicate with both lay and professional personnel.

Professional background. In order to qualify for a position of this scope, the individual must have a broad background of training and experience. Requirements similar to the following have been proposed:

1. College Permanent Certificate and evidence of 3 years of successful teaching experience.
2. Doctor's Degree or 70 hours of graduate study including a Master's Degree.
3. Included in the requirements for the Doctor's Degree or the 70 hours, there should be a minimum of twenty (20) semester hours related to elementary and secondary school curriculum, instruction, supervision and group process and a minimum of fifteen (15) semester hours in the humanities, including fine arts, social studies or natural sciences, or any combination of these subject areas.[12]

The authors would amend the above requirements and require teaching and/or administrative experience on both the elementary- and the secondary-school level.

RELATIONSHIP OF ASSISTANT SUPERINTENDENT TO OTHER ADMINISTRATIVE PERSONNEL

The assistant superintendent in charge of instruction is directly responsible to the superintendent and subordinate to him. As his right-hand man in charge of instruction, he serves in a line relationship to other administrative and supervisory personnel in carrying out his responsibilities. The assistant superintendent in charge of instruction is the recognized official head of the instructional leadership team. However, in working with other officials, he respects their leadership role in improving the instructional program and the curriculum. He considers district-wide coordination of the educational program kindergarten through grade twelve an important part of his assignment. In accomplishing this, he serves in a line relationship to the coordinators of elementary and secondary education and to other assistants. The assistant superintendent is an important member of the administrative council.

---

[12] *Teacher Certification Regulations* (Harrisburg: Commonwealth of Pennsylvania, Department of Public Instruction, State Council of Education, February 1961), p. 103.

COORDINATORS OF ELEMENTARY AND SECONDARY EDUCATION

These supervisory personnel are directly responsible to the superintendent in small districts and to the assistant superintendent in charge of instruction in intermediate- and large-size school districts.

Job Analysis

In intermediate- and large-size districts, the coordinators are the right-hand men of the assistant superintendent in charge of instruction. As coordinators in their respective fields, they function as line personnel on a district-wide basis; however, they operate only in a staff relationship to principals when they work in the individual buildings. When there is no assistant superintendent in charge of instruction, the coordinators assume his responsibilities and duties. Even in an organization which has an assistant superintendent, many of the duties of the coordinators are similar to those of their immediate superior except that the coordinators work only on their respective levels of the school system.

Duties and responsibilities. Although they may vary from district to district, the following types of duties and responsibilities may be performed successfully by the coordinators.

1. Assist in the development of a consistent philosophy of elementary or secondary education.
2. Provide leadership in developing a continuous program of curriculum improvement on their respective levels.
3. Work with the staff in the development of goals in the various curriculum areas on their respective levels.
4. Assist the principals in a staff capacity in evaluating the quality of teaching and learning.
5. Aid the principals as consultants on discipline, guidance, diagnosis of learning problems, and psychological referrals.
6. Aid the principals as consultants in the organization of instruction, teaching procedures, and experimentation.
7. Assist the principals, upon request, in supervising the work of teachers.
8. Aid the assistant superintendent and principals in the recruitment, selection, orientation, and assignment of new teachers.
9. Aid the assistant superintendent and the principals in the development of a sound program of evaluation.
10. Assist the assistant superintendent and principals in developing and

executing procedures relative to pupil classification, marking, reporting, and promoting.

11. Aid the assistant superintendent and principals on curricular needs, and in formulating and administering the budget in the areas of curriculum and instruction.

12. Aid the assistant superintendent and the principals in determining the need for instructional staff specialists and in directing and supervising their work.

13. Aid the assistant superintendent and principals in developing a comprehensive policy and program of in-service education for all professional staff members.

14. Aid the assistant superintendent and principals in the establishment and execution of policies relative to promotion, transfer, and dismissal of instructional personnel.

15. Assume responsibility for keeping up to date professionally.

16. Aid the assistant superintendent and principals in the selection, procurement, and distribution of textbooks, library books, and all categories of instructional supplies and equipment.

17. Aid the assistant superintendent in the establishment of a districtwide curriculum materials, audio-visual, and professional library center.

18. Assist in the editing and publishing of curriculum bulletins, guides, courses of study, and pamphlets.

19. Aid in the preparation of adequate reports and materials to provide the assistant superintendent, superintendent, and board of education with summary information relative to the instructional program.

20. Aid in the preparation of materials relative to the instructional program for distribution to lay groups.

Qualifications

The qualifications of the coordinator of elementary or secondary education should be similar to those of the assistant superintendent in charge of instruction, except that the coordinator should have extensive graduate work in curriculum and teaching on the level on which he expects to serve as a coordinator. His teaching experience also should have been largely in the division in which he will be serving as a coordinator.

RELATIONSHIP OF THE COORDINATORS TO OTHER ADMINISTRATIVE PERSONNEL

The coordinators are directly responsible and subordinate to the assistant superintendent in charge of instruction in districts employing this official. In districts without assistant superintendents, coordinators assume this relationship with the superintendent. As it has been stated elsewhere in this handbook, coordinators serve in a line relationship in carrying out district-wide responsibilities, but they function in a staff capacity when providing service and assistance to principals. Consequently, all requests for coordinators to work in individual schools should be made through the principal. The coordinators also are members of the administrative council.

SUMMARY

The superintendent of schools is the key individual in the improvement of the curriculum and the instructional program. This leadership role calls for a person who is intelligent, perceptive, and decisive. He must be able to visualize the whole picture and see each problm in its broader context. He must possess excellent physical and mental health and have great skill in working with people.

He must be broadly educated, with a knowledge of society and the forces that play upon it. He must have a sane, forward-looking philosophy of education and a respect for and knowledge of research.

The assistant superintendent in charge of instruction has numerous and varied responsibilities in connection with the curriculum and the instructional program. In addition to the usual characteristics necessary for educational leadership, this individual must possess a high degree of creativity.

He also must be broadly educated and have expert knowledge of the curriculum on all levels of the elementary and secondary school. Teaching and/or administrative experience on both the elementary- and secondary-school level seem(s) to be a desirable prerequisite.

Coordinators of elementary or secondary education have important roles to play in the improvement of the curriculum and the instructional program. With qualifications similar to those of the assistant superintendent, they can be of great assistance to him and to the principals in their respective fields.

SUGGESTED ACTIVITIES AND PROBLEMS

1. Secure the certification requirements from four states and examine the requirements for each of the positions discussed in this chapter. Write a paper illustrating how these requirements qualify each of the individuals for their respective positions.

2. Interview three chief school officials to ascertain what they consider to be the most significant contributions they make to the improvement of instruction and the curriculum. Evaluate their responses in light of current research and authoritative opinion.

3. Write a case study that illustrates the roles of the superintendent, assistant superintendent, and coordinators in the solution of a specific instructional problem.

4. Select a school system in which there is an assistant superintendent in charge of instruction. Interview this official, a principal, a teacher, and a parent to determine the different viewpoints held concerning the role of the assistant superintendent in the improvement of the instructional program and the curriculum.

5. Write a letter of application to the superintendent of schools that will convince him of your fitness for the position of elementary or secondary curriculum coordinator. Include some supporting evidence if you do not wish to incorporate it all in the body of the letter.

SELECTED READINGS

American Association of School Administrators, *The Superintendent as Instructional Leader*. Thirty-fifth Yearbook. Washington, D.C.: National Education Association, 1957.

American Association of School Administrators, *Professional Administrators for America's Schools*. Thirty-eighth Yearbook. Washington, D.C.: National Education Association, 1960.

Becker, James W., "Processes Used by Superintendents for the Improvement of Education in Selected School Districts" (Doctoral dissertation, Temple University, 1958).

Halpern, Andrew W., *The Leadership Behavior of School Superintendents*, The School Community Development Study, Monograph No. 4. Columbus: College of Education, The Ohio State University, 1956.

Swearingen, Mildred E., *Supervision of Instruction: Foundations and Dimensions*, Chap. 5. Boston: Allyn and Bacon, Inc., 1962.

Torrance, E. Paul, *Guiding Creative Talent*, Chap. 10. Englewood Cliffs, N.J.: Prentice-Hall, Inc., 1962.

chapter six

The Principal at Work in Supervision

The leadership role of elementary- and secondary-school principals has changed to a considerable extent in the past two decades. Unfortunately, boards of education, superintendents, other higher-echelon personnel, and the general lay public have not always recognized the importance of the principal's role. On the other hand, some principals have refused (or have not been qualified) to assume this new, greatly expanded leadership role. In these instances, the vision of the principal's role has not risen beyond clerical minutiae, paper-clip counting, and the disciplining of uncooperative students.

FACTORS INFLUENCING THE ROLE OF THE PRINCIPAL

What are the major factors that have been responsible for the increased prestige of the principalship? One basic cause has been the urbanization and consolidation of school districts, resulting in larger administrative units, but even more fundamental has been the new concept of the role, objectives, and purposes of the principalship. This broader concept has resulted from the gradual acceptance and practice of democratic procedures in school administration.

The involvement of pupils, parents, and teachers in the solution of educational problems has created a need for a kind of leadership that is skillful in the use of group processes in the improvement of the curriculum and the instructional program.

Other factors that have broadened the scope of the principal's job are: (1) population explosion, (2) increased complexities of the American way of life, (3) changes in society, (4) automation, and (5) the inadequately defined line between the role of the school and other community agencies. In respect to the latter factor, the school has assumed more and more of the responsibilities formerly carried by the home and other community agencies, as, for example: health services, psychological services, guidance services, speech therapy, special education, adult education, driver education, safety education, and recreation.

THE JOB AND THE MAN

The thesis of this handbook is that, irrespective of the type of school organization, a good supervisory program is more likely to result if specifications are prepared for each position and if the qualifications desired for personnel to serve in those positions are stipulated. These qualifications and specifications, the authors believe, may vary somewhat from school district to school district, because the essential outstanding characteristic of a superior supervisory program is that the staff operates as a smoothly coordinated team. This team concept and the role of the principal in the team will be discussed later in this chapter.

Job Analysis

The principal in present-day public school organization is the chief school administrator's representative in the actual day-to-day administration and supervision of the school system's building units. As the administrative head of a building unit, the principal in effect is the local superintendent of schools. Therefore, if the principal does his job effectively, he will assume on the local building level many of the same responsibilities and duties carried by the central office staff on a district-wide basis. In assuming his leadership role, then, the principal must accept responsibility for the following major tasks: (1) instructional leadership and curriculum improvement, (2) personnel administration, (3) business management, (4) plant management, (5) school-community relations, (6) administration of routine duties, and (7) professional, personal, and cultural growth.

This handbook is concerned mainly with the first task, namely, instructional leadership and curriculum improvement.

Instructional leadership and curriculum improvement. Writers in the field of educational administration have been saying for years that the improvement of the instructional program and the curriculum is the most important task of the principal. Several writers have recommended that at least 60 per cent of the principal's time should be devoted to this important role.[1] Not only does current practice fall far below the above recommendation, but even the aspirations of members of one level of the profession miss the mark by a considerable margin. A recent status study revealed that elementary-school supervising principals devoted only 35 per cent of their time to supervision and the curriculum, and that their preference was to increase this to 49 per cent.[2] It seems safe to suggest that very few principals, if any, devote enough time to the improvement of the instructional program and the curriculum.

The following duties and responsibilities of the principal belong in this supervisory category:

1. To work with the staff in the formulation and execution of an adequate philosophy of education consistent with the district-wide philosophy.

2. To assume leadership for providing, within his building unit, a continuous program of curriculum improvement which will at the same time contribute to district-wide curriculum improvement.

3. To work with the staff within his building unit in the development of instructional goals consistent with district goals for the various levels and curriculum areas.

4. To work with the staff in the development and execution within his unit of a system-wide program of evaluation and appraisal.

5. To work with the staff in the development, application, and supervision within his unit of programs for atypical children.

6. To work with the staff in the formulation and execution within his

---

[1] Ellwood P. Cubberley, *The Principal and His School* (New York: Houghton Mifflin Co., 1923), p. 43.

[2] Department of Elementary School Principals, *Elementary School Principalship—A Research Study*, Thirty-seventh Yearbook (Washington, D.C.: National Education Association, 1958), p. 98.

unit of district-wide policies relative to pupil classification, marking, reporting, and promoting.

7. To ascertain the need for instructional staff specialists in his unit and to direct and supervise their work.

8. To assume responsibility for a continuous program of supervision within his unit.

9. To assume responsibility, within the framework of the district plan, for a continuous program of in-service education for the staff members in his unit.

10. To keep abreast of new educational developments on the local, state, and national levels and to inform his staff concerning them.

11. To provide for the interchange of information and ideas among teachers and other staff personnel.

12. To see that the necessary facilities, equipment, books, and supplies are available when required.

A comparison of the above list of duties and responsibilities with those given for central office personnel in Chapter V reveals that they are quite similar. In fact, many of them are identical. The main difference is the level on which the leadership role is exercised.

Qualifications

The leadership role of the elementary- and secondary-school principal in instructional improvement and curriculum development requires a broadly educated and thoroughly experienced individual with the personal characteristics that will fit him for this role. Professional requirements similar to the following have been proposed in one state:

Elementary or Secondary Principal's Certificate. The Provisional Elementary or Secondary Principal's Certificate will be issued on the following basis—an applicant shall:

1. Hold a Pennsylvania College Certificate.
2. Have three years of successful teaching experience.
3. Complete forty-five (45) semester hours of graduate study, including a Master's degree with the following minimum requirements:
   (1) Twelve (12) semester hours in an academic field other than psychology.
   (2) Graduate study in developmental and remedial reading.
   (3) Fifteen (15) semester hours distributed among (1) administrative processes, (2) curriculum and instructional processes, and (3) the history and role of the school in society.
   (4) Documentary evidence of proficiency in English.

RENEWAL

The Provisional Principal's Certificate is valid for five (5) years. This certificate may be renewed for two additional five (5) year periods upon satisfactory completion of six (6) semester hours of additional graduate study for each renewal period. This graduate study may be applied toward permanent certification.

PERMANENT CERTIFICATION

1. The Provisional Elementary Principal's Certificate shall be made permanent when the holder of the Provisional Elementary Certificate has completed five (5) years of successful experience as a principal.

2. Has completed at least fifteen (15) semester hours of approved graduate work in addition to the graduate work required for the Provisional Elementary Principal's Certificate. Of these fifteen (15) semester hours of graduate work some time shall be devoted to a study of representative problems in education, of national, state, and local significance.[3]

The following personal attributes also will prove valuable in the principalship:

1. Possessor of above-average intellectual ability.
2. Possessor of sound mental and physical health coupled with abundant energy.
3. Demonstrated ability to exercise sound, mature judgment.
4. Possessor of a personality that encourages others to respect his professional competence and to seek his counsel and assistance.
5. A sane, workable, consistent philosophy of education and the ability to translate it in terms of instructional purposes, programs, and procedures.
6. An individual who derives great satisfaction from assisting others to develop their potential and who is skillful in motivating others to realize their greatest potential.
7. Demonstrated ability in democratic leadership and effective decision-making.
8. Ability to work well with others in a peer-group relationship.
9. Ability to communicate effectively through the use of both the written and spoken word.

The manner in which the principal uses these attributes in the improvement of the instructional program and the curriculum will be described in some detail in Chapters VIII, IX, X, and XI.

The Instructional Leadership Team

It should be readily apparent to the reader that the principal performs as a member of a team. The job of educational leadership is so immense

[3] Adapted from: *Official Notice of the State Council of Education and Superintendent of Public Instruction.* (Harrisburg: Commonwealth of Pennsylvania, Department of Public Instruction [Adopted May 23, 1962 to become effective October 1, 1964].)

today that it no longer can be accomplished successfully by individuals working independently. The more successful chief school administrators surround themselves with a corps of well-prepared specialists and likewise see that principals are provided with sufficient assistance. The ability to work with individuals and to utilize their special skills and talents thus becomes a top priority in the qualities essential for dynamic educational leadership.

Elementary- and secondary-school principals serve as valuable members of the school district's instructional leadership team, and, in addition, they are the responsible leaders of their own teams.

Team and *teamwork* are well-known, commonly understood terms. Because they are central to the vocabulary of every sport, individuals learn quite early in life that good teamwork wins games. Although star athletes often execute spectacular plays, every coach knows that behind each star stands the teamwork of the supporting players.

The application of these terms to the industrial, scientific, and political world is a less understood but equally important concept best typified by research teams that have made possible the many new wonders of the scientific age. By tapping the creative genius of many persons working cooperatively as research teams, the life span of man has been increased, many diseases have been wiped out, thousands of new products and labor-saving devices have been invented, the marvels of television and air travel have been made possible, and the comforts and luxuries of man have been multiplied a thousand-fold.

In the field of government, the team concept has long been practiced. In fact, our democratic system of government provides for participation in decision-making by teams of individuals. This is one of the distinctive features of our form of government. Decisions are formulated by groups, not by individuals. True, individuals exert a powerful influence, but they must secure the support of the other members of the team before a decision is finally made.

Unique aspects of educational administration. The team concept has been explored briefly in relation to the sports, industrial, scientific, and political world. There are, however, certain unique aspects of educational administration which influence the way that teamwork functions in this sphere. The reader should note that, in the ensuing discussion, the term *educational administration* is used in its broadest sense to encompass both supervisory and administrative functions. This handbook is, of course, concerned with the improvement of instruction and the curriculum, although the authors have emphasized several times that it is difficult to draw a fine line between supervisory and administrative functions. Campbell ably describes the following peculiarities that he believes make educational administration (and, consequently, instructional leadership) a special case:

1. School administrators have almost no legal status.
2. They are responsible to lay boards of education which know little about education.
3. School administrators cannot choose their own clients.
4. Many staff members have had as much formal education as the administrators.
5. Many teachers have tenure, and they can resist direction from school administrators without being guilty of outright insubordination.
6. Nonprofessional personnel are in the minority.
7. There are wide differences in the professional worker's perception of the role of administration in education.
8. School administrators are directly responsible to a large number of diverse sub-publics.
9. An educational administrator has to serve as the administrative officer of his school, and he needs constantly to reshape his organization in order that it shall achieve its purposes more adequately.[4]

Although all of the above items may not necessarily influence the formation and functioning of administrative teamwork, some of them, such as items 4, 5, 7, and 9, are particularly crucial and make the job of the educational administrator more difficult than that of administrators in other fields. For example, the fact that most teachers probably know more about their jobs than the principal does has many serious implications for the team concept. Likewise, item 7 presents a difficult challenge to the administrator who desires to use the team approach to school administration. Unless the majority of the professional staff have similar images of the role of the principal, little success will be achieved in the development of a professional team.

Essentials of teamwork. A recent text in administration raises the following questions and lists five essentials of teamwork:

> Why do some teams win and others lose? What elements are present in good teamwork and absent in poor? How can the creativity in each team member be tapped and utilized to the fullest extent? These, and others, are questions to which satisfactory answers must be found. What, then, are the essentials of good teamwork? First, the team must have a goal, purpose, cause, or objective identified, accepted, understood, and desired by all members of the team. Second, the team must have spirit,

[4] Adapted from: Roald F. Campbell, "What Peculiarities in Educational Administration Make It a Special Case?", in *Administrative Theory in Education,* ed. by Andrew W. Halpin (Chicago: The Midwest Administration Center, University of Chicago, 1958), pp. 173-184.

morale, and the desire to win even at considerable individual sacrifice. Third, the lines of authority and responsibility must be both clearly defined and understood. Fourth, channels of communication must be established. Fifth, leadership must discover and utilize to the fullest extent the creative abilities of each of the individuals and weld them into a smooth working team.[5]

The Principal Works in His Building Unit

The principal of even a small school has a large number of individuals with whom he has to work, and the larger the school, the more complicated the human relations problem becomes. As an essential prerequisite for providing in his school the best possible educational program for the boys and girls under his charge, the principal must build a team that will cooperatively develop and work to achieve a set of objectives and outcomes. He must assist a group of persons with widely different backgrounds to work together for a common cause. This is no mean achievement and requires leadership of a rare type.

Assistant principal. According to a recent study, only 15 per cent of 2,008 elementary supervising principals reporting indicated that services of an assistant principal were available to them.[6] This would seem to indicate that the position of assistant principal is not very common in the elementary schools of the United States. On the secondary level, many principals have assistant principals.

If carefully selected, the assistant principal can become a valuable member of the team. Rather than assigning him routine clerical responsibilities or placing him in charge of attendance or discipline, the wise principal will pick an assistant who can complement him and thus help to build a stronger team. Usually, there are areas in school administration and supervision in which the principal is not so proficient as in other areas. The selection of an assistant principal with these particular skills will greatly strengthen the team.

Regardless of his special areas of responsibility, the assistant principal should be given opportunities to participate in all aspects of school administration. When the principal is out of the building, the assistant principal is the logical person to be placed in charge.

The position of assistant principal not only affords valuable assistance to the principal, but it provides a much-needed training ground for the

---

[5] James B. Burr, William H. Coffield, T. J. Jenson, and Ross L. Neagley, *Elementary School Administration* (Boston: Allyn and Bacon, Inc., 1963), p. 402.

[6] Department of Elementary School Principals, *The Elementary School Principalship—A Research Study,* Thirty-seventh Yearbook (Washington, D.C.: National Education Association, 1958), p. 67.

principalship. In this capacity young men and women can receive excellent experience in school administration.

The scope of activities and responsibilities of the assistant principal should be clearly defined in writing and made known to all staff personnel, pupils, and parents.

Regular classroom teachers. Although by virtue of his title and responsibilities the principal will be assigned an authoritarian role in the minds of most of the staff, he should do everything possible to develop a peer working relationship with teachers. This is a goal toward which the principal should work, and yet he should not be discouraged if he fails to achieve it. Past experiences of staff members with autocratic principals, images of the role of the principal dating from their own elementary-school days, and concepts developed as they observed the actions of persons in authority in various walks of life are difficult to eradicate.

Morphet, Johns, and Reller emphasize the fact that:

> The organizational plan lays the basis for the procedures by which the principal works with his staff, both instructional and noninstructional. Therefore, all members of the staff should participate in the development of the plan of organization. They should understand it and accept it.[7]

The following list of suggestions, although incomplete, characterizes the team concept of working with staff members:

1. The principal recognizes that leadership is a function shared by many persons rather than the sole prerogative of the status individual.
2. Staff members are encouraged to participate in the administrative and supervisory activities of the school.
3. The talents and special abilities of staff members are utilized to the fullest extent.
4. Faculty meetings and staff committees are chaired by faculty members.
5. Faculty members participate in making all decisions of policy that affect them.
6. The principal assumes a peer relationship when he participates in staff discussions.
7. Decisions are made by consensus rather than by majority rule.
8. The principal clearly defines with staff members the limits of their operation. That is, they know when they have the authority to make a decision ("budget of power") and when they can only recommend.
9. The principal never vetoes "budget of power" decisions, and when

[7] Edgar L. Morphet, Roe L. Johns, and Theodore L. Reller, *Educational Administration: Concepts, Practices, and Issues* (Englewood Cliffs, N.J.: Prentice-Hall, Inc., 1959), p. 288.

recommendations cannot be implemented, he sees that staff members understand the reasons.

10. Suggestions and recommendations are freely made by staff members.

11. The principal believes in the democratic process, but he realizes that, in the final analysis, he is the responsible leader of the school.

Other professional personnel. This category would vary considerably from school to school, with the greatest differences to be noted between elementary and secondary schools. The size of the school and the school district, as well as the type of organization, would determine whether or not some of the specialists were central office personnel or regular members of the staff of a particular school. Special personnel are found in the following categories on both the elementary- and secondary-school levels: (1) nursing, (2) library, (3) art, (4) music, (5) physical education, (6) home economics, (7) industrial arts, (8) guidance, (9) audio-visual, and (10) reading. In addition, secondary schools may have department heads, roster chairmen, and vocational teachers. Recently, with the introduction of team teaching, new categories of personnel have appeared, with various titles such as *team chairman, master teacher, divisional principal,* and others. Some of the larger elementary schools also have speech, foreign language, and science specialists assigned as regular members of a principal's staff; however, these are usually central office personnel.

These special personnel are all members of the principal's instructional leadership team; consequently, he must learn to work effectively with them individually and in groups. Several suggestions for the principal to follow in working with special personnel on his staff seem appropriate here:

1. Special personnel should be given the same privileges, rights, and responsibilities as regular classroom teachers. Care should be exercised that they do not appear to be a favored group.

2. Wherever possible, the principal should coordinate the work of the special personnel with the work of regular classroom teachers and the central office resource staff.

3. The principal should give the special personnel opportunity to interpret their work to the entire staff and to learn about the work of all the other members of the staff.

4. Special services should be scheduled so that there will be a minimum of conflict with regular teachers' programs and with each other.

5. The principal should provide leadership to insure that special services that are coordinated, for example, guidance and health services, do not duplicate their efforts but rather function as a team in attacking a problem.

6. The principal should see that special personnel are involved in curriculum revision and other professional-growth programs.

Nonprofessional personnel. The important contributions made to the school program by the nonprofessional personnel are common knowledge. It is sufficient to emphasize here that the school secretary, custodian, bus driver, cafeteria manager, and all other nonprofessional personnel should be treated as equals and the importance of their work continually stressed. As in the case of professional staff, these persons should have the opportunity to participate in making policy decisions that affect them and their jobs. They should be invited to attend staff meetings when matters that concern them are being discussed. As part of the school team, they and their families should be welcome at social events sponsored by the school staff.

Pupils. The enlightened principal spends as much time as possible with children. He learns to know them and to understand their problems. Many principals who have been in a given school for a number of years know all their pupils by name. This is a valuable asset to the principal and the staff if they truly believe in democratic administration and supervision and, consequently, consider the pupils part of the team.

The principal who: assists the teacher by working with pupils when he enters the classroom and even relieves teachers occasionally, prefers to talk with pupils in the corridors rather than to shout at them, eats with them in the cafeteria instead of patrolling the lunchroom, and mingles with children on the playground rather than spying on them from a classroom window has the basis for building a strong working relationship with pupils. In addition, the example he sets may be followed by other members of the staff.

If this kind of working relationship with pupils has been established, they, too, can become valuable members of the instructional-leadership team. Pupils of all ages can, on their level, make a contribution to the improvement of the curriculum and the instructional program. In the past, children and youth have not been given enough opportunity to assist in these important activities. In addition to the contributions they can make, it will be a valuable learning experience for the contributors.

Lay individuals. Gone are the days when a principal could completely ignore the wishes and desires of parents in respect to the educational program. Today, education is discussed so freely on so many different fronts that in every community there are lay individuals who desire to be involved in some way in improving the educational program of their own community. The successful principal is well aware that lay individuals must now be considered as members of the team.

> . . . studies have shown that the way a principal works has a vital influence on the climate for the total educational program. His working pattern must be consistent in his relationships with teachers, pupils, and parents if he is to attain maximum effectiveness as a leader. No group can be ignored.[8]

From time to time the principal will want to involve representative lay persons in an advisory capacity to assist in the solution of educational problems. Several instances of how lay persons may assist the principal are in the revision of a reporting system, the development of a philosophy of education, and assisting in the over-all evaluation of the school. They also can make many worthwhile contributions as members of curriculum-revision committees and as resource persons in the actual instructional program.[9]

The Principal Works with the Central Office Staff

The number of central office staff personnel with whom the principal works varies considerably from school district to school district. As systems become larger, more central office personnel doubtless will be added. The personnel most likely to be found on the central office staff includes the superintendent, assistant superintendent for instruction, assistant superintendent for business, school psychologist, and an array of special teachers, supervisors, and/or consultants.

Superintendent of schools. The principal is a valued and trusted member of the superintendent's team. It should be remembered that, in districts employing an assistant superintendent in charge of instruction, this official will be responsible for directing the activities of the instructional-leadership team. It is the principal's responsibility to see that the policies of the board of education and the rules and regulations handed down from the central office are carried out. As the responsible leader of his school, he is expected to support the superintendent and interpret policies and rules and regulations to his staff. This does not mean that he should not try to see that policies are improved and rules and regulations changed; but, as long as they are in effect, he must support them. Disloyalty to the superintendent is unprofessional and can only lead to disaster and even professional ruin.

If the principal finds himself in the unenviable position of disagreeing with the superintendent or the assistant superintendent in charge of instruction, he has only three constructive courses of action left open to him,

---

[8] Morphet, Johns, and Reller, *Educational Administration, op. cit.*, pp. 290-291.

[9] Committee on Human Resources of the Metropolitan School Study Council, *Fifty Teachers to a Classroom* (New York: The Macmillan Company, 1950).

namely, (1) he can try to change the position taken by his superior, (2) he can resign, or (3) he can support the position taken by his superior.

As a member of the administrative council, the principal is expected to help develop policies and to make recommendations for the improvement of the educational program in the district. He also is expected to utilize the talents and abilities of his staff in the solution of district-wide problems.

Assistant superintendent for instruction. The relationships of the principal to the assistant superintendent for instruction depend upon whether or not he is a line or staff official. Usually, this is a line and not a staff position. If this is the case, the principal is responsible to this assistant in all matters relating to instruction. Most of what has been said concerning the principal's relationship with the superintendent also applies here, but only in matters dealing with instruction.

Assistant superintendent for business. The relationships of principals to this official may vary tremendously from school system to school system. Under the preferred, unit-control organizational plan, the assistant superintendent for business affairs is in a subordinate position to the chief school official. The principal serving in a school system with the unit-control organizational plan should preferably not deal directly with the business manager in matters pertaining to the instructional program but instead should work through the superintendent or the assistant superintendent in charge of instruction.

Coordinators. Coordinators on either the elementary- or secondary-school level assume a line relationship with principals in respect to the instructional program. They have no authority over the principal in purely administrative matters. Working with the coordinator can prove to be one of the most difficult assignments of the principal. Because of their responsibility for the over-all elementary- or secondary-school program in a district, coordinators may at times appear to be usurping some of the authority of the building principal. To prevent friction from developing, it is essential that limits of operation be drawn and understood. In most cases, if the principal is doing an effective leadership job in the improvement of the instructional program and the curriculum, the coordinator will work with and through him. However, if the principal is weak in this respect, he has only himself to blame if the coordinator takes over.

Resource personnel. The number of resource personnel with whom the principal must work is very large in some school districts and very small in others. Most of these resource personnel may be considered as central office staff, with the exception of those previously discussed in this chapter.

If the principal is to be successful, he must learn to work effectively with as many of these resource personnel as are made available to him. Griffiths states: "The problems that the administrator faces in working with specialists are of two varieties: (1) those involved in the *services* that the specialists bring to the school, and (2) those involved in the *limitations* of the specialists themselves." [10] In discussing these two problems, he emphasizes the difficulty of scheduling and evaluating the services of specialists and their inability to see their "own field of endeavor in proper perspective." [11] Other limitations cited by Griffiths are:

> . . . the tendency of many specialists to identify with other specialists and to ignore the arguments of nonspecialists . . . to confuse the importance of their knowledge with the significance of what they recommend, . . . and the specialists' aversion to new ideas, particularly if these ideas come from outside the specialist group.[12]

Space here does not permit a discussion of the principal's relationship with each of these individuals, but a number of generalizations will be made for consideration by the principal or future principal.

1. All resource personnel should be accorded the same courtesies as regular staff members.
2. The use of the title "supervisor" should be avoided in the case of specialists in the various curriculum areas, including the special areas of music, art, and physical education. Use instead the title "coordinator" or "consultant" (see Chapter VII).
3. Coordinators preferably should have staff rather than line-authority relationships to the principal when they are working with his staff. Principals should be the instructional leaders of their schools, and coordinators should give them assistance when needed.
4. Resource personnel should attend staff meetings and be involved in making any decisions that affect their work.
5. Adequate space and materials should be provided by the principal so that resource personnel can do their most effective job.
6. The principal should be familiar enough with the work of the resource personnel so that he can support and interpret their work to the staff and the public.
7. The principal is responsible for seeing that the best possible use is being made of the special abilities of resource personnel during the times

---

[10] From: *Human Relations in School Administration* by Daniel E. Griffiths, p. 283. Copyright © 1956, Appleton-Century-Crofts, Inc. Reprinted by permission of Appleton-Century-Crofts.

[11] *Ibid.*, p. 284.

[12] *Ibid.*, p. 285.

they are available. Failure to provide clerical assistance for the librarian, so that she spends a large segment of her time in cataloging books, is an example of uneconomical use of the librarian's time.

8. School time must be provided for resource personnel to work and plan with the teaching staff so that they may become more proficient in these areas and skills.

The following ideas summarize the relationship of the principal to the central office: All relationships of the principal to the central office staff should be clearly defined and understood. The lines of communication between the principal and the superintendent should be direct, and there also ought to be direct functional communication between the principal and all other central office services. The principal, however, must always be recognized by the central staff as the responsible head of the school he administers. Under no conditions should any member of the central staff have direct control over the employees under the principal's direct supervision. The principal is administratively responsible for the educational program in his school. However, this must not be stressed to the point where relationships become strained. Friendly and cooperative relationships between the principal and the central office staff are essential for instructional improvement. The principal does not operate alone—he is a member of a well-organized team.[13]

The Principal Works with Other Principals

Although the principal is almost autonomous in his own school, he does not work in isolation. Principals periodically are called together by the chief school official to share experiences and discuss common problems. It is during these meetings that district-wide policies concerning education are developed and their implementation discussed. The principal must be prepared to face conflicts, and he must learn to resolve differences of opinion that may arise between himself and other principals in the district. Unless he functions as a good team member, his value to the district will be lessened. This does not necessarily mean that he must compromise his beliefs, but he must learn to respect the opinions of others that may be quite different from his own.

Elementary- and secondary-school principals must learn to cooperate to a greater degree than they have in the past, because they have many problems in common. For example, a district-wide educational philosophy

---

[13] Adapted from: Morphet, Johns, and Reller, *Educational Administration*, *op. cit.*, pp. 285-286.

is essential if children are to benefit from a continuous educational program. Curriculum development also should be pursued on a kindergarten-to-grade twelve basis. Common systems of marking, reporting, and promoting ought to be agreed upon. School evaluations might advantageously be conducted simultaneously on both the elementary- and the secondary-school level.

Another mutual problem of vital importance is that of assisting the elementary-school pupil painlessly to make the transition from the elementary to the secondary school. This requires teamwork of the highest type.

In some school districts, elementary- and secondary-school principals may be required to share common services and facilities. Here is a real opportunity for the elementary principal to demonstrate high-level leadership ability. Not only must he cooperate with the secondary-school principal, but he must insure that the elementary-school pupils do not come out second best.

The wise principal is aware of the fact that he can learn a great deal from principals outside the district, and that he has a responsibility to share his knowledge and experience with them. Consequently, he will hold membership in the local, state, and national elementary principals' associations, and he will actively participate in their meetings and the other activities sponsored by them.

SUMMARY

The role of the principal as an instructional leader has increased in prestige during the past decade. A number of factors concerned with the setting, the man, and the job have been influential in bringing about this change. Foremost has been the recognition that the individual school faculty is the most logical unit for improving instruction. This has been a natural consequence of the increasing realization that democracy in educational administration requires the involvement of pupils, parents, and teachers in the solution of educational problems. The increased importance of the principal's job has made it necessary to raise the requirements for entering the principalship.

The principal is a valuable member of a team. As a team member, he must learn to work skillfully with professional and nonprofessional staff, a host of central office personnel, pupils, lay individuals, and other principals. While working with individuals, alone and in groups, he will endeavor to use the democratic processes because he realizes that in this way he can be assured of the highest degree of success.

SUGGESTED ACTIVITIES AND PROBLEMS

1. Examine school board policies and rules and regulations that are concerned with curriculum or the improvement of instruction. Select five significant rulings of the board and discuss their implications with respect to the principal's job of instructional leadership.

2. Assume that you are the principal of an elementary or a secondary school with an enrollment of 1,000 pupils. You have been authorized to look for an assistant principal. Knowing your own capabilities and interests, for what kind of person would you look, and how would you utilize his services? Justify your choice and the division of the work load.

3. Using anecdotes freely, describe how a principal you know well works with *one* of the following groups: (a) professional staff, (b) nonprofessional staff, (c) central office staff, (d) pupils, or (e) lay persons. Confine your study to procedures affecting the instructional program. Make recommendations for the improvement of these procedures.

SELECTED READINGS

American Association of School Administrators, *Staff Relations in School Administration.* Thirty-third Yearbook. Washington, D. C.: National Education Association, 1955.

Burr, James B., William H. Coffield, T. J. Jenson, and Ross L. Neagley, *Elementary School Administration,* Chap. 4. Boston: Allyn and Bacon, Inc., 1963.

Corbally, John E., Jr., T. J. Jenson, and W. Frederick Staub, *Educational Administration: The Secondary School,* Chaps. 5 and 14. Boston: Allyn and Bacon, Inc., 1961.

Griffiths, Daniel E., *Human Relations in School Administration,* Chaps. 11 and 13. New York: Appleton-Century-Crofts, Inc., 1956.

Jordan, William C., *Elementary School Leadership,* Chap. 5. New York: McGraw-Hill Book Company, Inc., 1959.

Morphet, Edgar L., Roe L. Johns, and Theodore L. Reller, *Educational Administration,* Chap. 13. Englewood Cliffs, N. J.: Prentice-Hall, Inc., 1959.

chapter seven

Specialists, Department Heads, Team Leaders, and Helping Teachers

One of the unresolved dilemmas of the elementary school organized on the self-contained classroom plan is the problem of how to use specialists most effectively. Although the number of specialists employed varies from district to district, they are most commonly engaged to work in the fields of art, music, and physical education. Some districts also employ special personnel in one or more of the following areas: (1) handwriting, (2) speech, (3) remedial reading, (4) foreign language, (5) home economics, and (6) industrial arts. Helping teachers and curriculum collaborators also are being employed in some school districts. The department head still plays an important leadership role in the secondary school, and some districts have begun to employ guidance specialists to work in the elementary school. The increasing popularity of team teaching has made it necessary to supply team leadership.

USING SPECIALISTS IN ELEMENTARY SCHOOLS

The discussion in this section will be confined to the use of specialists in the areas of art, music, and physical education in the elementary school. Over the years, these specialists have served in the elementary school in a variety of ways which roughly fall into the following three patterns:

(1) The specialist serves as a special teacher in his area of the curriculum.

(2) The specialist serves as a supervisor in his area of the curriculum.

(3) The specialist serves as a consultant in his area of the curriculum.

The remainder of this section will be devoted to a discussion of the advantages and disadvantages of each of these roles of the specialist.

The Specialist as a Teacher

For many years individuals specially trained in the fields of art, music, and physical education have taught their subjects one or more periods a week in each elementary classroom. Working on a regular weekly schedule, these special teachers have taken over the classes of regular elementary teachers and taught their particular specialty to the class. In some instances, the regular classroom teacher remains as an observer or an assistant teacher. In others, he uses this as a free period.

Advantages. Advocates of this role of the specialist claim the following advantages for it:

1. The specialist is much better qualified to teach his area of the curriculum than is the regular classroom teacher.
2. Having regularly scheduled periods taught by specialists insures that these areas of the curriculum will not be slighted in the programs of regular classroom teachers who feel incompetent in the special areas.
3. All pupils on a given grade level are assured of similar experiences in these areas.
4. It provides free time for the regular teacher.
5. Pupils enjoy a change from their regular teacher.
6. If at least one specialist is a male, it insures that boys will have some contacts with a male teacher.

Disadvantages. Educators who are opposed to having specialists used largely as teachers of these areas maintain that it is a violation of the concept of the self-contained classroom. They give the following arguments against this role of the specialist:

1. Specialists cannot learn to know and understand the large number of pupils they are expected to teach.
2. Specialists may use different control techniques from those accepted and practiced by the regular teacher. Under this situation, the specialist may become a disturbing influence in a normally well-ordered classroom.
3. The necessity for tightly scheduling the specialist results in the disruption of the highly desirable "large block of time" approach to teaching.
4. Pupils are forced to participate in activities for which they are not ready and, in the case of a physical education class immediately after lunch, at a time that is undesirable from a health standpoint.
5. Specialists are frequently off schedule five or ten minutes and sometimes fail to show up at all. This results in the disruption of the regular teacher's program and the loss of valuable teaching time.
6. This use of the specialist makes it more difficult to relate the special areas to the other areas of the curriculum.
7. Frequently, pupils receive no experiences in the special areas other than those which they have under the guidance of the specialists.
8. Regular teachers who have a particular interest in the special area prefer to teach it themselves.

The Specialist as a Supervisor

In schools that define the role of the specialist as a supervisor, the individual also may do a considerable amount of teaching. However, in this instance the teaching is considered to be demonstration teaching, and regular teachers are expected to provide their pupils with additional experiences in the special areas.

Advantages. Defenders of this role of the specialist advance the following arguments:

1. The special areas should be a regular part of the daily curriculum experiences of children.
2. Regular classroom teachers require a lot of supervisory help in the special areas of the curriculum in order to provide these daily experiences.
3. Regularly scheduled periods for the specialist to visit each classroom and a cooperatively planned curriculum insure a balanced program in each special area.
4. Because the program is planned under the supervision of a specialist, pupils can be assured of continuity of learning in the special areas as they progress through school.

Disadvantages. Some of the disadvantages of using the specialist as a supervisor are similar to those listed in the previous section, namely, items 3, 4, and 5. The following additional arguments are also used against the practice of giving the title of "supervisor" to the specialist.

1. Because specialists are usually no better prepared in their specialty than regular classroom teachers are in theirs, considerable resentment is shown by classroom teachers when the specialists are given the title of "supervisor."

2. Even with the help of specialists, many regular classroom teachers are not competent to teach the special areas of the curriculum.

3. Although the specialists have worked out with the regular classroom teachers a teaching plan for the week, there is no guarantee that the plan will be executed.

It should be noted that in some school districts the specialist is given the title of "supervisor" but in actual practice performs as a teacher of his special subject, and in other districts a specialist might assume the role of a helping teacher and actually be performing the role discussed in the section above. Apparently, the title of a position does not define the job.

The Specialist as a Consultant

The role of the specialist as a consultant is a rather recent development. One authority in the field of supervision describes it as follows:

> The new approach makes use of the specialist as a resource person, a consultant, and a helper to the teacher in his work and teaching activities; at times the specialist helps a group of teachers in some joint project of a larger nature, as with a chorus from several rooms, or in a display of children's art for parents.[1]

In the last decade, increasing support has been given to the role of the specialist as a consultant. However, as is the case in the other two roles, this one also has its strengths and weaknesses.

Advantages. The following arguments have been given for assigning to the specialist the role of a consultant in the self-contained classroom plan of organization:

1. The concept of the completely self-contained classroom is preserved under this plan.

2. Flexible scheduling of the special subject areas is possible because it is completely under the control of the regular classroom teacher.

---

[1] J. Minor Gwynn, *Theory and Practice of Supervision* (New York: Dodd, Mead and Company, 1961), p. 286.

3. Expert assistance is available on an "on call" basis at all times.
4. The most economical use can be made of the time and talents of the specialist, because he can devote the bulk of his energy to assisting teachers who need the most help.

Disadvantages. Opponents of this procedure for utilizing the services of the specialist point out that it has several of the same weaknesses inherent in the plan that assigns the role of supervisor to the specialist. The following weaknesses have been observed in this plan:

1. Some teachers do not recognize that they need help in the special areas and, consequently, do not ask for help.
2. Complete utilization of the services of the consultant is rarely accomplished. This is particularly true in the early stages of this arrangement.
3. The special areas may be neglected by teachers who do not consider them important and who have no desire to improve in teaching them.
4. Some teachers may monopolize the services of the specialists and thus make them unavailable for other teachers.
5. The specialists are not always available when they are needed; for example, several teachers might require the help of the art consultant at the same time.

The authors take the position that school organization serves no purpose except to facilitate learning. Regardless of whether or not the specialists serve as teachers, supervisors, or consultants, the principal must ensure that all pupils regularly have a balanced educational program including all areas of the curriculum. However, the authors believe that, under the self-contained classroom plan of organization, a balanced educational program is more likely to result if the specialists serve as consultants.

THE DEPARTMENT HEAD

For many years the department headship has been a respected position in most of our larger secondary schools. In some schools it is a permanent appointment; in others, a department chairman is elected; and in still others, the headship is rotated. Regardless of the title of the position or the procedure used in selecting the individual to fill the post, the department head can play a valuable role in the supervisory program.

Because the department head has teaching responsibilities, it is easy for him to maintain a peer relationship with the other members of the department. Inexperienced new teachers readily come to him for counsel, advice, and assistance, and most teachers respect his ability as a teacher and leader.

The following instructional and supervisory duties and responsibilities have been suggested for this position:

1. Sets a good example by his own teaching and on request conducts demonstration lessons.
2. Supplies information and materials that can contribute to the improvement of teaching.
3. Visits classrooms, works with teachers, and brings to their attention special resources, possible field trips, and appropriate audio-visual aids.
4. Works cooperatively with his staff in developing meaningful curriculum materials.
5. Assists in the orientation of new teachers.
6. Recommends, secures, orients, and assists substitute teachers.
7. Assists with the student teaching program, if one exists.
8. Confers with teachers on personal and professional matters that might affect their morale and teaching efficiency.
9. Recognizes, encourages, and stimulates professional growth and initiative on the part of the staff.
10. Regularly holds departmental meetings.
11. Assumes responsibility for intra-departmental communication.
12. Assists his staff in identifying and carrying out successful action research.
13. Assists in the selection, encouragement, and implementation of special informal activities, such as club activities, assembly programs, and career conferences.
14. Serves as the first recourse in assisting teachers who are having discipline problems.
15. Makes decisions concerning the placement of students in courses within his department.
16. Assists in the guidance program.
17. Provides leadership in planning the testing program.[2]

Recently, changes in school organization have resulted in the appointment of department heads or area chairmen to supervise closely related areas of the curriculum such as science and mathematics. This, in turn, has paved the way for a kind of divisional leadership based on groups of pupils rather than subjects. This new leadership role will next be discussed.

---

[2] Adapted from: Benjamin J. Novak, "The Department Headship To-Day," *Educational Administration and Supervision,* 44, No. 2 (1958), pp. 92-95.

THE TEAM LEADER

Currently, on both the elementary- and secondary-school levels, team teaching has been attracting considerable attention. As is frequently the case when innovations in education are introduced, there are a considerable number of variations in actual practice. Although there are leadership possibilities in other types of teacher-team organization, the one that assigns a major role to the team leader will be discussed here. Anderson describes it as follows:

> The essential ingredients of team teaching are not only co-operation and collaboration in the planning and presentation of the program, but also the assignment of specific leadership and responsibility (with the accompanying prestige and recognition) to career-oriented teachers of superior training and competence.[3]

Although theoretically two teachers working with the same group of pupils could constitute a team, the composition and characteristics of the Claremont Teaching Team seem to make it a desirable model to describe. The Claremont Teaching Team consists of a distinct student group, four to six faculty members with complementary talents and specializations, and certain auxiliary personnel who assist the teachers and children.

"A *Team Leader* is a mature, experienced, licensed teacher of unusual talent and extensive training who has been elected or appointed to serve as the leader of a teaching team. . . ."[4]

The role of this important functionary is further classified by Brownell in the following manner:

> The elected or appointed leader of a faculty team assumes responsibility for the general performance of his team. In order to carry out his responsibility adequately, he is given an extra period, in addition to the common conference period, to plan and to coordinate team activities. Furthermore, he is paid a stipend above his normal pay for his leadership. The primary functions of the leader are his classroom teaching and his leadership of the team in improving instruction, counseling, and the performance of other tasks required for optimum development of team students.[5]

---

[3] Robert H. Anderson, "Team Teaching," *NEA Journal,* 50, No. 3 (1961), p. 52.

[4] John A. Brownell and Harris A. Taylor, "Theoretical Perspectives for Teaching Teams," *Phi Delta Kappan,* XLIII, No. 4 (1962), p. 151.

[5] John A. Brownell and Roland P. Shutt, *The Claremont Teaching Team Program, A Research Project* (Claremont, Cal.: Claremont Graduate School, 1961), p. 11.

What, then, are the specific duties and responsibilities associated with this new leadership role? Essentially, they are quite similar to many of those previously suggested for the department head on the secondary-school level or the helping teacher (to be discussed later) on the elementary- or secondary-school level.

A brief description of how one team leader functions will illustrate some of the advantages of this organizational plan for assisting teachers to grow professionally.

Miss X, who was chosen to head a team consisting of one senior teacher, five regular teachers, and a group of approximately 185 pupils, is an expert in subject matter as well as in educational theory. She has had over ten years of teaching experience, holds a master's degree, and has completed most of the requirements for the doctorate.

Because of large-group lessons and flexible scheduling, Miss X has one full day and several mornings free for observing her team members in action. She also has sufficient time to coordinate the team's activities by a series of conferences and memorandums.

The following are a few brief excerpts from recent notes she has circulated to team members:

> Parent Conferences
>
> Team members have been informed of the week in which to initiate parent-teacher conferences. Other team members should participate if necessary.
>
> Think-abouts
>
> Handwriting: Miss Y is interested in teaching handwriting—how can the schedule be changed to capitalize on her interest?
>
> Art: Are the periods of sufficient length? Could we schedule one-hour periods?
>
> Rainy Mornings: Can we plan better activities for pupils on rainy days when teachers have meetings?
>
> Music: Miss Z mentioned the fact that she had conducted large music groups in camp. Can we arrange for her to take several groups to sing at one time?
>
> Creative Writing: Miss A has shown considerable ability in helping pupils to write creatively. If she is willing, can it be arranged for her to take charge of a series of large groups instead of several other assignments? [6]

If careful appraisal should reveal that pupils learn equally well under the team teaching plan without affecting their mental health adversely, an avenue will be open to attract and retain individuals of superior talent. There are doubtless many teachers who enjoy helping others to improve

---

[6] Adapted from: Arthur D. Morse, *Schools of Tomorrow—Today!* (Garden City, N.Y.: Doubleday and Company, Inc., 1961), pp. 12-18.

professionally but do not wish to leave the classroom themselves. Serving as a team leader may prove to be the solution for hundreds of individuals who are qualified for administrative and supervisory positions but cannot be placed because of insufficient demand. It also may provide teachers with the opportunity to discover whether or not they would like to prepare for a full-time supervisory position.

THE HELPING TEACHER

Many of the larger school systems have inaugurated the practice of using "helping teachers." These individuals are successful teachers who become attached to the central office staff for the purpose of helping other teachers. They have no responsibility for evaluating teacher performance but are concerned only with assisting teachers to improve in the classroom.

The following duties have been performed by "helping teachers" on the elementary-school level:

1. Holding professional conferences.
2. Helping in summer workshops.
3. Becoming "floating" teachers.
4. Giving television courses for teachers.
5. Encouraging individual schools to engage in studies.
6. Providing programs to strengthen instruction in certain subjects.
7. Offering extension courses.
8. Participating in research projects.[7]

> In Santa Monica, California, five master teachers provide materials, aids, methods, and inspiration for other teachers. Their rooms serve as distribution stations for classroom materials. If these consultant teachers see some excellent materials in one school, they may reproduce them for use in other schools.[8]

Philadelphia (Pa.) selects teachers who are outstanding in a particular area to serve as curriculum collaborators. They assist teachers in interpreting curriculum guides, demonstrating methods, presenting new ideas, and suggesting instructional materials. In addition, they assist in the writing and revising of new guides and serve as group leaders in workshops or in-service courses. Curriculum collaborators must be prepared to teach any grade at any time. After serving a three-year term as a col-

---

[7] U.S. Office of Education, *Fourth Conference for Supervision of Elementary Education in Large Cities* (Washington, D.C.: U.S. Department of Health, Education, and Welfare, March 24-27, 1959), p. 6.

[8] American Association of School Administrators, *The Superintendent as Instructional Leader*, Thirty-fifth Yearbook (Washington, D.C.: National Education Association, 1957), p. 70.

laborator, they return to regular classroom teaching or, in some cases, are promoted to administrative and supervisory positions.

Gary (Ind.) uses "helping teachers" on the secondary-school level. These individuals serve as consultants in the various subject areas and perform many of the functions listed previously in this chapter in the section dealing with the department head.

SUMMARY

Specialists in the areas of art, music, and physical education serve in a variety of relationships to the teacher in the self-contained classroom of the elementary school. Some specialists serve as teachers of their area, others as supervisors, and some as consultants. Each of the above relationships has its advantages and disadvantages. When specialists are provided to assist regular classroom teachers, they should be used in the manner that is most likely to result in a balanced educational program for each child.

Although the department head may still perform an important supervisory function on the secondary-school level, imaginative kinds of staff organization and utilization are responsible for creating new posts with titles such as "area chairman," "division leader," and "team leader." These new positions hold much promise for the improvement of instruction.

Larger school districts also are releasing superior teachers from their regular classroom duties to serve as helping teachers and curriculum collaborators.

SUGGESTED ACTIVITIES AND PROBLEMS

1. Interview five elementary-school teachers to determine how they would prefer the art, music, and physical education specialists to work with them. Attempt to determine to what extent each of these five teachers provides his pupils with experiences in the special fields during the days when the specialists are not available.

2. Interview an art, a music, and a physical education specialist to determine the manner in which each of them believes his services can be used most effectively in the elementary school. Ask each of them to give the reasons for his statements.

3. Locate and read several references dealing with the use of specialists in the elementary school. Assuming the role of an elementary principal, write a detailed recommendation to the superintendent for the most

effective utilization of these staff members. Describe the steps that you took before arriving at your decision, and include the arguments that influenced you.

4. Interview a department head in the secondary school to determine how he perceives his instructional-leadership role. Compare his perception of this role with the competencies and functions of the department head as listed in this chapter.

5. Make an intensive study of a teaching team to determine the role of the team leader. Interview the team leader to determine how he perceives his instructional-leadership role. Compare his perception of this role with the role of this position as described by experts. Attend at least one team meeting to observe the leader in action.

SELECTED READINGS

Barkan, M., *Through Art to Creativity: Art in the Elementary School Program.* Boston: Allyn and Bacon, 1960.

Brownell, John A., and Roland P. Shutt, *The Claremont Teaching Team Program, A Research Project.* Claremont, Cal.: Claremont Graduate School, 1961.

Brownell, John A., and Harris A. Taylor, "Theoretical Perspectives for Teaching Teams," *Phi Delta Kappan,* XLIII, No. 4 (1962), 150.

Gwynn, J. Minor, *Theory and Practice of Supervision,* Chap. 13. New York: Dodd, Mead and Company, 1961.

Marvel, L., *The Music Consultant at Work.* New York: Bureau of Publications, Teachers College, Columbia University, 1960.

Novak, Benjamin J., "The Department Headship To-Day," *Educational Administration and Supervision,* 44, No. 2 (1958), 91.

chapter eight

Factors that Influence Change

For any supervisory technique or device to accomplish its purposes, change must be brought about in the understandings, attitudes, appreciations, and practices of individuals. Too frequently we concentrate on the device or the technique for effecting change and pay little or no attention to change itself and the factors that influence it.

Before the factors that influence change can be understood, it is essential that certain misconceptions about the phenomenon of change be corrected and a positive approach adopted. The following suggestions should prove helpful to the supervisor in this respect:

1. Approach change with an attitude of "let's see."
2. Realize that the most fundamental change is a gradual steady growth.

3. Recognize that change is natural.
4. View change not as a threat, but as an opportunity for growth.
5. Recognize that acceptance of change is not vacillation.
6. Realize that understanding and accepting change requires more than factual knowledge.[1]

Change is everywhere about us. It is, perhaps, like birth and death, one of the few certainties in life. Because of its complexities, it would seem appropriate to briefly discuss here some of the elements of change in respect to changes in the educational process.

THINKING VERSUS DOING

In educational circles the argument over which comes first, thinking or doing, is as bitter as the long-debated question concerning which came first, the chicken or the egg. Do teachers change their instructional practices because their thinking has been changed by a vicarious educational experience, or does their thinking change only after they have actually used an educational procedure or technique successfully?

Reeder labels this as a false dichotomy when he writes:

> It seems obvious that when in asking whether one should change the doing of teachers by changing their thinking, or change their thinking by changing their doing, one has created another of the false dichotomies which has been the curse of our educational thinking. The only sensible answer is that one should change both. But when one has said that, it does not follow that the analysis made above is futile. On the contrary, it shows that in the case of producing change in any significant area of behavior, thinking and doing are inextricably interwoven. Progress in the two must proceed not only simultaneously but in close relationship to each other.[2]

It should, therefore, be apparent that anyone concerned with improving instruction must take into account both the thinking and the doing of the members of the staff.

Translating Thinking Into Doing

It is not too difficult to understand how doing may be translated into thinking, since the eating is the proof of the pudding; but the factors that prevent the translation of thinking into doing are frequently subtle and

---

[1] Department of Elementary School Principals, *The Flexible School* (Washington, D.C.: National Education Association, 1957), pp. 14-16.

[2] Edwin H. Reeder, *Supervision in the Elementary School* (Boston: Houghton Mifflin Company, 1953), p. 19.

obscure. In the first place, the thinking of individuals concerning a particular educational practice may be on several different levels. To illustrate the point, on the same faculty Teacher A might reject the concept of team teaching with little or a great amount of knowledge concerning it, Teacher B might passively accept it on a verbal level, Teacher C might actively accept it on a verbal level, and Teacher D might believe in it implicitly as a superior way to organize for instruction. If the school had been reorganized for team teaching, you would expect four distinct types of performances from the above staff members. Teacher A, if he remained in the district, would begrudgingly comply but he would be likely to use every opportunity to criticize and, perhaps, jeopardize the success of the new procedure. Teacher B would respond with little enthusiasm and probably attain only mediocre success in team teaching. Teacher C might be so occupied with selling the idea to other staff members that he would never develop much proficiency in the procedure himself. Teacher D you would expect to be eminently successful from the start. How does an individual working in a supervisory capacity help teachers to bring about changes in themselves that will result in more of them reacting in the same manner as Teacher D? Perhaps the biggest step is the one from the position of Teacher C to that of Teacher D.

Whether or not thinking comes before or after doing, it is a widely accepted psychological fact that human beings tend to find time for and learn to do those things which they understand, believe in, and value as important. The task of the supervisor, then, is to assist teachers in the examination of their present beliefs and of the values they hold, and to assist them to modify these beliefs and values in light of the changing needs of children and society and the findings of research in child growth, development, motivation, and learning.

FACTORS INFLUENCING CHANGE

An essential prerequisite to success in helping teachers to bring about changes in their thinking and doing is an awareness and understanding of some of the forces that encourage or obstruct change in beliefs and values that teachers hold. Knowledge and understanding of these forces and factors enable the supervisor to bring about change more readily. Cognizance of these facts also helps him to maintain a more sympathetic attitude toward staff members who are struggling with change and consequently are slow in showing signs of improvement. In addition, he will be more tolerant of individuals who reject change in a completely similar fashion to the case of Teacher A previously cited.

No claim is being made here that the following list of factors influencing change is all-inclusive, but rather that it is representative. The following factors will be discussed briefly: (1) individual differences, (2) insecurity, (3) shadows of the past, (4) fear of the new, (5) resistance to change, (6) lack of understanding, (7) lack of skill, (8) too much work, (9) too much time required, (10) different philosophies of education, (11) adult impatience, (12) desire for approval, (13) sense of accomplishment, and (14) discontent.

Examination of the above list gives the reader the impression that most of the factors impede change rather than encourage it; however, the discussion which follows will emphasize both aspects where applicable.

Individual Differences

School administrators for years have been insisting that teachers must make provisions for individual differences in children; then they have treated teachers as if they were all alike. *Readiness* is another term that is applied to children and seldom, if ever, thought of in connection with teachers. However, there are great differences in teachers' readiness for change, owing to factors such as age, health, energy, motivation, and educational background and experiences. The wise supervisor knows all staff members well, understands their individual differences, and gauges the growth of each teacher in terms of his own peculiar growth pattern rather than by comparing it with that of the group or with an ideal held by the supervisor. This is what good teachers are expected to do with children. Why should we ignore individual differences when we work with adults?

Insecurity

Security is one of the basic needs of mankind. We know that too much insecurity in childhood can result in poor mental health and even neurosis in adult life. Much of our striving in life is for security now and in our old age. Billions are being spent for defense in order that we may feel more secure as a nation. Teachers are fearful of giving up practices with which they are familiar. This is true particularly if they have felt secure in using these practices for many years.

Individuals who serve in a supervisory capacity must do everything possible to assist teachers to feel secure in the new situation. Each case will be different, but taking steps similar to the following should prove helpful.

(1) Encourage the teacher to change procedures gradually, taking one step at a time.

(2) Help the teacher to evaluate each step taken before moving to the next one.
(3) Assist the teacher to discover the similarity of the old and new procedures.
(4) Sincerely praise each accomplishment.
(5) Be readily available to render assistance when needed.
(6) Let the teacher know that he is not alone in his feeling of insecurity.

Shadows of the Past

Very often the longer a teacher has taught, the more he is swayed by the influence of the past. The supervisor must recognize that it is difficult for a teacher who, for example, has successfully taught arithmetic to seventh-grade youngsters for thirty years to admit that the team teaching approach might be superior. In the mind of the teacher (perhaps at a subconscious level), this is tantamount to admitting that his work for the past thirty years has been inferior.

The supervisor has all around him examples of progress in other professions and areas of living to use in helping teachers to understand that one's past performance is not to be condemned when newer and better ways are found to accomplish an objective. Present-day automation does not mean that the millions who are now being replaced by machines have labored in vain.

Fear of the New

Basically man, except for the adventurous few, is fearful of something new and different. Part of this fear, of course, has to do with his sense of insecurity previously discussed. In addition to the steps suggested in that section, supervisors should encourage the pioneering spirit. Education needs more adventurous people. Teachers should be encouraged to experiment—to try new things. Too many teachers with twenty-five years of teaching experience have in reality taught one year twenty-five times. If this spirit of inquiry, investigation, and experimentation is to prevail, teachers must not be penalized for making mistakes. Thomas Edison performed hundreds of experiments before he developed the incandescent light bulb. Teachers must learn that success usually comes as the result of a number of failures.

Resistance to Change

Man is a creature of his habits. The daily routine of the average individual changes little during a lifetime. Many teachers day by day, month by month, and year by year go through the same motions. As one observes them teach, the impression is received that much of their teaching has become automatic. These teachers are "in a rut" instead of being "in the groove." How does the supervisor help teachers to overcome these old habits? The simplest answer is to form new and more desirable habits to replace the old ones. The suggestions given under the two areas discussed immediately above also may be applied effectively in this case. In fact, all three factors are closely interrelated.

Lack of Understanding

Too frequently, supervisors assume that teachers understand a certain procedure or process and later on find out that there is considerable misunderstanding. An example of this occurred some years ago when one of the writers was a supervisor in a school district that was attempting to move to a "less regimented" program of instruction. One day he visited a second-grade class that resembled a three-ring circus. During the conference which followed the observation, it soon became apparent that the teacher believed that she was successfully conducting a "less regimented" program. Upon further analysis of the learning situation based on criteria that previously had been developed, the teacher was shocked to discover that, instead of the desired freedom, she was encouraging license in the classroom.

What is the cue for the supervisor when lack of understanding prevents a teacher from following a new technique or procedure? The answer to this question is obvious. The good supervisor does everything possible to see that all teachers understand the change that is to be effected. One way to ensure that this happens is to move slowly. Evolution is preferable to revolution, even though it takes a considerably longer period of time. Teachers should be discouraged from trying a new procedure until they thoroughly understand the purpose of what they are attempting to do as well as the correct manner in which it is to be done. For example, teachers should not be encouraged to employ such child-study techniques as the keeping of anecdotal records or the using of sociometric techniques until they have had considerable competent instruction in these areas.

Lack of Skill

It is quite possible for a teacher to thoroughly understand a process and its purposes and at the same time lack the necessary skill to use the process effectively. Here again the individual differences found in teachers must be given consideration. These differences in teachers were quite evident in one school district which was attempting to change from a basal reading system to an experience approach. It soon became apparent to the supervisor that some teachers made the transition easily, that others made the move with varying degrees of success, and that a few teachers were unable to make this change at all. In this particular instance, the district continued to supply sets of up-to-date basal and co-basal readers if teachers desired to use them. However, teachers were encouraged to employ the experience approach to the degree in which they felt comfortable in using it.

Too Much Work

Many of the new procedures being advocated today require the additional expenditure of energy. The already overburdened teacher is reluctant to try new techniques if it requires a heavier load than he is now carrying. The trend of the times is toward less work and more leisure. Teachers should not be expected to willingly increase their work loads when everyone else is lightening theirs.

In attempting to counteract this impediment to change, the supervisor must look for ways of reducing the clerical and supervisory duties of teachers before the instructional load is increased. There are many duties performed by teachers that can be done equally well by less-qualified personnel.

Too Much Time Required

Quite frequently teachers equate work and time, but these are actually of different dimensions. One of the most serious points of conflict has to do with the definition of a teacher's day. For some reason boards of education and school administrators have been unwilling to designate what constitutes a teacher's day. As a consequence, a teacher's work day varies considerably from school district to school district. Because there has been no common agreement, most teachers and the general lay public assume that a teacher's day consists of the hours during which the pupils are in school. Any demands made by the school on the teacher's time after the pupils leave is resented by many teachers. For years, secondary-school teachers have expected additional remuneration for certain services performed after school hours and, more recently, elementary teachers also have received extra pay for similar assignments.

One school district that recently introduced team teaching on the elementary-school level has received considerable opposition from the teachers because team meetings are held after school several evenings a week.

With this attitude on the part of teachers, great success in the new type of organization can hardly be expected.

As was suggested in the previous section, if teachers are expected to carry additional responsibilities because of the changes desired, they must be relieved of part of their work load. In this instance, the essential element is time. In the case just cited, unless boards of education are willing to define a teacher's day as extending beyond the time when pupils are present, time for team meetings will have to be found during the pupil-attendance day. This may necessitate the employment of additional personnel.

Different Philosophies of Education

Many teachers hold strong beliefs about educational procedures and cannot honestly support practices which are contrary to what they believe. For example, a teacher who strongly believes in the merits of the core program in the junior high school may find himself in a situation where a decision has been made to return to a completely departmentalized type of school organization. Instead of a teaching assignment that includes the teaching of English and social studies to two core groups, his assignment under the departmentalized organization would consist of teaching English to five sections of seventh-grade pupils. He honestly believes that it is essential for a teacher to know his pupils well and that English can be taught best by relating it to other areas of the curriculum. Under the core plan of organization he has 60 different pupils to work with each day, while under the departmentalized plan his pupil load will be 150 pupils each day.

Under the above circumstances, could the teacher be blamed for resisting the change and giving the departmentalized organization only half-hearted support? What procedures can the supervisor follow in situations similar to the one cited above? Should teachers be required to work under conditions that make it necessary for them to engage in practices that are in conflict with their philosophy of education? The authors believe that generally it is not good educational practice to require teachers to change under these circumstances. If there is reliable research to prove the superiority of the new procedure, the supervisor should do everything possible to help the teacher to "see the light." If he fails, the teacher should be given the opportunity to accept within the district another assignment that does not conflict with his philosophy. If this is not possible, the administration should assist the teacher in locating elsewhere a position that is consistent with his beliefs.

Unfortunately, too frequently these changes are an administrative expediency or a "band wagon" tactic, neither of which can be justified under any circumstances. Consequently, if the supervisor meets strong resistance to change because of differences in philosophy, it might be a cue for him to examine more carefully the contemplated change.

Adult Impatience

This characteristic of the adult which may result in resistance to change is described as follows in a recent publication:

> The typical adult learner is an *impatient learner*. After he has worked a few years and acquired the normal number of adult responsibilities—a home, a family, a lawn to mow, household bills to pay, a monthly bank statement to check—he has less time to be patient. With so many tasks competing for his limited supply of time, he has the least patience with those things he does not have to do. Usually an out-of-school project can be classified as one of the things he is not forced to do. He may feel compelled to attend the meeting but he cannot be forced to produce in a discussion.[3]

The adult learner shows his impatience in other ways. If he can't learn quickly, he may stop trying. Because of his status, he often considers it a reflection on his ability if suggestions for improvement are made. He violently defends the *status quo*.

In dealing with this trait of the adult learner, the supervisor must react to impatience with patience. He must help the teacher to realize that new patterns of action are not easy to acquire. Every small gain must be consolidated. The motto must be, "the less haste, the greater the speed."

Desire for Approval

Another strong basic human need is the desire for approval. This basic need can influence change both positively and negatively. Teachers will change their practices in order that they may receive the approval of their peers, parents, pupils, and supervisors. They also may resist change if they find that their friends are not in favor of the innovation. Many a principal has wondered why a teacher who in private conversation spoke enthusiastically in support of a contemplated change voted against it with the majority in a subsequent staff meeting. If one of these bewildered principals could have followed that teacher in the interim, he would have noted the strong influence of friends as they rejected the new idea.

---

[3] American Association of School Administrators, *Staff Relations in School Administration*, Thirty-third Yearbook (Washington, D.C.: National Education Association, 1955), pp. 91-92.

The enlightened supervisor capitalizes on this desire for approval by working with groups to arrive at group decisions. In addition, as previously suggested, approval and recognition are sincerely given for every little achievement.

Sense of Accomplishment

A sense of accomplishment spurs the doer on to even greater efforts. Each step upward widens the horizon of the climber and urges him on to greater heights. Conversely, there is very little motivation for the climber who tries to reach the second floor by using a "down" escalator.

Successful supervisors know that teachers must be urged regularly to evaluate their accomplishments. They must be encouraged to aim high but often should be satisfied with small gains. Sometimes teachers are so close to their jobs that they do not recognize the progress that they have made. They welcome the assistance of the supervisor in assessing their accomplishments.

Discontent

Discontent is one of the most valuable allies that a supervisor can enlist to bring about change.

> Any conscious change in an individual's method of teaching or his selection and use of instructional materials starts when he becomes discontented with what he is doing. Discontent is the first phase of the process of change and improvement, and discontent results from the more or less continuous assessment every professional person makes of the effects of what he is doing. When these effects indicate too great a difference between what he sees happening and what he believes should happen, he becomes uneasy. He is moved to begin to change his practice in order to bring the *is* and the *ought* closer together.[4]

The authority quoted above believes that, when the dissatisfaction is great enough, the teacher will search for new procedures that will reduce the gap between present and desired practices. Eventually new practices will be selected (sometimes unwisely), a design worked out, the procedures tried, and finally an evaluation made.[5]

It should be evident to the reader that the supervisor has an important role to play in each one of the above steps. One of the most difficult tasks

---

[4] American Association of School Administrators, *The Superintendent as Instructional Leader,* Thirty-fifth Yearbook (Washington, D.C.: National Education Association, 1957), pp. 30-31.

[5] *Ibid.,* p. 31.

is to help teachers to overcome their complacency. The supervisor can encourage continuous assessment, which is prerequisite to discontent, but how can he be certain that teachers will be displeased with what they find? The real leadership role here is to assist teachers to set their sights high enough so that they are never completely satisfied.

Chapters IX and X are concerned with individual and group techniques that the reader can use in assisting teachers in the assessment, search, selection, design, trial, and evaluation steps.

SUMMARY

The supervisor who wishes to develop competency in producing educational change must know and understand the factors that influence change. As his knowledge and experience increase, he will learn that, among others, the following elements encourage or impede change: (1) individual differences, (2) insecurity, (3) shadows of the past, (4) fear of the new, (5) resistance to change, (6) lack of understanding, (7) lack of skill, (8) too much work, (9) too much time required, (10) different philosophies of education, (11) adult impatience, (12) desire for approval, (13) sense of accomplishment, and (14) discontent.

As he works with teachers, the supervisor will become increasingly more skillful in eliminating or ameliorating the factors that retard change and more adept at utilizing those elements that are favorable to change.

SUGGESTED ACTIVITIES AND PROBLEMS

1. Interview five teachers who have been in positions where it was necessary for them to adopt new teaching procedures. Keeping in mind the factors discussed in this chapter, attempt to find out which of them influenced each of the teachers for or against the innovations. Write a paper in which you report the findings from the interviews and the conclusions you have drawn.

2. Compare and contrast change as it operates in the teaching profession with the way it takes place in medicine, government, and industry.

3. Agree to make a radical change (for the better) in the area of your job in which you are the least proficient. During a minimum period of six weeks, keep a record of your trials, tribulations, and successes in effecting this change. Write a final report in which you recount your experiences and relate them to the information in this chapter.

SELECTED READINGS

Department of Elementary School Principals, *The Flexible School.* Washington, D. C.: National Education Association, 1957.

Lucio, William H., and John D. McNeil, *Supervision—A Synthesis of Thought and Action,* Chap. 8. New York: McGraw-Hill Book Company, Inc., 1962.

Swearigen, Mildred E., *Supervision of Instruction: Foundations and Dimensions,* Chap. 12. Boston: Allyn and Bacon, Inc., 1962.

Kumpf, Carl H., *The Adaptable School.* New York: The Macmillan Company, 1952.

chapter nine

Working with Individuals to Improve Instruction

The improvement of the instructional program in a school results from changes that take place within each individual staff member. Some of these changes take place as a result of group experiences and others, as an outcome of individual experiences; moreover, individual and group techniques are not mutually exclusive. In fact, operationally they reinforce each other. In addition, there are some techniques that could be placed in either category, depending upon whether the emphasis is on the individual or the group. For example, if a teaching demonstration is conducted in a given teacher's classroom to assist him in the solution of an instructional problem, this type of demonstration lesson would belong in the category of individual techniques. On the other hand, if a demonstration lesson is taught before a group of teachers to introduce a new teaching procedure—for example, teaching the new mathematics—it would be considered a group technique. Therefore, for the purpose of discussion, the authors have arbitrarily assigned the various supervisory techniques to one or the other of the two categories. Tradition supports a majority of the assignments, but in several cases the writers have departed from it. The individual techniques will be discussed in this chapter and the group techniques in Chapter X. In addition to a discussion of devices to be used in working with individuals, this chapter will deal with creative teachers, problem teachers, and teachers who have personal problems.

INDIVIDUAL TECHNIQUES

For convenience of discussion, the following devices or techniques will be classified as supervisory procedures to be used largely in working with individuals: (1) assignment of teachers, (2) classroom visitation and observation, (3) classroom experimentation, (4) college courses, (5) conferences (individual), (6) demonstration teaching, (7) evaluation, (8) activities and conferences of professional organizations, (9) professional reading, (10) professional writing, (11) selection of instructional materials, (12) selection of professional staff, (13) supervisory bulletins, (14) informal contacts, and (15) other experiences contributing to personal and professional growth.

Assignment of Teachers

Many school administrators would consider the assignment of teachers an administrative function, but in reality it can be the one supervisory move that affects not only the immediate success but the entire career of the teacher. If a teacher is given an assignment for which he is not qualified emotionally as well as academically, he may be a complete misfit and beyond any real supervisory help.

Here, again, administrators should take a cue from their own educational clichés. "Place a child in the situation in which he has the greatest opportunity for success," they say. However, in the assignment of teachers, they frequently give inexperienced and other teachers new to the district the worst teaching situations. The best assignments are awarded to staff members on a seniority basis or, in some cases, as a reward for conforming (*cooperating* is the term most frequently used.) On the other hand, rarely do the senior citizens (those within five years of retirement) receive the consideration they should have. Certainly, teachers who are approaching retirement should be permitted to ease up gradually rather than be expected to run full steam ahead until the very end and then come to a full stop.

As a supervisory technique, then, the qualifications of each teacher should be carefully studied before an assignment is made. Teachers should be placed, with their consent, in positions for which they are best qualified, taking into consideration all their characteristics as well as their education and years of teaching experience. In making assignments, the concept that all teachers must be treated in an identical manner should be discarded. In its place the belief that individuals should be treated in terms of their needs should be substituted in order that an effective teaching force may be developed.

Classroom Visitation and Observation

Probably no area of supervision has been discussed in greater detail, with more conflicting opinions, than the conditions under which observations are to be made and the procedures that are to be used. Early texts in supervision gave the supervisor a blueprint for entering the classroom and conducting the observation. Later texts advised against the use of this unpopular technique, and present-day writings emphasize that classroom observations should be made only after the supervisor has established rapport with the teacher, and then largely on an "on call" basis.

Beliefs held about visitation. Currently there are a number of beliefs concerning procedures to be followed in classroom visitation that are rather commonly held by authorities in the field of supervision. There are, of course, those who take exception to one or more of the statements. It will become clear later that the authors will have to be placed in this group of dissenters. The following list is representative of these beliefs and not a complete list:

1. Good rapport should exist between the teacher and the supervisor.
2. Visitation should be largely on an "on call" basis.
3. The supervisor should carefully prepare for each classroom visit.
4. The visitor should enter the classroom as unobtrusively as possible.
5. The supervisor should not participate in the activity in progress.
6. A conference should precede the visit.
7. A conference should follow the visit.
8. Notes for use in the conference should be kept of each extended classroom observation, but they should not be made during the visit without the approval of the teacher.
9. The observer should concentrate on the total learning situation.
10. The supervisor should attempt to discover the strong points in the learning situation.

11. Suggestions for the improvement of the lesson should not be made unless the teacher asks for them.

12. The supervisor should not remain in the classroom if his presence is disturbing either the pupils or the teacher.

13. There is no established minimum and maximum time for a visit.

14. Details of room management are important to observe.

15. Records of supervisory visits should be kept.

16. During the visit, the supervisor should not in any way show disapproval of what is happening in the classroom.

17. The supervisor should make a complimentary remark before leaving the classroom.

Although each of the above suggestions has merit under certain conditions, they must be followed intelligently in respect to a particular set of circumstances. Perhaps the first suggestion has the most universal application. The authors concur with those authorities who stress the importance of rapport between supervisor and teacher. However, they believe that, after rapport has been established, there is no single set of classroom visitation procedures that is applicable under all circumstances. They agree with Jordan when he writes: "Actually teachers differ so much, classrooms differ so much, and methods differ so much that it is almost impossible to determine the protocols of visiting." [1] Therefore, it would seem logical to suggest that it is no longer possible to generalize concerning the correct procedures to use under all circumstances in classroom visitation and observation. The visitor, the purpose of the visit, the teacher visited, and the type of activity observed condition the procedures to be used. It would be impossible in a work of this dimension to demonstrate all the variables, but several illustrations will be given to clarify the point made above.

Assisting an inexperienced teacher. Miss Willing is in her first month of teaching English to a tenth-grade class of general students. She has been having difficulty in getting her students interested in Shakespeare's *Twelfth Night.* Miss Willing had an unusually good relationship with her critic teacher during her practice teaching; consequently, she has no fear of the supervisor but looks upon him as someone who can assist her in solving her problems. Miss Willing has informed the supervisor of her problem and invited him to drop in at any time and as often as it is possible for him to come. In this favorable climate, which of the above suggestions apply?

Assisting an experienced teacher. Mr. Oldster has been teaching gen-

[1] William C. Jordan, *Elementary School Leadership* (New York: McGraw-Hill Book Company, Inc., 1959), p. 195.

eral science to eighth-grade pupils for thirty years. During that period his instructional procedures and the content of his science curriculum have changed very little. With the new emphasis on science in the elementary school, much of the material which Mr. Oldster presents is now learned in the elementary school. As a consequence, pupils are bored in his classes and refuse to cooperate. A constant stream of pupils are sent to the office. Mr. Oldster has always resented classroom visitation by any school official. If you were a new principal in this situation, which of the above suggestions would you consider important to observe in attempting to improve this learning situation?

Assisting non-certificated teaching personnel. Because of a short supply of certificated teachers, Mr. Smart, a graduate of a liberal arts curriculum, has been engaged to teach a self-contained classroom of fifth-grade youngsters. Although he seems to enjoy working with pupils in this age group, Mr. Smart has some decided opinions concerning instructional procedures. By the end of the second week of school, you have received several reports from parents that Mr. Smart is conducting his classes largely by the lecture method. You know that he needs help. Which of the suggestions would be pertinent in this situation?

Implementing a group study project. An elementary-school staff has undertaken an in-service education project concerned with the use of programmed instruction in the teaching of arithmetic in grades four, five, and six. The principal has taken a summer workshop dealing with this topic and is serving as the consultant for the project. Classroom visitation and observation are necessary to the success of the project. Which of the suggestions would apply in this situation?

Purposes of classroom visitation. The above anecdotes illustrate four different classroom situations in which visitation and observation may be used as one procedure for improving instruction. It should be noted that, in the first three anecdotes mentioned above, teacher status is the most crucial variable that must be considered. In the fourth one, this is not an important factor.

Although the list is not complete, the following additional purposes are worthy of note: (1) to observe a substitute teacher in action, (2) to hear a resource person make a presentation, (3) to view small- and large-group instruction under the team teaching plan of organization, (4) to observe an outstanding lesson by invitation of the teacher, and (5) to assist in the evaluation of an audio-visual presentation.

It should be apparent to the reader that the four purposes included in the anecdotes and the five purposes listed above roughly fall into the following two (although not mutually exclusive) categories: (1) observations made to obtain an over-all picture of the instructional program and (2) observations performed to acquire information that can be used in the solution of instructional problems. Most writers on the subject emphasize the second category almost to the exclusion of the first. The authors believe that the first category is equally important. They support this belief with the ensuing discussion of the necessity for individuals in a supervisory capacity to have an accurate over-all picture of the learners, the learning environment, and the instructional program.

Observation as a basic supervisory technique. It is impossible for the principal or other staff personnel to serve effectively in a supervisory capacity without seeing the pupils in action. If the objective of supervision is to improve the learning situation, the supervisor must spend a great deal of time in the places where the learning is taking place. If he is to assist in the development of a curriculum that will meet the needs of the children or youth in the particular building or school district in which he serves, he must observe these youngsters—all of them—at work and play. He must be aware of their activities in the classroom, library, auditorium, gymnasium, and cafeteria, and on the playground and athletic field. He must see them in study halls, in co-curricular activities as participants and spectators, and at social events. No activity should escape his notice.

As he observes his charges, the supervisor gathers a lot of information about them. He learns something about their homes and their state of health from the way they look, act, and speak. He acquires a good understanding of the learning situation. He notes whether or not they are enthusiastic or disinterested, unchallenged or over-extended, cooperative or overly competitive, active or passive, independent or overly dependent, secure or insecure, and happy or unhappy.

He checks to see whether or not they are improving in their work habits, growing in their ability to think critically and creatively, becoming more proficient in using research techniques, and learning how to get along better with each other. These things and others the supervisor learns about the pupils through visitation and observation.

Although his attention is on the children and the learning situation, the supervisor gets some cues from the teacher as part of the learning environment. He soon knows whether or not the pupils like and respect the teacher, how the teacher feels about the pupils, and something about the effects of the teacher's personality on the pupils. He learns how the teacher feels about the area of the curriculum being taught and the extent to which the teacher is providing for individual differences. He notes the teacher's skill in classroom management, and he soon becomes aware of the more obvious strengths and weaknesses in the instructional program.

The supervisor who spends sufficient time in the classroom also learns much about the curriculum. Crosby makes this point clear when she writes:

> Observation throws new light upon the quality of the learning experiences present in a teaching situation. The kinds of experiences provided, the relationships between and among the various experiences, the roles of the teacher and children in planning and evaluating their experiences, and the quality of planning revealed are factors which must be analyzed when teacher and supervisor work together to help the teacher provide for more effective curriculum building with children.[2]

Through classroom visitation the supervisor learns how effectively the teaching tools are being utilized. Are pupils using reference materials other than the basic text? How effectively are workbooks being employed? To what extent and how effectively is programmed learning being used? Are audio-visual materials being utilized to the greatest advantage? What is the quality and quantity of homework that is being assigned? Complete answers to these and other similar questions cannot be obtained except through classroom visitation and observation.

Finally, classroom visitation is necessary to determine the physical learning environment in which pupils and teachers are working. In recent years much research has been conducted in order to discover the effect of the physical environment on learning. The effects of the thermal, visual, and sonic environments on learning have all been the subject of investigation. In spite of the findings of research in these areas, hundreds of thousands of children and youth attend classes in rooms that violate all known principles of a good learning environment. During the past year the authors visited over a hundred elementary- and secondary-school classrooms in buildings ranging in age from some that were 100 years old to others that were being used for the first school term. In classrooms old and new, children were working in thermal environments ranging from 60 to 90 degrees, in visual environments varying in light intensity from 20 foot-candles to 200 foot-candles, and in sonic environments that ranged from rooms that were adequately sound-conditioned to those in which sounds within the room and outside reverberated at a distracting level.

In addition to the above, the furnishings of the room and their arrangement influence the learning of pupils. Whether or not desks are too large or too small, in straight lines or grouped, light- or dark-colored, defaced or unmarred, screwed to the floor or movable, all tell their story about the learning environment.

In the case of the physical environment, the authors are not suggesting

---

[2] Muriel Crosby, *Supervision as Co-operative Action* (New York: Appleton-Century-Crofts, Inc., 1957), p. 52.

that, just because the supervisor is aware of any undesirable situations, these can be improved immediately. However, they are stating that, unless the supervisor visits all classrooms frequently, these conditions may not be discovered. Unfortunately, teachers are prone to continue year after year in classroom environments that are undesirable for learning. In fact, they frequently are responsible for this undesirable physical environment. By their own poor classroom management and through unreasonable requests to the custodian, teachers keep their classrooms too hot or too cold, too light or too dark, and too neat or too untidy. They place movable furniture in straight lines and keep it there, or they are constantly shuffling their furniture. Yes, teachers must accept some responsibility for the physical environment of their classrooms.

Visitorial and observational procedures. It has been the thesis of this section that the individual who serves in a supervisory capacity must spend a great deal of time in classroom observation under many different conditions and sets of circumstances. It also has been suggested that, because of the variety of circumstances, no hard-and-fast set of rules and regulations for classroom visitation can be drawn up and followed on every occasion. However, the remainder of this section will offer suggestions that show how the visitorial and observational patterns of the supervisor might vary, depending upon whether he is observing to obtain an over-all picture or to assist in the solution of a problem.

There are at least three different types of observational visits that the supervisor might use in obtaining an over-all view of the educational program. One of these is the classroom visit made in the morning before the teachers and pupils arrive or in the late afternoon when they have departed. Much can be learned about the educational program from an empty classroom, particularly on the elementary level. The observer should note whether or not the classroom is neat and attractive and at the same time has the earmarks of a workshop. The use that is being made of the bulletin boards also should be observed. Is there any evidence that special projects are being carried on in the classroom? Projects and displays are quite revealing. Other pupils' work may be in evidence for examination. Writing on the blackboard or on charts may be quite informative. If an elementary classroom is visited, the observer should note whether or not the room has work centers and if it is homelike in appearance. He should also pay particular attention to the arrangement of the furniture. This often gives cues concerning the extent to which informality is encouraged in the learning environment. Finally, the observer should check to determine whether or not the classroom is well equipped with supplies, books, maps, charts, pictures, and other audio-visual materials.

A second and somewhat similar procedure is to make a series of short visits during the school day. Five- or ten-minute visits to a large number of classrooms during a span of several days will make it possible not only to get answers to the above questions but also to gather a considerable amount of information concerning teacher-pupil relationships and the general climate of learning.

A third type of observation in this category consists of visiting a number of classrooms on different grade levels and becoming a participant in the activities in progress. Some authorities frown upon this procedure, maintaining that it is very poor visitation etiquette. The authors disagree with this attitude. They firmly believe that individuals who work in a supervisory capacity (particularly principals) are not visitors, but part of the instructional team. For years they have entered classrooms and pitched right in, working with pupils at their seats or in work groups while the teacher was conducting some other small-group activity. One of the authors gauged his rapport in a given classroom in terms of whether or not pupils approached him for assistance when the teacher was otherwise occupied. To hear one of the following salutations as soon as you enter the classroom is music to the ears of a supervisor: "Mr. Jones, we are writing an original play; please come over and help our group." "Miss Smith, our group is trying to set up an original experiment to prove how evaporation takes place—please, won't you give us some guidance?" A supervisor then is no longer an outsider in that classroom.

On other occasions, the supervisor may assist the teacher in correcting papers or workbooks, help pupils who are working on a frieze, make suggestions to pupils who are working on a social studies project, join in the singing, participate in playground activities, and engage in numerous other activities which demonstrate to pupils and teachers that the supervisor is there to help. This is not only one of the best procedures to keep in touch with the total program, but it is more likely to insure a welcome for the supervisor at other times when problems arise that need to be solved cooperatively.

The reader will note that the authors have not suggested that the supervisor under any circumstances should take over the class. The *teacher is in charge* of the class at all times. The supervisor is merely assisting pupils who need and desire help which the teacher cannot give at the moment because he is working with other pupils. It is important to emphasize again that the rapport between the supervisor and the teacher must be excellent for this type of visitation to take place.

Observations made for the purpose of gathering information to use in the solution of a problem may be of the "on call" type or they may be scheduled by the supervisor in cases where the teacher is not aware of the problem, unable to accept the problem, or unwilling to admit that it exists. Observational visits made for this purpose would have to take place at a time when the activity to be studied was in progress or the condition to be observed was present in the classroom.

Careful preparation is required for this type of visit, including a conference with the teacher before the visit in some instances. The supervisor under these circumstances would be likely to work most efficiently as a passive observer, at least at first. In some instances it may be highly desirable to take notes, if it is agreeable to the teacher. The teacher may even be willing to have parts of the activity recorded on tape. Doubtless, in the future, both sight and sound reproduction will be employed as an aid in the solution of classroom problems, as equipment becomes less expensive and more readily available.

A number of visits of varying length, followed by conferences, may be necessary before a plan for a solution to the problem can be cooperatively agreed upon. It may take a long time to improve some situations. The supervisor who expects speedy improvement in all instances is doomed to disappointment.

Throughout the years, authorities in the field of school administration and supervision have developed various types of check lists, observation forms,[3] and observational procedures to assist the observer in appraising the teaching-learning situation. The opponents of these devices frequently have been as loud in their condemnation as the exponents have been in their praise. The authors maintain that any device that assists the observer to improve his observation techniques can be of value at certain times and under certain conditions. If the use of such a device destroys the rapport between the teacher and the supervisor, it should not be used.

One very promising procedure, the Flanders system of interaction-analysis observation,

> . . . has been found to be an effective way to supply to the teacher objective and reliable information about his role in the classroom. It is a procedure which may be used by observers who may collect data systematically in his classroom, or it may be used by the teacher himself as a method of analyzing tape recordings of his own teaching. It is a method of summarizing what he actually does in the classroom where he is free to make his own judgments of value about it.[4]

These examples of several different kinds of visitorial behavior, together with the other discussion provided, should be sufficient to convince

[3] Dwight E. Beecher, *The Teaching Evaluation Record* (Buffalo, N.Y.: Educators Publishing Co., 1956).

[4] Edmund J. Amidon and Ned A. Flanders, *The Role of the Teacher in the Classroom, A Manual for Understanding and Improving Teachers' Classroom Behavior* (Philadelphia: Temple University, College of Education, Group Dynamics Center, June 1962), p. 4.

the supervisor or prospective supervisor that each individual must determine his own pattern of classroom visitation in keeping with his unique situation. Finally, the authors hope that they have convinced the reader that this is a very important technique if it is used properly.

Classroom Experimentation

Teachers should be encouraged to originate new approaches, new techniques, and new materials for teaching. For years schools have been reluctant to experiment because they were fearful of unfavorable public reaction. The answers received in opinion polls in three rather diverse areas involving, respectively, 2,201, 1,253, and 769 parents indicated that from 75 to 80 per cent of the parents favored experimentation in the teaching of arithmetic and reading.[5] This should give us some encouragement to experiment.

Experimentation may vary from small changes in teaching practices to large-scale research projects that include the use of control groups. One third-grade teacher with whom the writer worked as a supervisor actually had her class write a third-level reader, claiming that adults could not write books for children. Another teacher experimented with *individualized reading* ten years before it became a popular topic in the literature in the field. A third teacher taught eighth-grade science on an individual basis with every pupil working in areas of his own interests.

However, experimentation also has its dangers. Gwynn suggests the following cautions in using classroom experimentation as a supervisory technique:

1. The new method that is tried out should be judged to be as good and as effective as the old method and should not harm the pupil or hinder his learning.
2. Both children and parents should be made aware of the experimentation and the reasons for it, and their co-operation should be secured in carrying it out.
3. The teacher should not be blamed if the experiment is not as successful as was hoped. Not all experiments succeed.[6]

College Courses

If they are going to prove helpful to the teacher in his present teaching situation, supervisors should assume a more active role in assisting teach-

---

[5] Educational Service Bureau, Temple University, *A Survey of the Neshaminy Joint Schools, An Evaluation of the Easton-Forks Elementary Schools,* and *A Survey of the Cornwall-Lebanon Schools* (Philadelphia: The Bureau, 1962). (Mimeographed)

[6] J. Minor Gwynn, *Theory and Practice of Supervision* (New York: Dodd, Mead & Company, 1961), pp. 339-340.

ers to select courses offered on campus and in extension centers. The writer has advised hundreds of students in planning their graduate programs, and he has found only a small number of students who actually recognize their strengths and weaknesses. This awareness seems to increase somewhat with experience. Too many teachers (particularly men) take graduate work to prepare for another type of educational position instead of to improve themselves for their present assignment.

Another manner in which supervisors can help in this respect is to sponsor college or university extension classes in their school buildings or districts. Quite frequently the educational institution can be persuaded to offer a course especially tailored to fit the needs of a particular faculty if sufficient registration can be assured.

Conferences with Teachers

Next to classroom visitation and observation, the supervisory conference is the most direct procedure to assist the individual teacher. Because conferences frequently precede and almost always follow all but general classroom observations, they are commonly thought of as companion techniques.

As was the case in the discussion of classroom visitation and observation, the authors are reluctant to prescribe hard-and-fast rules for conferencing. Here, again, the situation to a great extent determines the course of action.

Reasons for a conference. Various reasons have been given for holding conferences with teachers. After teachers have been observed, they naturally are anxious to know how the supervisor feels about what he saw and heard. If a conference is not held, the teacher frequently begins to worry and is fearful that the supervisor was not pleased. On the other hand, some teachers know that the lesson observed was a good one, and they are eager for words of praise. However, the basic reason for holding a conference is that it is a valuable technique for improving instruction. Observations to assist inexperienced teachers, non-certificated teachers, and experienced teachers with problems would not prove very helpful unless one or more conferences were held to plan a program for improving the situation.

Suggestions for conferencing. In keeping with the philosophy that the supervisor-teacher relationship should no longer be a superior-inferior relationship but instead a peer relationship, Burton and Brueckner define a conference in the following manner:

> An individual conference is (or should be) a meeting between two persons equally interested in improving a situation. The views and facts of each party are necessary to complete the picture. Exchange of facts and

ideas is focused on problem-solving and not on one of the persons in the conference.[7]

If the reader keeps in mind the fact that each conference is unique, and follows or adapts the suggestions that fit his situation, the following list should prove helpful.

1. The individual supervisory conference should be looked upon as part of a problem-solving technique.
2. Conferences should be thoroughly prepared for by both the supervisor and the teacher.
3. The conference should be held as soon after the classroom observation as possible.
4. The conference should be held on school time, or within the teacher-day as defined by district policy.
5. The conference should be as informal as possible and held in a place where both the teacher and the supervisor feel at ease.
6. The discussion must be in light of a common, district-wide philosophy of education understood and accepted by both parties.
7. A plan of action should be drawn up in writing, including a summary of points agreed upon by both parties and the assignment of responsibilities.
8. A written summary should be kept of all conferences, and copies should be given to both participants.
9. The conference should be evaluated by both participants with the idea in mind of improving the conferencing technique.

Demonstration Teaching

As was indicated in the introduction to this chapter, demonstration teaching may be used as an individual or a group supervisory technique. Although it is true that, under the modern concept of supervision, a supervisor would not take over a teacher's class unless he requested it, demonstration teaching has an important place in a supervisory program. Spears highlights its role when he writes:

> There is nothing old-fashioned about demonstration teaching in a supervisory program. From the point of view of the one receiving the help it is observation, and the observation of the good work of other teachers is a sound practice in teacher training that begins in the undergraduate school and continues throughout the professional career of a teacher.[8]

---

[7] From: *Supervision: A Social Process,* by William H. Burton and Leo J. Brueckner (New York: Appleton-Century-Crofts, Inc., 1955), p. 168. Copyright © 1955, Appleton-Century-Crofts, Inc.

[8] Harold Spears, *Improving the Supervision of Instruction* (Englewood Cliffs, N.J.: Prentice-Hall, Inc., 1953), p. 273.

The procedures for planning and conducting teaching demonstrations as part of a supervisory program should be adapted to the particular situation. If the reader keeps this in mind, the following list of suggestions should prove helpful when they are used with discretion:

1. Careful preparations should be made for the demonstration by the demonstrator and the observer(s).
2. Demonstrations are more effective if they are conducted in the classroom of the participating pupils.
3. The demonstration should be as similar to a normal classroom situation as possible.
4. During the demonstration, emphasis should be placed on the particular skill or procedure in which the observer(s) desire(s) help.
5. Demonstration teaching should be largely, if not entirely, on an "on call" basis.
6. If the demonstration is conducted by individuals other than supervisory personnel, these persons should not be imposed upon too frequently.
7. The same group of pupils must not be used so often for demonstration purposes that it interferes with their regular planned learning program.
8. A conference including the demonstrating teacher should be held as soon after the demonstration as possible to raise questions and to clarify procedures.
9. The demonstration should be evaluated by observers and participants.

If a school is organized for team teaching, supervisors should capitalize on the possibilities of using large-group instruction as a form of demonstration teaching. As the other team members observe the large-group presentation, they should be learning and benefiting from the material presented and the techniques used. One of the strong arguments for team teaching is the many opportunities for professional growth that can be inherent in this plan of organization.

Evaluation

Evaluation is an essential process in the improvement of the learning situation. Self-evaluation,[9] evaluation by peers, evaluation by supervisory

[9] For example, see Herbert F. A. Smith, "A Self-Analysis of Classroom Teaching," *The Bulletin of the National Association of Secondary-School Principals*, 42, No. 236 (1958), pp. 182-184, and Richard P. McLean, "Teacher, How Do You Rate Yourself?" *New York State Education*, 47, No. 4 (1960), p. 32.

personnel (which actually should be a peer relationship), and evaluation by pupils should all be encouraged. Evaluation of the administrative and supervisory activities by other professional staff members also should be invited. (See Chapter XII.) Individuals serving in a supervisory capacity should attempt to create an atmosphere in which everyone is constantly on the alert to improve himself, to assist others to grow professionally, to enrich the curriculum, to upgrade the materials of instruction, to better the physical facilities, and to enlarge the scope of the special services. This is not to imply that evaluation is only negative. To evaluate and acknowledge that something is good may result in greater improvement in the learning situation than to concentrate on the weaknesses. This idea is not new; authorities for a number of years have suggested that a good supervisory program emphasizes strengths rather than weaknesses.

No attempt will be made here to discuss all aspects of evaluation as it relates to the improvement of instruction; however, several less evident aspects will be highlighted.

Evaluation by pupils and teachers. The authors have found that the evaluation of the instructional program by the pupils can be quite revealing and at the same time stimulates teachers to improve their programs. Administrative and supervisory personnel also benefit greatly from having their effectiveness evaluated by the staff. These procedures are more likely to be of value if the instruments to be used in evaluation are cooperatively formulated and then anonymously filled out by the evaluators. It is asking too much to expect pupils to identify themselves when they are evaluating their learning experiences. If their honest opinions are desired concerning their teacher(s) and other aspects of the school program, they must have the protection of anonymity. The same protection should be given teachers when they are asked to evaluate the administrative and supervisory services. It is somehow easier to be frank in making evaluations when you know that your future relationships with the individuals whose services are being evaluated are not likely to be affected.

Participation in total evaluations. Too frequently the diagnostic aspects of evaluation are considered to be the end results. As a technique for improving instruction, the evaluation process itself is a valuable professional growth experience. For approximately thirty-five years, many secondary-school personnel have periodically participated in the self-evaluation of their educational units. In this process, standardized evaluative criteria have been used which provide check lists for each aspect of the educational enterprise.[10] More recently, a number of evaluative cri-

[10] *Evaluative Criteria* (Washington: National Study of Secondary School Evaluation, 1960).

teria have been developed for use in elementary schools.[11] In keeping with the trend that views the educational process as a continuous K to 12 enterprise, the authors recommend that the application of evaluative criteria be made on a K to 12 basis. Committees for the various areas to be evaluated should include membership from both the elementary- and secondary-school faculties.

Any staff that spends six months to a year (longer if necessary) in an exhaustive evaluation of all aspects of their educational enterprise is bound to grow professionally. Individuals who see only accreditation as an objective in over-all school evaluation are short-sighted indeed.

Many school personnel will have the opportunity to serve on a visitation committee to another school as part of a total evaluation process. Although this necessitates making provisions for the absent teachers' classes, principals and other supervisory personnel should encourage teachers to serve on visitation committees. In fact, the principal should contact the proper authorities to see that his school is represented from time to time on visitation committees. Many teachers who have had this experience place it high on the list of activities that have contributed to their professional growth.

Professional Activities and Conferences

Teachers should be encouraged, but not forced, to engage in activities, meetings, and conferences sponsored by the various national, state, and local educational groups. In recent years the quality of programs presented at these meetings has steadily increased and so has the caliber of their publications. By maintaining a liberal travel budget, administrators should make it possible for staff members to attend these meetings. This is usually accomplished by sending representatives to the meetings of the various organizations on a rotating basis. These representatives should be encouraged to share their experiences with the staff by making an oral or written report. In some instances, both types of reports may be desirable. Supervisors should follow similar procedures when they attend professional meetings.

Some school districts have considered it desirable to have their entire staffs attend certain educational meetings. Typical of this are the Annual Schoolmen's Week Meetings held in Philadelphia, Pennsylvania, each year and sponsored by the School of Education, University of Pennsylvania. Most of the Philadelphia suburban schools close for one or two days so that their staffs may attend these excellent educational meetings.

---

[11] James F. Baker, *Elementary Evaluative Criteria* (Boston: School of Education, Boston University, 1953).

Professional Reading

One of the best ways to keep abreast of the profession is regularly to read several professional magazines and representative books in the field of education as they are published. However, so much is being written that it is impossible for any one person to be thoroughly acquainted with even the literature of his special interest. How, then, can the supervisor make professional reading serve as an individual supervisory technique? First, every school should subscribe to several good professional publications. Second, a strong professional library should be organized in every building. Third, procedures should be cooperatively formulated that will encourage extensive use of these books and magazines. The routing of articles and books to staff members who might benefit from reading them, brief reports on books at staff meetings, and book circles organized for the purpose of discussing current works on education have all proved helpful under certain circumstances. If the supervisor reads widely, he can, during a conference, for example, recommend certain books or articles that have a bearing on the problem to be solved.

Staff members should also be encouraged to build up their own professional libraries and to share books with each other. The supervisor might set the example in this respect. At least one book club for educators is in existence.[12]

Professional Writing

The self-discipline required to write for publication results in a kind of professional growth that is not a by-product of any other educational experience. To encourage a teacher to read widely on a topic, to investigate it further through observation and, if necessary, experimentation, and then to organize the findings into a lucid, written discussion that may prove helpful to others is a valuable individual supervisory technique. Supervisors, therefore, have the responsibility to encourage teachers to write for publication. The writer has read many fine research papers that are worth publishing, but unfortunately most of them never appear in print.

Not only does the writer benefit from his experiences, but through publication individuals who read the article share the fruits of the author's labors.

Here, again, the supervisor can set the example by submitting articles

[12] Educator's Book Club, Englewood Cliffs, N.J.

for publication or even engaging in a more ambitious undertaking. An excellent way to interest teachers in writing is to invite them to collaborate in a writing project. One acquaintance of the writer, while serving as a supervisor in a suburban school district, involved a number of teachers in writing an elementary language series.

Selection of Textbooks and Other Instructional Materials

It should be apparent to the supervisor and prospective supervisor that textbook selection offers many opportunities for the professional growth of teachers and other participants. Determining need, developing criteria, examining sample copies, attending textbook exhibits, applying score cards, and conferring with book-company consultants all can be made to contribute greatly to the in-service growth of the staff. However, this will necessitate wise leadership by the supervisory personnel. At each step of the way, as many teachers as possible should be involved in the selection process. This means that time must be provided. If the main objective is to select one or more series as rapidly as possible so that the textbook order will meet the deadline set by the central office, little opportunity will be provided for professional growth. The search for new textbooks and other teaching materials should be a continuing one. As the curriculum is under constant scrutiny in its entirety, and as areas of it are up for revision periodically, concurrent studies should be conducted to find the necessary texts and other instructional materials that seem to fit the needs of the pupils best. If this procedure is followed, not only will better textbook selection result, but the entire staff will benefit immeasurably as a result of their involvement in the process.

Representatives of publishing companies are always ready and willing to discuss their publications with principals, supervisors, textbook committees, and individual teachers. They are usually familiar with competing books in the field and, consequently, they are in a position to point out the strengths and weaknesses of their textbooks as well as those of competing series. This is usually a valuable educational experience.

> School authorities and publishers have a common purpose in studying the problem of textbook selection: to determine those procedures which best assure a fair and objective evaluation of every textbook under consideration. This means an understanding not only of what each book contributes to good teaching, but also of how well it meets the school's objectives for the grade and subject. Obviously such an understanding benefits both children and schools; it also works for better textbooks by making the publisher an active partner in the teaching profession.[13]

---

[13] The American Textbook Publishers Institute, *Textbooks Are Indispensable* (New York: American Book-Stratford Press, Inc.), p. 65.

Although, as has been suggested, it is possible to involve an entire faculty in certain phases of textbook selection, the actual selection committee might profitably consist of five or six teachers together with administrative and supervisory personnel. Members of the committee should be selected because of their experience, proven teaching competence, individual judgment, and resourcefulness. Other desirable attributes are the ability to recognize imaginative teaching and to appreciate the contribution that good textbooks can make to the learning process when they are used properly.[14]

The following policies concerning the work of the textbook committee are worthy of serious consideration:

1. The membership of the committee should be announced.
2. The membership should be small.
3. The committee's assignment should be reasonable.
4. Adequate free time should be made available.
5. The selection period should be long enough.
6. Publishers should be informed of pending adoptions.
7. Time for interviews with textbook representatives should be provided.
8. Textbook hearings should be arranged if necessary.
9. Opportunities for prudent consultation with other staff members should be provided.
10. All aspects of the publisher's program should be studied.
11. The selection of textbooks and the development of a course of study should be coordinated.
12. Individual subjective judgment should be stressed in selection.[15]

If the informal method of selection is followed, some of the above policies also apply, and these should be observed in the selection process.

When the field finally has been narrowed to two or three basal series, the assistance of the publishing companies can be solicited once more. These firms all employ educational consultants who will be glad to work with your staff in appropriate ways.

Developing criteria for selection. A continuous program of textbook evaluation based on a set of written criteria developed locally and a subjective appraisal as books are used day by day make the task of selecting new textbooks a less complicated one. Too frequently, textbooks are examined critically only at adoption time. All materials of instruction, as well as methods of instruction, should be under constant scrutiny at all times. Evaluation is a continuous process.

Criteria for selection are of both a quantitative and a qualitative nature. Some of the most commonly used quantitative measures are: vocabulary

---

[14] *Ibid.*, p. 66.
[15] *Ibid.*, pp. 67-70.

LANSDOWNE-ALDAN JOINT SCHOOL SYSTEM
ELEMENTARY SCHOOL TEXTBOOK EVALUATION SCORE CARD
LANGUAGE TEXTBOOKS OR WORKBOOK TEXTS

		Rating of Book
Title ______________	Superior	______
Author ______________	Good	______
Publisher ______________	Average	______
Copyright date ________ Price ________	Poor	______

Scale for rating each item: 3-Superior; 2-Acceptable; 1-Not acceptable; 0- Not included

ITEM	RATING 3	2	1	0
A. Authorship and Point of View				
1. Are the authors well qualified in training and experience?				
2. How acceptable is the underlying philosophy of the series?				
3. Is the philosophy clearly and consistently demonstrated in the presentation and use of the contents?				
4. Does the textbook follow and interpret the objectives of the course of study?				
5. Is the series based on important research?				
B. Content				
1. Does the material arouse the interest of the children?				
2. Is it related to the children's experiences in speaking, writing, reading, and spelling?				
3. Is there adequate emphasis on fundamental English skills?				
Is enough functional grammar provided?				
4. Are stories, poems, and children's literature appropriate and of high quality?				
5. Is there correlation with the other subject areas of the curriculum?				
6. Is there proper balance between oral and written expression and listening experiences?				
7. Are the vocabulary and sentence structure well adapted to the grade level?				
8. Are ideas developed skillfully?				
9. Is the development of social competence emphasized?				
Are the social amenities taught in due perspective to the communicative skills?				
10. Is there provision for creative work in language?				
C. Presentation of Material and Organization				
1. Is readiness developed for each new topic?				
2. Are skills developed in natural settings and with purposeful practice?				
3. Is the presentation clear, understandable, and stimulating?				
4. Is the organization flexible?				
5. Is the development of content easy to follow by pupils and teacher?				
D. Practice and Drill Material				
1. Is practice preceded by careful development?				
2. Is the book adequately equipped with practice material?				
3. Is sufficient practice provided for initial mastery of new processes or understandings?				

Fig. 7. Textbook Score Card.

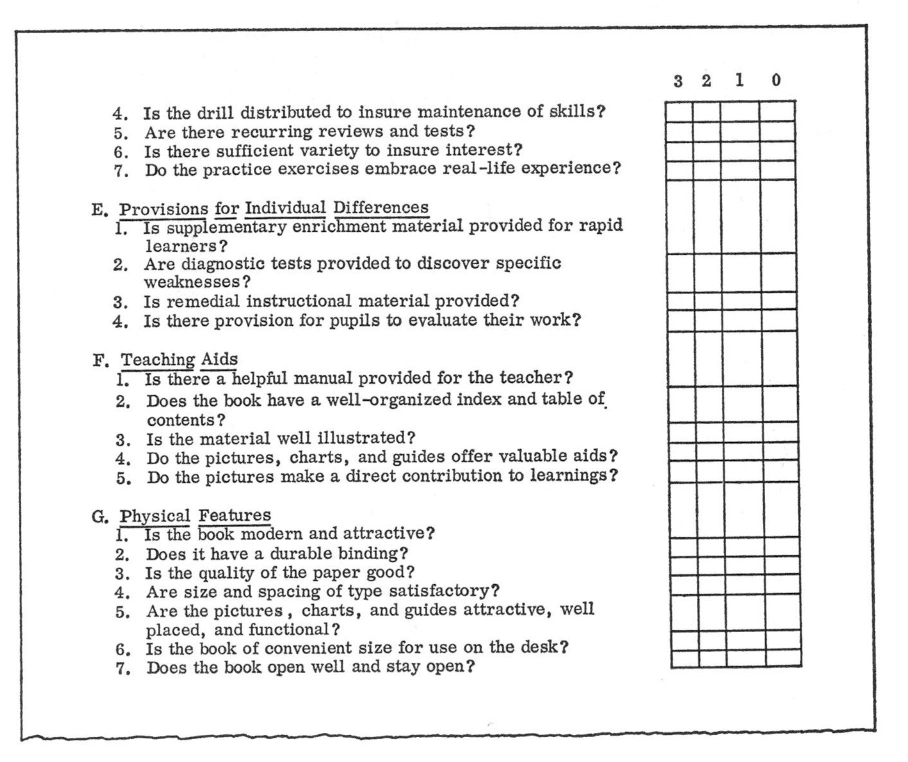

	3	2	1	0
4. Is the drill distributed to insure maintenance of skills?				
5. Are there recurring reviews and tests?				
6. Is there sufficient variety to insure interest?				
7. Do the practice exercises embrace real-life experience?				
E. Provisions for Individual Differences				
1. Is supplementary enrichment material provided for rapid learners?				
2. Are diagnostic tests provided to discover specific weaknesses?				
3. Is remedial instructional material provided?				
4. Is there provision for pupils to evaluate their work?				
F. Teaching Aids				
1. Is there a helpful manual provided for the teacher?				
2. Does the book have a well-organized index and table of contents?				
3. Is the material well illustrated?				
4. Do the pictures, charts, and guides offer valuable aids?				
5. Do the pictures make a direct contribution to learnings?				
G. Physical Features				
1. Is the book modern and attractive?				
2. Does it have a durable binding?				
3. Is the quality of the paper good?				
4. Are size and spacing of type satisfactory?				
5. Are the pictures, charts, and guides attractive, well placed, and functional?				
6. Is the book of convenient size for use on the desk?				
7. Does the book open well and stay open?				

Fig. 7. (Continued)

counts, number of illustrations, length of sentences and paragraphs, number of exercises included, number of teaching aids, and so forth.

The qualitative judgments, naturally, are of a subjective nature. Criteria concerned with format, quality of paper and illustrations, and general attractiveness are not too difficult to apply. However, the more important subjective judgments, such as the way ideas are developed, appropriateness of content material for the curriculum area and the age level for which they are selected, and program balance are much more difficult to determine. These, however, may be the crucial ones. The old adage, "You can never tell a book by its cover," applies here.

If used in the correct manner, score cards can be of some value in textbook selection. A well-organized score card calls attention to the important elements to be considered in comparing several series of textbooks. It is quite common for publishers to make score cards available for evaluating a particular text series of theirs, such as, for example, a reading, arithmetic, or language series.

If a publisher's score card is used to evaluate, for example, several series of language texts, the score card may favor the series for which it was designed. This, of course, is to be expected, but it must be kept in mind when the scores are being compared. For this reason, some schools have developed their own score cards. Under the proper leadership, this exercise can prove to be a valuable learning experience for the participants. A facsimile of a locally developed score card for evaluating language textbooks and workbook texts may be found on pages 144 and 145.

Sharing in the selection of other instructional materials can be equally valuable as part of the professional-growth program of teachers. Teachers should be given opportunity to attend educational exhibits during the various educational meetings. A number of school districts within a 70-mile range of Atlantic City, New Jersey, consider this type of exhibit so valuable for teachers that they provide transportation by school bus to the exhibits of the American Association of School Administrators during the annual meeting. Similar but much smaller exhibits are usually set up in conjunction with other educational gatherings.

Distributors can frequently be prevailed upon to demonstrate the use of supplies and equipment in the local school system. Demonstrations on the use of handwriting materials and workshops on the use of art media are frequently run by companies that supply these materials. The same is true in respect to the newer teaching materials in arithmetic and science. Distributors of devices for use in programmed learning also are eager to demonstrate, and purveyors of foreign-language teaching materials will gladly give demonstrations.

Selection of Professional Staff

The selection of the professional staff is related to the improvement of instruction in several ways. In the first place, a well-qualified staff will render a higher level of professional services than will a less-qualified corps of teachers. Some teachers also are capable of infinitely greater professional growth than others.

In the second place, if present staff members have a part in setting up the qualifications desired for teaching positions and if teachers are actually involved in the selection of co-workers who have these qualifications, then a great potential exists for professional growth on the part of those faculty members who participate. As faculty members draw up these qualifications and search for individuals who meet them, a process of self-examination is certain to take place. This should result in some professional growth on the part of each staff member involved.

Supervisory Bulletins

The supervisory bulletin can be made a valuable aid in the improvement of instruction if it is a well-written document that is used properly.

Types of supervisory bulletins. Usually the supervisory bulletin assumes one of three different forms. In certain instances it is a device used to prepare staff members for another type of activity, as, for example, a field trip or a demonstration lesson. The second form of supervisory bulletin is the summary, supplementary, or follow-up type. This form of bulletin may be concerned with generalizations resulting from many classroom observations, conclusions, and recommendations reached at a staff or in-service meeting, the summary of the highlights of a school-visitation program, or the significant conclusions drawn from a demonstration lesson.

The third category includes bulletins, handbooks, and guides, preferably prepared by a group of teachers working with the principal, other supervisory personnel, or a specialist. For example, a bulletin on child study would require the assistance of a guidance specialist and/or the school psychologist. Bulletins of this nature may be only several pages in length if they deal with a subject as specific in nature as the one on Bulletin Boards, excerpts of which appear on page 148; or they may be quite long, representing weeks and even months of research and study. Among others, the authors have seen excellent examples of supervisory bulletins on the following subjects: (1) audio-visual aids, (2) child study, (3) discipline, (4) field trips, (5) guidance, (6) instructional-materials center, (7) parent-teacher conferences, (8) programmed instruction, (9) school library services, (10) team teaching, (11) ungraded primary organization, and (12) the unit method. Bulletins of this type are also issued on all phases of the curriculum, but they are distinguished from the regular curriculum bulletins by the fact that they emphasize new approaches and specific techniques.

Teachers' handbooks may also be considered in the category of supervisory bulletins in view of the fact that they frequently include much valuable information that enables the teacher to do a more effective job. For example, the section on evaluation in a teachers' handbook may be so complete that it serves the same purpose as a separate guide on the topic.

The writing and illustrating of a good supervisory bulletin require skill and practice. The following suggestions should prove helpful in perfecting this technique:

1. A sharp distinction should be made between educational bulletins

IDEAS For Your Classroom

A BULLETIN FOR TEACHERS, PRINCIPALS AND SUPERINTENDENTS

PUBLISHED BY THE PHILADELPHIA AREA SCHOOL STUDY COUNCIL, SOUTHERN NEW JERSEY GROUP

EFFECTIVE BULLETIN BOARDS

HERE'S WHY THEY'RE IMPORTANT!!!!!

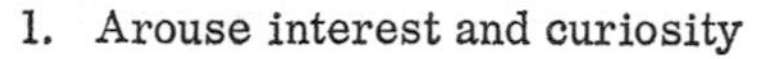

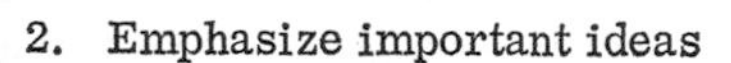

1. Arouse interest and curiosity
2. Emphasize important ideas
3. Bring out relationships
4. Introduce a unit
5. Make abstract ideas more concrete
6. Encourage extra student activity
7. Sharpen the sense of observation

HERE'S WHAT THEY DO!!!!!

1. Show contrast and comparison
2. Show central idea
3. Show development of events
4. Show relationships
5. Show sequence
6. Show progress in student work

HERE ARE YOUR TOOLS!!!!!

1. Staple gun
2. Bulletin Board Wax
3. Pin On Letters
4. Miracle Discs
5. Thumb tacks
6. Construction paper
7. Project Rolls
8. Bristol Board
9. Cotton
10. Mica Snow
11. Poster Paint
12. Day glo Paint
13. Wall Paper
14. Metallic Paper

Fig. 8. Effective Bulletin Boards.

and notices, summaries of regulations, routine announcements, news notes, and the like.

2. A supervisory bulletin should be written to meet a specific need.
3. The scope of a bulletin should, preferably, be confined to one problem, issue, or item.
4. Supervisory bulletins may result from individual action but, preferably, they should be issued as an outcome of cooperative group study, discussion, and summary.
5. Supervisory bulletins should be used only when their unique values serve better than any other technique.
6. Bulletins should be dynamic in tone, stimulating both thought and action. (They should include questions, suggested activities and procedures, study guides, and references.)
7. The vocabulary, style, and tone of the bulletin should be lively and interesting.
8. Provisions should be made for individual and group actions.
9. Provisions should be made for continuity of study on the given and related problems.[16]

Mechanical details. The following mechanical details abstracted from the same source are worthy of note. The supervisory bulletin should carry a provocative title and an attractive format. Cartoons and other decorative devices may be used to advantage on the title page. The organization should be clearcut and definite, with the problem, issue, or purpose stated clearly and concisely at the beginning. Explanation and background should be reduced to a minimum. Illustrative material should be used freely. Conclusions or summaries should be included in numbered, outline form. Credit for quotations and contributions from staff members should be properly acknowledged.[17]

Informal Contacts

Supervision is a continuous process. The supervisor must realize that he is never free of his responsibility for improving instruction. By the same token, his being on the job at all times offers many opportunities to assist teachers to grow professionally. Supervisors should never forget that a valuable part of their college education was obtained in "bull sessions," "kaffee-klatches," and heart-to-heart talks with individual students or faculty members. Opportunities for supervision, then, are pre-

---

[16] Adapted from: *Supervision: A Social Process,* by William H. Burton and Leo J. Brueckner (New York: Appleton-Century-Crofts, Inc., 1955), p. 159. Copyright © 1955, Appleton-Century-Crofts, Inc.

[17] *Ibid.,* p. 159.

sented each time the supervisor comes in contact with a teacher. In fact, this influence is felt each time that the teacher observes the supervisor, even though the supervisor may not see the teacher. For example, the writer vividly recalls the time that a teacher came to her mailbox for her keys a few minutes late and went to her classroom in tears when the writer (at that time her supervisor) failed to say "Good morning" because he did not see her. Even after an explanation and an apology, this sensitive teacher believed she had been snubbed because she was late.

Another supervisor, who is very congenial when he interviews teachers for positions but rarely notices them during informal contacts after they are appointed to the staff, quickly destroys the illusion that his is a friendly school. He thus loses many opportunities to assist teachers. It is unfortunate when individuals spend years learning and perfecting the formal techniques of supervision and ignore completely the informal contacts.

Informal contacts with pupils also can prove valuable in a supervisory program. The writer regularly ate lunch with different groups of pupils, mingled with children on the playground, and talked with them before and after school. During classroom visitation, the supervisor is encouraged to focus his attention on the pupil. He sometimes learns more about the program by observing pupils during informal contacts than he does in more formal situations. He can observe how they conduct themselves and hear what they say when they are free to discuss the topics they choose to talk about. If interest in a classroom activity spills over into the lunch or play period, the supervisor knows that good things are happening to these children. If they appear eager before school to attack the day's work, he is aware that they have been highly motivated in some way.

One word of caution seems appropriate. Although the supervisor should be a good listener, he must not interrogate pupils for the purpose of obtaining derogatory information about their teachers. This is an unethical practice that can place the entire supervisory program in jeopardy.

Other Experiences

There are many different kinds of experiences usually not discussed in a work of this nature that can contribute to the personal and professional growth of teachers. Some years ago the writer had the privilege of serving on a state committee to recommend procedures for the renewal of teaching and administrative certificates. The committee began with the premise that any activity that contributed to the personal and/or professional growth of an individual ultimately contributed to the improvement of the instructional program. As a result of this committee's work, the following procedures for certificate renewal, in addition to the usual ones, were recommended to the State Council on Education, approved by this body, and kept in effect for a number of years:

Complete Special Methods for Renewal, to be undertaken only after careful counseling and the approval of the teacher's immediate supervisor and the State Department Special Committee to be appointed by the State Superintendent, of which the following are suggestions:

1. Active participation in self-evaluation in preparing for accrediting by a recognized educational agency.
2. Participation in a curriculum revision of major proportions.
3. Participation in an in-service program of recognized importance whether connected with a college or university or independently conducted by the local school.
4. Courses in Human Relations.
5. Courses in Personal Grooming, Social Usage, and Personality.
6. Extended critical attendance and evaluation of musical or art events, movies or theatrical performances.
7. Extended independent critical evaluation of current printed matter.
8. Acquisition and consistent pursuit of new avocational interests.[18]

Some of the above suggestions may appear bizarre to the reader; however, thoughtful examination of each of them should convince the supervisor that they have a great deal of merit. How many times have teachers been accused of being dull, uninteresting individuals with one-track minds? How many teachers has the reader known who could benefit greatly from a few sessions on personal grooming and/or personality development? What would learning to bowl, swim, or play golf do for Mr. Stout or Miss Plump? How much more interesting might Mr. Flat's elementary-school music program become if he attended a few operas, orchestral concerts, recitals, or even "jam sessions"? What enthusiasm, new ideas, and information can teachers bring back from a tour of Europe or visits to historical landmarks in our own great country?

Working with the Creative Teacher

Interest in the creative individual is a comparatively recent phenomenon. For years the creative child has been ignored and the creative teacher misunderstood. Important recent research and a review of past research indicate that creativity can be discovered and measured. The individual in a supervisory capacity must learn to work with creative

[18] *Certification Rules and Regulations* (Dover: State of Delaware, Department of Public Instruction, Bulletin No. 5-52, February, 1952), p. 22.

teachers and to assist all teachers to work with creative children. In order to do this effectively, he first must learn to recognize the creative individuals. The following characteristics have been attributed to them:

1. They are highly sensitive individuals with a great amount of resourcefulness, flexibility, and willingness to explore new fields.
2. They have unusual capacity to establish rapport with their creative students.
3. They like to tackle difficult tasks, some of which may be beyond their capacity, and, consequently, they may fail at times.
4. They may possess some odd characteristics, refuse to conform, and at times display childish tendencies.
5. They at times may seem discourteous, uncultured, primitive, unsophisticated, and naïve.
6. They are not concerned with being sociable or socially skilled because of their absorption in assisting children to grow and develop.
7. They outwardly may appear bashful, withdrawn, and quiet.
8. They are accustomed to having others laugh at their ideas and, consequently, question the genuineness of the friendly advances of other teachers.
9. They at times may seem haughty and self-satisfied because of their independence in thinking.
10. They frequently appear to be discontented and critical of the *status quo* as a result of their ability to recognize problems and defects. However, they may readily be distinguished from the malcontents because creative teachers always have constructive suggestions for improving the situation.[19]

Because a number of the above characteristics are objectionable to the average individual, the supervisor must assist the creative teacher so that he does not become obnoxious but at the same time retains his creativity. The following suggestions given by Stein to creative research chemists so that they would be less obnoxious should prove equally valid for creative teachers:

1. Maintain assertiveness without showing hostility or too much aggressiveness.
2. Become more aware of superiors, peers, and subordinates as persons. Adopt the human touch.
3. Work alone at times, but do not become isolated, withdrawn, or uncommunicative.

---

[19] Adapted from: E. Paul Torrance, *Guiding Creative Talent,* © 1962 by Prentice-Hall, Inc., Englewood Cliffs, N.J., pp. 195-196. By permission.

4. In school, be congenial but not sociable; outside of school, be sociable but not intimate.

5. "Know your place," but don't appear timid, submissive, or acquiescent, and give your opinions without being domineering.

6. In making a point, be subtle without being cunning or manipulative.

7. In all human relationships, be sincere, honest, purposeful, and diplomatic.

8. Intellectually, be broad without spreading yourself too thin, deep without seeming "bookish" or "too pedagogical," and "sharp" without being overcritical.[20]

In addition to the suggestions that may be given to creative teachers to assist them to become better members of the professional team, the individual who serves in a supervisory position takes the following steps in guiding creative talent:

1. Lets teachers know that he respects creativity and creative teaching.
2. Uses some regular system for obtaining teachers' ideas.
3. Tolerates disagreement with his own ideas.
4. Encourages experimentation.
5. Avoids loading teachers with too many extra duties.
6. Makes it possible to try out new ideas without failure being "fatal."
7. Makes school atmosphere an exciting, adventurous one.
8. Avoids *overemphasis* on teamwork.
9. Holds meetings in which ideas are evaluated honestly.
10. Helps develop sound but exciting ideas from failure experiences.
11. Exposes teachers to the creative work of other teachers.
12. Makes it easy for new teachers to generate new ideas and stimulate the staff.
13. Facilitates communication between teachers in his school and teachers elsewhere working on related problems.
14. Occasionally questions established concepts and practices.
15. Carries on a continuous program of long-range planning.
16. Recognizes and tries to relieve tension when frustration becomes too severe.
17. Maintains frequent communication with individual teachers but lets them make most decisions alone.[21]

---

[20] M. I. Stein, "A Transactional Approach to Creativity," in Calvin W. Taylor (ed.), *The 1955 University of Utah Research Conference on the Identification of Creative Scientific Talent* (Salt Lake City: University of Utah Press, 1956), pp. 176-177, and in Calvin W. Taylor and Frank Barron (eds.), *Scientific Creativity: Its Recognition and Development* (New York: John Wiley & Sons, 1963), p. 224.

[21] E. Paul Torrance, *Guiding Creative Talent, op. cit.*, p. 206. As adapted from E. Paul Torrance, "The Creative Teacher and the School Team: Problems and Pleasures of the Principal," in *Professional Growth for Principals,* April 1961 (Arthur C. Croft Publications), and used by permission.

In assisting teachers to improve their procedures for working with creative pupils, the supervisor can help them to adapt many of the procedures suggested for helping creative teachers to the operational level of creative pupils. However, as was true in the case of the supervisor, teachers must be given assistance in learning to recognize and identify pupils with creative talent. Through study they will learn that creative pupils manifest characteristics similar to those mentioned earlier in this section. Consequently, these pupils may be just as obnoxious as creative teachers. Unfortunately, not only do creative pupils offend their peers but, if misunderstood, they annoy their teachers and are rejected by them. Thus, the creative pupil may become a bored, unchallenged student, a discipline problem, or a withdrawn, ineffectual individual. In these days of struggle for our very survival, schools dare not fail to develop the creative talent of our children and youth. To assist teachers in developing creative talent effectively may prove to be one of the supervisor's most important tasks.

Much of the supervisor's time is spent working with problem teachers and assisting teachers with problems. The remainder of this chapter will be devoted to these topics.

Working with Problem Teachers

Teachers, like children, come in assorted sizes, dispositions, personalities, and physiques. They vary greatly in ambition, motivation, state of health, vitality, interest, voice, and any other characteristic you choose to name. There is even a considerable range in their intelligence. The supervisor must recognize these differences and understand each teacher so well that he can help him individually to capitalize on his assets, overcome many of his liabilities, and minimize the remaining ones.

In a fairly comprehensive discussion of teacher personality, Bartky writes:

> There are sick teachers and their illnesses do influence their teaching behavior. There are also a very few nonintelligent teachers who make the efforts of their supervisors seem almost futile. There are lonely teachers. There are queer teachers of all types, seclusive, hardboiled, artistic, grouchy, radical, or suspicious. There are frustrated teachers with neurotic doubts, fears, anxieties, obsessions, or compulsions. There are moody teachers, some highly optimistic and some always pessimistic; there are perverse teachers, sadists, masochists, sexual perverts, all suffering from antisocial drives. These teacher personalities each demanding its own therapeutics are the responsibility of the supervisor.[22]

---

[22] John A. Bartky, *Supervision as Human Relations* (Boston: D. C. Heath and Company, 1953), pp. 68-69.

It would be presumptuous to suggest procedures for dealing with the diversified personalities mentioned above; however, there are several types of individuals that a supervisor most certainly will have to work with many times during his professional career. Wiles includes the following teachers in this category: (1) the "lazy" teacher, (2) the "colorless" teacher, (3) the older teacher, (4) the "undemocratic" teacher, and (5) the "disagreeing" teacher.[23]

The "lazy" teacher. The "lazy" teacher has lost the zest for teaching. His satisfactions are being derived from activities outside of his job. The task of the supervisor is to assist this teacher to rediscover the joys and rewards of teaching. The following suggestions for accomplishing this end should prove helpful:

1. Attempt to build the teacher's confidence in himself and pride in his profession through the enlistment of staff members in a total school evaluation program.
2. Include the "lazy" teacher in a professional reading program.
3. Involve "lazy" teachers in the work of the teacher-welfare, self-evaluation, or program-planning committees.
4. Try to interest this type of teacher in some new procedure or action research, as, for example, programmed learning, team teaching, aero-space education, or new trends in his own field. (A summer workshop in the area of the teacher's assignment might do the trick.)

The "colorless" teacher. This type of individual is found teaching on every academic level. Strangely enough, there is something about teaching that attracts the person with the colorless personality. This teacher is drab in appearance and speaks in a monotonous voice. He lacks a sense of humor and is overly conscientious about his work. He follows the school's rules and regulations meticulously. Socially he is withdrawn, and he is unable to be friendly with his pupils or colleagues. He is a loner.

Assisting this individual to develop a more colorful personality is a difficult assignment. Prerequisite to any personality change is the recognition by the individual of a need for the change. How can a supervisor help this teacher to face the facts of life? The following suggestions have proved to be of value in helping the "colorless" teacher:

1. Involve him in a program of faculty social activities. (Square dances, masquerade parties, and glee clubs are excellent means of releasing participants from their inhibitions.)

---

[23] The five teacher categories and many of the ideas in this section on "Problem Teachers" have been adapted from Kimball Wiles, *Supervision for Better Schools: The Role of the Official Leader in Program Development* (2nd ed.) (Englewood Cliffs, N.J.: Prentice-Hall, Inc., 1955), pp. 114-130. By permission of the publisher.

2. Assist the teacher in developing an interest in a recreational activity involving groups of individuals. (One school found a faculty dramatics club helpful in this respect.)

3. Encourage the "colorless" teacher to participate in workshop experiences. (A group dynamics or human relations workshop would be particularly valuable.)

4. Encourage the teacher to make tape recordings of his voice and assist him in working out a program of voice culture.

5. Courses in personal grooming and personality development would be valuable here but difficult to recommend to the individual.

6. Assist the teacher in grasping a better understanding of the fact that it is possible to have informality in the classroom without losing the pupils' respect.

7. Encourage the teacher to bring humor into the classroom.

The older teacher. The problem of the older teacher was discussed briefly in this chapter in the section dealing with teacher assignment. However, the authors consider the topic of sufficient importance to elaborate here on other aspects of the problem.

The older teacher is not always an individual who is old in years. Old age comes not only as a result of living but from the way one lives. Some teachers are old at fifty; others remain young after retirement and begin new careers. The discussion here is concerned with teachers who retire on the job. Wiles describes them in this manner:

> Some seem to be seeking the easiest way to complete the last few years. They have reached maximum salary and make no attempts to improve their teaching. They have not attended any in-service course or read any of the newer publications in education. Others seem to want to prevent change. They have commitments to certain values which keep them from adapting their courses of study to meet the broad range of abilities present in the modern school. They try to keep the rest of the staff on the right path by attempting to dictate on the basis of seniority.[24]

The following suggestions have been made for dealing with the older teacher:

1. Capitalize on the experience of the older teacher by using his leadership.

2. Provide opportunities for him to share his skills, information, and abilities with the other staff members.

3. Stress the fact that progress results from different types of contributions.

---

[24] Wiles, *Supervision for Better Schools* (2nd ed.), *op. cit.*, p. 118.

4. Emphasize that the child's needs should be the criteria for judging ideas, not their source.

5. Provide opportunities for younger teachers to work with older teachers but discourage domination by the latter group.

6. Encourage the older teacher to experiment and share his findings with the staff.

7. Fit the teaching schedule to the physical condition of the older teacher.

The reader will recognize that some of the suggestions given for helping the "lazy" teacher also apply here.

The "undemocratic" teacher. It is a strange coincidence that in a democratic society the agency that shapes and is shaped by society is frequently one of our most undemocratic institutions. Although administrators and supervisors must assume some of the blame for this situation, many teachers do not hold democratic values or believe in democracy in educational practice. There are also educators and lay persons who would like to see schools become even less democratic than they are by making them more teacher-centered.

Individuals in a supervisory capacity, then, must be prepared to deal with "undemocratic" teachers. In order to work with them, it is necessary to identify them by their patterns of behavior, which are as follows: The "undemocratic" teacher dominates the classroom completely, and the pupils have no opportunities to participate in classroom management, express their opinions, or plan learning activities. This teacher is the fount of all wisdom and believes that education is the acquisition of knowledge rather than the development of democratic attitudes, skills, and values. In this teacher's classroom, pupils are not given the opportunity to learn to discuss issues and to think for themselves.

In his relationship with the administration, he may expect undemocratic leadership, and he opposes democratic participation of the staff in school administration. On the other hand, he may, through undemocratic procedures, attempt to dominate the decision-making. He frequently becomes the leader of the vociferous minority.

The following suggestions have proved to be helpful in dealing with the "undemocratic" teacher:

1. Examine your own pattern of behavior to ascertain whether or not you are truly democratic in your actions, and encourage others to do likewise.

2. Recognize that some individuals were raised in autocratic homes and were educated in autocratic schools. As a consequence, they do not understand or feel comfortable in democratic situations.

3. Begin "where teachers are" in using the democratic processes. Develop a readiness on their part and encourage small beginnings.

4. Encourage the "undemocratic" teacher to visit (preferably in another school) the classroom of a teacher who is skillful in using democratic procedures.

5. Bring to the staff materials that emphasize democratic practices and individuals who stress democratic values.

The "disagreeing" teacher. In every group of people you find individuals who seem to enjoy disagreeing with others. Irrespective of the point of view expressed, they take the opposite one, regardless of how untenable their position may be. They thrive on argument.

The following suggestions should receive consideration in working with the teacher who disagrees:

1. Recognize that disagreement can be healthy. Without disagreement there would be little discussion, and issues would be decided without sufficient study and consideration.

2. Do not take disagreement as a personal affront. Work as closely with those who disagree as with those who agree.

3. In dealing with the teacher who disagrees, place the professional growth of the teacher above winning an argument.

4. Remember that the teacher might be correct in his viewpoint. Many of the great advances in all fields of knowledge were made because an individual or small minority opposed the majority.

In dealing with problem teachers, the supervisor must remember that each individual is unique. The suggestions that have been made may work in some situations and be ineffective in others. As a student of human nature, the supervisor knows that there are no pat formulas that fit all situations. Much of the time he will be "playing by ear."

Assisting Teachers with Personal Problems

There are only a few problem teachers in each school, but all teachers have problems. Like all other human beings, teachers have financial problems, marital difficulties, and worries about their offspring. They become ill, lose loved ones, run afoul of the law, and suffer from disasters of various types. Any of the vicissitudes of life are bound in some way to affect the quality of teaching. Some few individuals become stronger and better individuals as a result of these experiences; others may be defeated by them. Although some supervisors may be reluctant to become involved in the solution of teachers' personal problems, those who do know that the results are infinitely rewarding. Some of the best supervision may be done through these channels.

Teachers want a supervisor who cares. The writer learned this fact early in his career as a supervisor. When he requested teachers to make an anonymous rating of the supervisory services, a number of them suggested that the supervisor should show more interest in the personal lives of teachers. They accused him of never discussing anything but educational matters with them. One teacher expressed the sentiment of the group when he wrote: "Make conferences pleasant occasions in which pleasant topics are discussed. Learn to know the teacher as a friend at such times. Forget school once in a while."

As a result of experience, the authors believe that good personnel administration and supervision require that administrators and supervisors show interest in teachers' personal problems and assist in their solutions whenever it is possible. However, good rapport must exist between the supervisor or administrator and the teacher before this type of assistance is welcome or even approved. After rapport has been established, some teachers will come to the supervisor for help with personal problems. If a feeling of mutual respect does not exist, any assistance offered to the teacher may be misconstrued as meddling in affairs that are of no concern to the supervisor.

Supervisors who believe that helping teachers with their personal problems is an important part of their job have assisted in many different ways. In the experience of the writers, the following situations have arisen and some assistance has been rendered: (1) helping teachers out of debt, (2) matchmaking, (3) testifying for a teacher wrongly accused, (4) arranging for funerals of loved ones, (5) locating living quarters, (6) comforting them in time of grief or illness, and (7) assisting them with problems concerning their children or spouse.

Sometimes all that teachers need is the sympathetic ear of someone who is interested in them personally and can be depended upon to keep in confidence what he has heard.

SUMMARY

In their efforts to improve instruction, individuals serving in a supervisory capacity spend a large segment of their time working with individuals. In order to do this most effectively, they utilize the following techniques to assist teachers in their personal and professional growth: (1) assignment of teachers, (2) classroom visitation and observation, (3) classroom experimentation, (4) enrollment in college courses, (5) conferences with teachers, (6) demonstration teaching, (7) evaluation, (8) professional activities and conferences, (9) professional reading, (10) professional writing, (11) selection of textbooks and other instructional materials, (12) selection of professional staff, (13) supervisory bulletins, (14) informal contacts, and (15) other experiences that may in any way contribute to the improvement of the teacher as a person.

In working with individuals, the supervisor becomes more sensitive to the fact that teachers differ from each other in many ways. He is particularly anxious to assist creative teachers to realize their greatest potential. He also realizes how important it is to assist all teachers to work more effectively with creative children. Finally, he learns to work with problem teachers and to become interested in the problems of teachers. As a result, these individuals benefit greatly from their association with him.

SUGGESTED ACTIVITIES AND PROBLEMS

1. Secure permission to visit three classrooms when the teachers and pupils are not present. Carefully examine the physical environment and look for signs of learning activities as suggested in this chapter. Write a description of the learning environment and indicate the kinds of learning that you believe take place in each classroom, giving the reasons for your tentative conclusions. Check your tentative conclusions by observing the teacher in action or interviewing the teacher, or both.

2. Secure permission to observe a teacher make a large-group presentation under the team teaching plan of organization. Interview the teacher to find out his objectives and purposes for the lesson and the procedures he used in preparing for it. Interview three pupils and secure their reactions to the lesson. On the basis of this information, make recommendations for improving the lesson.

3. Collect five supervisory bulletins and evaluate them on the basis of the nine criteria and suggestions concerning mechanical details given in this chapter. Select the poorest of the five bulletins and rewrite it so that it meets the criteria and suggestions for mechanical details.

4. Write a detailed case study of a "lazy," "colorless," or "undemocratic" teacher, illustrating the forces, experiences, and circumstances that may have contributed to developing this type of teacher. Using dialogue freely, describe how you would assist this individual to grow personally and professionally.

5. Interview several teachers to determine whether or not they are aware of creative talent in their pupils. Try to find out what procedures they use in working with these creative pupils.

SELECTED READINGS

Association for Supervision and Curriculum Development, *Leadership for Improving Instruction,* 1960 Yearbook. Washington, D.C.: National Education Association.

Bartky, John A., *Supervision as Human Relations,* Chaps. 4, 5, 6, 8, 10, 12. Boston: D. C. Heath and Company, 1953.

Gwynn, J. Minor, *Theory and Practice of Supervision,* Chaps. 3, 14, 16. New York: Dodd, Mead and Company, 1961.

Hicks, Hanne J., *Educational Supervision in Principle and Practice,* Chaps. 3, 4, 5, 6, 7. New York: The Ronald Press Company, 1960.

Torrance, E. Paul, *Guiding Creative Talent,* Chap. 10. Englewood Cliffs, N.J.: Prentice-Hall Inc., 1962.

chapter ten

Working with Groups to Improve Instruction

It is the purpose of this chapter to identify ways of working with professional groups to improve the instructional program. By definition, *group supervisory techniques* are those which involve the administrators and supervisors with a number of staff members, ranging from a grade-level committee of two teachers to the total teaching staff at times. Certain procedures aimed at the improvement of instruction can best be initiated and carried out through group interaction which involves the sharing of experiences, ideas, and the findings of educational research. Dynamic, democratic leadership and effective human relations, as discussed in Chapter I, are prerequisites to success in group techniques. Each staff member must be encouraged to play a significant and cooperative role in the evaluation and improvement of the teaching-learning situations in the school district.

GROUP TECHNIQUES

As discussed in Chapter IX, some supervisory methods may be considered either individual or group. The following have been identified by the authors as group techniques and are discussed in this chapter: orientation of new teachers, action research, development of professional libraries, visiting other teachers, coordination of student teaching, cooperative development of the testing program, new organizational patterns, and interpretation of the instructional program to the public.

Orientation of New Teachers

The substantial turnover of teachers which almost every school district currently experiences requires a carefully developed plan for the orientation of teachers new to the district. First of all, it is essential to recognize that there are at least five categories of new teachers:

1. The inexperienced teacher.
2. The teacher from another school system.
3. The teacher from another school in the same system.
4. The teacher assigned to a new department or level of teaching.
5. The experienced teacher who returns to teaching.[1]

Obviously, teachers in these categories have varying needs. The orientation program needs to be individualized and flexible. The following planning principles may help:

1. Human relations, as always, are most important. It is necessary for supervisors and administrators to be understanding, sympathetic, cooperative, and friendly.

2. Experienced teachers should be involved in planning, but should be compensated if they return early in the school term to participate in the orientation sessions.

3. Orientation is a continuous process, not a "one shot" program. However, the early emphasis will be on adjustment to the problems and concerns which the teacher must face immediately.

4. The orientation plan should be comprehensive but not overwhelming. If the new teacher gets too many regulations, booklets, and suggestions, for example, she will remember very little.

5. Each principal should have the new teachers in his building evalu-

---

[1] Research Division, N.E.A., *Orientation Programs for Teachers* (Washington, D.C.: National Education Association, October, 1957), p. 2.

ate the orientation program by the end of the first semester. Many helpful suggestions for improvement will be forthcoming.

6. As indicated later in this chapter, special in-service programs for new teachers should be arranged.

Several excellent guides are available to help the supervisor in planning teacher-orientation programs. These are listed in the selected readings at the end of this chapter.

Teacher orientation has been divided into four periods:

1. Contact to contract time.
2. Contract to reporting time.
3. Reporting and getting started.
4. Adjusting to the job.[2]

A comprehensive list of planning suggestions has been compiled by the American Association of School Administrators. The superintendent or the supervisor designated by him to coordinate the teacher-orientation program can select activities from this list which meet the needs of the new teachers in his district.

Understanding Terms and Conditions of Employment

1. Include full description of job with announcement of vacancy and application forms.
2. Take time for complete and honest discussion of job during interview.
3. Give full explanation of salary, certification, benefits, assignment (as nearly as can be determined), and other terms of employment at time contract is offered.
4. Review regulations governing rights, privileges, and restrictions at time of reporting and later as questions arise.

Becoming Acquainted with the Community

1. Enclose description of community with announcements and application forms.
2. Take time for more information and questions during interview.
3. Arrange for visit to community before hiring or between employment and reporting time.
4. Acquaint teacher with facilities for transportation, banking, shopping, and medical, dental, and other personal services.
5. Prepare and put in teachers' hands listings of housing, with descriptive information.
6. Arrange tours of the community to become acquainted with its business, cultural, and educational activities, for personal reasons and for teaching background.
7. See that invitations are extended to attend and take part in civic, religious, social, cultural, and recreational activities.

---

[2] American Association of School Administrators, *Off To A Good Start: Teacher Orientation* (Washington, D.C.: National Education Association, 1956), p. 9.

8. Enlist the help of organizations in arranging special events for introducing new teachers.

Getting to Know School System, Its People, and Its Organization

1. Provide information about organization of school system at time application is made and during interviews.
2. Furnish copies of rules and regulations, statements about policies, philosophy, and practices. (A number of school systems incorporate this and other information into a handbook for distribution.)
3. Describe help available, such as teaching materials, supervisory assistance, and special services.
4. Place copies of courses of study, textbook lists, and similar materials in hands of incoming teacher.
5. Put new teacher on mailing list for all bulletins, newsletters, and other publications sent to teachers.
6. Arrange for correspondence by superintendent, principal, supervisors, and fellow teachers prior to reporting.
7. See that new teachers meet and talk with superintendent.
8. Schedule conferences with supervisors and other staff personnel responsible for services to teachers prior to opening of school.

Learning About the School to Which Assigned

1. Take teacher on tour of building for becoming acquainted with layout and facilities.
2. Arrange meetings with building principal to learn about obtaining supplies and equipment, keeping records, making reports, handling problems of classroom management and organization, and the other details of school operation.
3. Assign an experienced teacher as a personal counselor and adviser.
4. See that there is time for getting acquainted with other members of the faculty and staff.
5. Allot time to work professionally with faculty in meetings before school opens.
6. Acquaint the new teacher with her professional organizations.

Adjusting to the Teaching Job

1. Set aside time of principal and supervisors to help in planning work, locating sources of materials, handling problems of classroom organization and management, making pupil evaluations, and preparing reports.
2. Make time freely available for talking over problems as they arise in private conferences with principal, supervisors, and others, as often as either party feels the need.
3. Assist the new teacher in getting to know pupils and parents.
4. Arrange opportunities for viewing demonstrations and observing experienced teachers at work.
5. Schedule meetings of new teachers for discussion of their own special problems.
6. See that the new teacher is given a reasonable and fair teaching load, commensurate with her training, skills, and experience.

7. Provide opportunities for continuing and expanding professional preparation begun in college, by offering in-service education activities specially designed to help new teachers.[3]

From the superintendent's initial letter of welcome, to the greeting from the new teacher's building principal, and finally to his full participation as an experienced member of the staff, the new teacher should feel that he is truly wanted and needed as a vital part of the instructional team.

Action Research

This term has been subject to many definitions in the literature. To some writers, a teacher who tries out new programmed learning materials with a group of pupils is conducting action research. To others, an experiment must be carefully set up and controlled, involving equated groups of pupils and an adequate sample, in order for it to qualify as action research.

There is considerable agreement that much more research should be conducted in the public school classroom, since here is the crucible where the findings of laboratory experimentation should meet the practical situations of the classroom teacher. Several obstacles, however, have retarded the development of significant research projects in many of the nation's schools.

1. Many administrators and supervisors, because of their limited training, experience, or vision, fail to appreciate the gains to education that can result from properly conducted studies. Some are afraid to have teachers engage in activities that might upset the *status quo*.
2. Teachers often lack the time, the interest, or the specialized abilities required for research in the classroom.
3. The loose concepts of action research held by some educators have resulted in a negative reaction by others.

Definition of the term. Corey says,

> Probably the most important characteristic that differentiates action research from more casual inquiry is that evidence is systematically sought, recorded, and interpreted. This is done to find out more definitely just what the problem is as well as to learn what happens when certain procedures are used to deal with it. Every kind of research involves accumulating and interpreting evidence, but action research focuses on

[3] American Association of School Administrators, *Off To A Good Start: Teacher Orientation* (Washington, D.C.: National Education Association, 1956), pp. 11-15.

evidence that helps answer the question, Did a particular action result in the desirable consequences that were anticipated? [4]

According to Franseth,

> In action research in education, the researchers are usually teachers, curriculum workers, principals, supervisors, directors of instruction, or others whose main function is to help provide good learning experiences for pupils. The hypotheses or theories are tested by the teacher in the classroom, the consultant in a curriculum study group, or some other educator in a practical situation. If, however, an on-the-job research project is not conducted under carefully controlled conditions, or if it is conducted only in a single classroom, the findings must be applied to other situations with extreme caution. . . . All types of research—basic, pure applied, or action—have one characteristic in common: all imply studious inquiry, systematic investigation, and a careful search for truth.
>
> The scientific principles of research are the same for all kinds of research: a problem is defined; a systematic method of collecting, organizing, and analyzing data is adopted; generalizations are made on the basis of the evidence collected; the results are used to guide future action or to improve practice.[5]

Action research, then, is carefully planned and controlled research in the classroom, which can be one of the best laboratories for the discovery of means to improve instruction.

Procedures for initiating and carrying out action research. If the administrator or supervisor is convinced of the possibilities of research in school situations, the following steps are suggested:

1. Using the techniques discussed in Chapters I and VIII of this handbook, continue to develop a climate that will free staff members to participate actively in group projects and to consider change.
2. Through group processes, decide on tentative areas for research, for example: "A Study of Certain Programmed Learning Materials in Modern Elementary Arithmetic." At this stage, an educational research professor from a nearby college or university could be helpful in selecting areas for study.
3. Seek professional help in structuring the research project according to approved methods. All interested teachers and supervisors should be involved.

Davison has outlined the following steps in action research and the methods of accomplishing them.

---

[4] Stephen M. Corey, *Action Research to Improve School Practices* (New York: Bureau of Publications, Teachers College, Columbia University, 1953), p. 26.

[5] Jane Franseth, "Improving the Curriculum and Teaching Through Action Research," *School Life*, XLII, No. 4 (December, 1959), 8-9.

Steps in Action Research	*Methods of Accomplishing These Steps*
1) There must be a clear need for the proposed research activity so that the staff involved can see why and how the study may directly help them.	1) The research coordinator must do some pre-study but must not act like an expert. A series of definite examples of the school problems should be presented for review by the school staff so that the participants can grasp the need for the study and then focus on the most essential elements to be included in their study. If there are no crisis problems a survey of the teachers' problems can give a starting point. The staff must know that the research will be sincere, and that they will have the opportunity to evaluate the whole outcome and make their contributions willingly rather than on the basis of pressure.
2) The problem and subordinate problems must be clearly defined with realistic limitations of such a nature that the research becomes actually feasible in that situation.	2) There must be review and restatements of the problems periodically. This enables the staff to look at the need and the stated problem to see if these are in harmony so that they will personally defend the choice of research problem.
3) The literature on the subject should be reviewed to help set the design of the proposed study. What methods have a chance for success? What curricular units are teachable? What do other current and prior research findings tell us that will assist us?	3) Assignments to review the literature and make group reports should be based on the individual interests of the staff members. School planning time, and if possible paid travel and materials, should be provided. The work should not be hurried, but there should be periodic checks on reading progress and staff morale. Reassignments may be necessary and deadlines may be required. The reports should be properly received and respected by all participants.
4) The procedure of the study requires initial and final evaluation so that effect or progress can be determined. The measures used must be designed to enable the acceptance or rejection of hypotheses at the end of the study.	4) The instruments of evaluation can have many forms: Pupil rating scales, teacher rating scales, achievement tests, judged projects with score cards, problem check sheets, inventories, projective techniques, internal and external criteria, case studies and follow-ups. The instruments used must be checked against the objectives of the hypotheses investigated with

Steps in Action Research	Methods of Accomplishing These Steps
	evaluation as to the procedure's effectiveness.
5) Part of the procedure will include progress reports so that the whole group of investigators can keep in touch with the study. Incorrect or misunderstood procedures that might lead to confusion at a later date should be cleared up.	5) This, with the design of the instruments above, is one of the difficult parts of the research. The administration needs to be alert to the need for group meetings. It is better for the research group to have many short meetings which clear the air immediately than to expose the teachers with the content and frustrations of long meetings.
6) Record keeping is the history of the evidence. The data and the notes from the meetings are both gathered. Materials are distributed and a schedule of events maintained. Diaries and classroom journals may be needed. All things issued to the participants should be ample so that steps can be retraced and all activities can be gathered into the retelling of the study.	6) One person should be delegated to keep track of where the study is and where it is going. In order to do this, ample clerical help and time are necessities.
7) Data analysis is the process of discovering possible meaning and principles in the evidence gathered. The interpretation of the data should be absolutely clear and should arrive after much reflection by the participants.	7) Graphs, flow charts, statistical comparisons, verbal evidence organized by some logic, and thoughts checked against criteria may form the basis for analysis. Data can be classified by logical groupings. Age, ability, interest, and experience groupings often point up the sense or usefulness of the data.
8) Conclusions for the research should accept or reject the hypotheses set up. The major problem of the study should be answered. A written and an oral report of the study should be given by the research group to the public or the school board.	8) There will need to be review and writing sessions on the part of the research team.
9) The written recommendations of such a report should have the unqualified endorsement of the research team. The recommendations should be put into operation in the school system according to a schedule agreed upon by the research staff and the school administration.	9) Conferences will be needed between the administration and the research team. It is possible that the board will require a private hearing before a public announcement of the results.

Davison concludes:

> If there is to be a revolution in educational research, it should come from the classroom teacher and the curriculum specialist. There are several reasons for this. The professional personnel have the basic tools for research: the children, the materials, and a large accumulation of experience with children in a school setting.[6]

An action research project. In the recent experience of the writer, the following research study was planned and conducted by supervisory and teaching personnel from several school districts in a three-county area, working cooperatively under the leadership of an assistant county superintendent.

With the great number and variety of programmed learning materials appearing on the market, it is difficult to determine which are appropriate for classroom use at different levels in the various subject areas. Consequently, the chief school administrators in three adjacent counties were surveyed to determine their possible interest in a joint research project to test available programmed materials in classroom situations. As a result, about 25 interested supervisors, administrators, and teachers met several times to identify subject areas and grade levels for experimentation. Between meetings, staff members in the several districts were involved in the planning. Finally, with the help of a research consultant from the state department of public instruction, the study was launched. The steps outlined above were followed; programmed learning materials were selected; and experimental groups were set up in the classrooms of cooperating teachers. The results of this action research project should make available to administrators and teachers information on the best use of certain programmed instructional materials.

Development of Professional Libraries

A most important supervisory technique is the establishment and maintenance of extensive professional libraries. Teachers should have readily available at both the building and the district level a wide selection of up-to-date books.

Certain books, because of the need for frequent referral, will be much more effective if they are available in the building library.[7] General

---

[6] Used by permission of Dr. Hugh M. Davison, Professor of Educational Research, Pennsylvania State University. From address to Department of Supervision and Curriculum Development, Pennsylvania State Education Association, November, 1961.

[7] For example, see Glenn O. Blough, Albert J. Huggett, and J. Schwartz, *Elementary School Science and How to Teach It* (New York: Holt, Rinehart, and Winston, Inc., 1958).

education books and those which would be of interest on occasion to individuals and groups will normally be housed in the district professional library.[8]

Some districts will have full-time librarians to handle the curriculum center and main professional library. In any event, it is essential that responsibility for the maintenance and distribution of these books be assigned to one of the district librarians. All staff members should be made aware of the volumes available and the procedures for using them.

At the building level, the school librarian, if there is one, should have charge of the professional books.

The coordinators of elementary and secondary education, the supervisors of special subject areas, and department heads may want to build up their own collections of specialized books in addition to the district and building libraries.

The following suggestions are designed to help the supervisor in establishing and maintaining professional libraries.

1. A general administrator or supervisor should be given responsibility for the central district library.

2. Each principal should coordinate with his staff and librarian, if any, the acquisition, placement, and distribution of the books in his building.

3. All staff members should be urged to suggest new titles for the several collections, and to join in the evaluation of new books.

4. A substantial sum must be budgeted each year to allow for the addition of current titles.

5. Potential usage of a book should determine its placement in the district.

6. A section of the district professional library could be set aside for the curriculum materials center. (See Chapter XI.)

Visiting Other Teachers

Intervisitation is one of the most neglected yet promising techniques for improving instruction. All teachers can profit from observing master teachers at work. The beginner can learn how to organize a classroom, how to manage a group of pupils, and how to plan effectively. The weak teacher can often be helped through observation of class management, good methods, and utilization of resources in his field. Even the master teacher can share ideas with another outstanding colleague, and through this experience the classes of both will be enriched.

---

[8] For example, see A.A. Lumsdaine and Robert Glaser, *Teaching Machines and Programmed Learning* (Washington, D.C.: National Education Association, 1960).

Careful planning must precede any visitation program. The district administrative council should develop, through its regular democratic procedures, a visitation policy. Such questions as these must be answered:

1. What are the purposes of staff intervisitation?
2. Should one or two days per year be established in the calendar for visitation by all professional personnel? Or should substitute teachers be hired during the year to permit flexibility in visits? (Some districts hire permanent substitutes for this purpose and for regular substitute teaching.)
3. Should all staff members participate in the program, or only certain persons, such as new teachers and those with special problems?
4. Should visitation be planned inside and outside the district?
5. Where can skillful teachers in the various subject areas and at all grade levels be found? Each principal will, of course, be able to identify some of his own teachers for a district list. All administrative and supervisory personnel must use considerable discretion in the preparation and execution of a plan for visiting within the district. Some experienced teachers will feel hurt or rejected if they are omitted.

The following ideas may help in building up a file of outstanding teachers in other districts.

A. All administrators and supervisors should use their contacts in principals' associations, curriculum study groups, and other organizations to identify master teachers in various fields.
B. The principals or the coordinators of elementary and secondary education can write to their counterparts in good school districts, requesting the names of teachers with certain identifiable skills. Don't ask for "your best teachers." Rather, make a specific request, for example, "a teacher who excels in social studies unit work at the intermediate level," or "one who uses the new CHEM approach in senior high school chemistry."
C. A card file can be maintained in each principal's or coordinator's office, listing superior teachers skilled in various techniques and subjects, both inside and outside the district.

Other suggestions on implementing a plan for intervisitation are:

1. Administrators and supervisors should plan to join their teachers on some classroom visits. Then follow-up discussions can be held back at school.
2. Standards and procedures for visiting should be established.
   A. Visitors should not interrupt class activities or speak to pupils without consent of the teacher.

B. All classroom visits should be a full period or lesson in duration.[9]
C. Visitors usually see the principal for orientation before entering the classrooms.

3. Experienced teachers should be encouraged to visit levels other than the ones they teach. It is most important that elementary teachers observe high school classes, and vice versa.

Many positive outcomes of intervisitation both inside and outside a district have been reported.[10]

1. Ideas for new teaching methods are shared.
2. Greater appreciation and understanding of other teachers and children result, especially when visiting a different level.
3. Specific goals may be achieved, such as learning the methods of handling pupils in team teaching.
4. Visiting staff members gain a broader understanding of the whole learning process in going beyond their own classrooms and schools. Too many professional educators get into a comfortable rut. Intervisitation raises sights and expands horizons in a healthy way if the program is carefully planned.

Coordination of Student or Intern Teaching in a District

It is the responsibility of schools located near a teacher-training institution to take student teachers or interns, if asked to do so. An increasing number of good classroom experiences must be made available to students as they move from educational theory into the practicalities of teaching a group of pupils. Prospective teachers should have opportunities to observe in their first and second college years, and should engage in real teaching experiences through the third and fourth years.

The alert supervisor realizes that a student teaching program is not a one-way street. Many advantages accrue to the receiving district that reflect themselves in an improved instructional program.

1. First of all, master teachers who agree to serve as student supervisors usually do an even better job in the classroom. They are often eager to assist a novice in the profession and to share their experiences.
2. The entire climate of the school can be enhanced by the freshness and vitality of the interns. Their knowledge of current theory and their earnest desire to succeed in the profession can often stimulate average

---

[9] Audrey M. Borth, George K. McGuire, Illa E. Podendorf, and James P. Rose, "Visiting Other Teachers in Your School: A Basis for Communication," *Elementary School Journal*, LVIII, No. 6 (March, 1958), 331-334.
[10] *Ibid.*

teachers more successfully than a number of techniques employed by the principal or coordinator. Enthusiasm is contagious.

3. While they will not always admit it, experienced teachers often learn new methods and approaches from students who have had the benefit of the latest research at college.

4. The district becomes known as a development center for the profession, as the interns leave to enter successful careers in teaching.

Procedures for accepting and training student teachers must be carefully developed. A handbook or duplicated pamphlet is suggested to summarize all important aspects of the intern program. The administrative council should prepare guidelines to be followed by all schools. Teachers would be consulted as the policy evolves. The following areas need clarification:

1. Are supervising teachers to be paid, and by whom? The trend is toward payment by the college, and at times by the receiving district.

2. By what criteria are supervising teachers to be selected? Here are some suggestions:

   A. Must be an above-average teacher with at least three years' experience in the public schools, one of which has been in the present district.
   B. Only volunteers should be accepted; no one should be asked to take a student against his will.
   C. The building principal has final authority in approving supervising teachers.

To implement the program, principals and coordinators should meet with the designated officials from the teacher education institution to work out cooperatively the assignment of students to classrooms.

The principal and teachers of a school should welcome interns as fellow staff members. In every sense they are regarded as a part of the team. Gone are the days when student teachers were considered clerical aides and servants in the classroom. As quickly as possible, the interns are encouraged to become familiar with the school and their specific teaching-learning situations. The skillful master teachers then lead them steadily into more and more responsibility with classes of pupils. From the beginning, student teachers should be peers of the supervising teachers in the eyes of the pupils.

The principal will sometimes be confronted with the lazy teacher who likes to have an intern so he can loaf on the job. Of course, there will be other evidences of such an attitude. Needless to say, teachers who do not want to make the necessary effort to become good supervisors should not be given students.

On occasion, older teachers will resent student interns in the school much as they are irritated by the new young teacher on the staff. The reason is usually jealousy, insecurity, or fear of change. The skillful principal will handle these situations through the practice of sensible human relations. The confidence of the older teacher must be maintained while the student teacher is given every opportunity to become a member of the team while he is there.

Cooperative Evaluation and Development of the Testing Program

Since tests represent one means of measuring the impact of the instructional program on pupils, they are a legitimate concern of the supervisor in the modern school. Testing programs today often are nonexistent, chaotic, or overburdening to students. In some districts, no attempt has been made to develop logical series of tests in the various areas of the curriculum. The result often is confusion, with each principal or teacher following his own program. Some pupils may receive no standardized tests; others may have a reasonable number. In other systems, test has been piled upon test over the years until pupils and teachers alike stagger under the weight of an unwieldy, inefficient, and overlapping program. Many school districts, of course, have tried to control the growth of their test patterns, keeping pace with the findings of research and curriculum development.

Here is a step-by-step process to enable administrators and supervisors to evaluate their present achievement testing programs and to formulate balanced and effective plans for the future.

1. The suggestion to examine the present testing program is placed on the agenda of the district administrative council for discussion.
2. Each principal then works with his own staff to identify the standardized and teacher-made tests now in general use throughout the district. If this compilation has not been done recently, the length and variety of the list will be surprising.
3. The district or county school psychologist or a testing expert from a nearby college or university should now be involved for consultation. Outdated, unreliable, or invalid tests should be eliminated immediately.
4. Considering the present curriculum in each subject area, the psychologist, supervisors, and teachers can begin to look for those standardized tests which most nearly measure the objectives of the courses of study. Some of those presently used will be retained as suitable. The programs from the various test producers can now be examined in light of the desired pupil outcomes.

Important leadership note: Tests should always be selected after the curriculum has been developed. Otherwise, there is a tendency to conform the course of study to the tests. Some teachers will teach the content of the tests if there is no cooperatively developed curriculum. (See Chapter XI for a plan of curriculum study.)

5. The achievement testing program must be planned in relation to the other tests administered in the district, such as those in aptitude and ability. Standardized testing should be spaced throughout the school year and be well balanced from kindergarten through high school. Above all, there should not be too many tests. Other methods of evaluation are just as important.

6. There should be many opportunities for teacher-made tests. Some of these may be adopted for use by more than one teacher. Others would be used once for a particular group of pupils. All available instruments should be listed if they might be helpful to a number of teachers.

7. The final list of tests should be continually revised as the curriculum changes from year to year. Pupil learning patterns are never static, and a testing program must always measure as accurately as possible desired pupil behavior. In this statement we see the danger of overemphasis on tests. Learning is a highly individual and complex matter. Any attempt to measure it will be grossly inaccurate. Our best tests merely sample the body of knowledge they purport to cover. In the proper perspective, achievement testing can add to our knowledge of the pupil and his progress. Tests, therefore, should be used but not abused as a supervisory technique.

Important leadership note: An overemphasis on the results of standardized tests and their relationship to teacher effectiveness can adversely affect teacher morale. It cannot be assumed that Miss Jones is not teaching arithmetic well just because her class median is below the national norm. Supervisors who look over test scores as an indicator of teaching success should be cognizant of the many other elements that must be considered, such as pupil ability, previous achievement, and other evidences of progress in learning.

Two recent research studies on elementary and secondary standardized testing programs offer additional guidance to the supervisor.[11]

---

[11] William F. Nye, "A Study of Standardized Test Programs in Selected Public Secondary Schools of Pennsylvania and the Attitudes of Secondary Classroom Teachers of Selected Subjects Toward Standardized Test Practices" (Doctoral dissertation, Temple University, 1962); John W. O'Brien, "Standard Test Programs of Selected Public Elementary Schools in Pennsylvania and the Attitudes of Elementary Classroom Teachers Toward Certain Standardized Test Practices" (Doctoral dissertation, Temple University, 1962).

Initiating and Carrying Out New Organizational Patterns

While mainly administrative in nature, the newer plans of organization, such as the ungraded school and team teaching, are being adopted to facilitate instruction. Consequently, they are of vital concern to the supervisor who is primarily interested in the improvement of learning opportunities in the classroom.

Supervisory personnel should be involved in each planning step as new organizational plans are introduced. For example, if the decision to inaugurate team teaching has been made in a district, the following steps are indicated to insure success of the instructional program.

1. The assistant superintendent in charge of instruction or the coordinator of elementary or secondary education usually would coordinate the planning. In the small district, the chief school official probably would direct the change.
2. The supervisory responsibilities of the following persons must be determined so that line organization is clear: the team teaching coordinator, the principal, and the team leader.
3. Team leaders and master teachers are identified and trained for their roles.
4. Each teaching team must be well balanced, considering the experience and major preparation of every teacher.
5. As the teams are organized and begin to plan, it is essential that some supervisory official attend every team meeting.
6. The principal works with all team leaders in his school to integrate the evolving instructional program. Experiments to date have shown that teams of teachers planning together actually evaluate and develop the curriculum as they proceed through the school year. It is imperative that the principal be a part of this supervisory activity.
7. If team teaching is being introduced at the same level in more than one school in a district, then the assistant superintendent or the general supervisor or coordinator must work with all principals and team leaders simultaneously.

In the introduction of any new organizational pattern, job descriptions must be outlined by the chief school official and the district administrative council to guide the staff and to assure continuity in the supervision of the instructional program. The table of organization should be clear in its designation of line authority and yet flexible enough to permit the most cooperative working relationships among staff members. As indicated in Chapter I, these are the most important ingredients in an effective supervisory program.

Interpretation of the Instructional Program to the Public

Without public acceptance of a school district's philosophy and curriculum, the finest supervisory program will be of little value. Therefore, all administrators and supervisors need to be vitally concerned with public relations as an aspect of the improvement of instruction.

The coordinator of secondary education and his teachers may be convinced that a new approach to mathematics is highly desirable in the senior high school. The superintendent may be prepared to recommend new courses and materials of instruction to the board of education. But the parents and other interested citizens of the community must also be prepared for this change. Indeed, they should be involved in it to some extent. Through P.T.A. discussions, citizens' council meetings, news releases, educational television programs, and service club talks, to mention a few, the newer research in high school mathematics could be presented in language that lay persons can understand. In other words, through an effective public relations program, improvements in the curriculum and funds to support them are made possible.

Several excellent guides to successful public relations are available, and the reader is referred to them for specific and detailed assistance in this vital area.[12]

IN-SERVICE EDUCATION

Many of the group supervisory techniques described above are often used as in-service training activities. When a definite program is organized, involving faculty members and utilizing group techniques, it is commonly designated "in-service education." Some researchers define any effort to improve instruction with the staff as in-service. For the purposes of this discussion, however, programs which involve the staff conference, workshop, or study-group approach are considered in-service by definition. The purpose always is to provide experiences for staff members which will enable them to work together and grow professionally in areas of common concern. The list of possible in-service programs is almost

---

[12] Leslie W. Kindred, *How to Tell the School Story* (Englewood Cliffs, N.J.: Prentice-Hall, Inc., 1960); Leslie W. Kindred, *School Public Relations* (Englewood Cliffs, N.J.: Prentice-Hall, Inc., 1957); American Association of School Administrators, "School-Community Relations That Promote Better Instruction," *The Superintendent as Instructional Leader*, Thirty-fifth Yearbook (Washington, D.C.: National Education Association, 1957).

infinite, since actual planning will be based on a number of factors, such as staff experience and training, nature of the pupil population and community, and the status of curriculum development in the district. However, some common group in-service activities are:

1. Curriculum study and development. (See Chapter XI.)
2. Self-evaluation by staff, using available evaluative criteria.
3. Workshops or institutes on various aspects of child study, the nature of the learning process, identification of pupil problems and needs, and the changing nature of society and the community.
4. Evaluation of school-district philosophy and general objectives.
5. Special programs or workshops for teachers new to the district.
6. Study of trends in reporting pupil progress.
7. Research project on grouping of pupils.
8. Study of newer organizational patterns, such as team teaching and the nongraded school.
9. Workshops on use of aids to instruction, including programmed instructional devices, language laboratories, and the various audio-visual aids.
10. Workshops on instructional techniques and new content in the subject areas.

How to Plan In-service Programs

Poor planning can ruin any in-service project before it is launched. Supervisors should be aware of significant research results to avoid mistakes. Burton and Brueckner report a study by C. A. Weber which lists the most serious obstacles encountered in programs of in-service education:

1. Lack of time, heavy teaching loads, heavy extracurricular loads, no suitable time of day.
2. Unprofessional attitudes of teachers.
3. Lack of money for providing professional books and magazines and suitable library facilities for staff.
4. Lack of planning.

In analyzing the second obstacle, "unprofessional attitudes of teachers," Weber found the following types of poor teacher attitudes:

1. Older teachers who have little interest in any kind of in-service education. (See Chapter IX for suggestions.)

2. Indifference, inertia, complacency of teachers.[13]

Some of Dreisbach's conclusions in his study of the opinions of principals and teachers regarding their in-service programs are pertinent:

1. . . . although the majority of respondents expressed their belief in democratic participation, there was evidence that democratic participation was invited and exercised in very few of the in-service programs held. . . .
2. The majority of respondents expressed satisfaction with the problem areas selected for study, but few of them could agree as to why those areas had been selected.
3. Although nearly all of the principals expressed the belief that the in-service programs had benefited the instructional program, there was no evidence to indicate that a majority of the teachers interviewed shared this belief.
4. Only in those school systems where teachers helped to plan the programs did the majority of teachers feel that any improvement in the instructional program had resulted. . . .
5. The lack of coordination in the curriculum . . . was not solved by most of the in-service programs.
6. Although nearly all of the respondents felt that the in-service programs could be improved, many of the teachers were interested in improving the programs through cooperative planning, whereas most of the principals were interested in devoting more time to the programs and in engaging the services of consultants.
7. There seemed to be a lack of communication between those who planned the programs and those who attended them. Many teachers did not know why the topics had been selected, nor did they know what to expect from the programs before they were presented.
8. Although the teachers reported that they enjoyed the in-service meetings, the programs apparently made no lasting impression on the majority of them.
9. The fact that a large majority of respondents felt that attendance at in-service programs should be compulsory and that teachers need not be reimbursed for time spent in in-service programs indicated that a majority of principals and teachers view in-service programs as being important professional obligations.[14]

Since a cooperatively planned in-service program will attract the interest and vital participation of more staff members, the following steps for action are suggested.

---

[13] William H. Burton and Leo J. Brueckner, *Supervision: A Social Process* (New York: Appleton-Century-Crofts, Inc., 1955), p. 525. Original source: C. A. Weber, "Obstacles to Be Overcome in a Program of Educating Teachers in Service," *Educational Administration and Supervision* (December, 1942). Copyright © 1955, Appleton-Century-Crofts, Inc.

[14] Dodson E. Dreisbach, "A Survey of the Opinions of the Supervising Principals, Elementary Principals, and Elementary Teachers Concerning the In-Service Programs Conducted in the Joint School Systems of Berks County, Pennsylvania" (Doctoral dissertation, Temple University, 1959), pp. 198-201.

1. The district administrative council tentatively identifies areas for in-service study.

2. Building principals and supervisors discuss suggested ideas with all staff members informally. A part of a school faculty meeting agenda can be devoted to consideration of in-service projects. Everyone should have an opportunity to take part in the initial planning, since this will help to insure success of the program.

3. The administrative council spells out objectives for the in-service work and decides on the topics for the year. These conclusions are made known to all staff members for their reactions.

4. The scope of the program is finalized by the administrative council and the following decisions are reached:

A. Format of the project—workshop, group discussion, total staff conference, or combination.

B. Time allotments and scheduling. For example, will the in-service program include curriculum study and development? (Details in Chapter XI.) In-service projects are scheduled as summer workshops, pre-school conferences in late August, and on early-dismissal days or full days throughout the year. Adequate time is essential to the success of any program. Teachers cannot be expected to react favorably to in-service work scheduled after a full teaching day. Furthermore, teachers should be paid for full in-service days placed in the calendar if these extend the total contract year.

C. Adequate funds must be budgeted by the district as recommended by the administrative council for such purposes as consultant fees, purchase of research materials, and compensation of staff.

D. All staff members are notified of the final plans for the year's in-service program, and each person has an opportunity to join a phase of the study which is of primary concern to him. (See Chapter XI for ideas.)

Additional Leadership Suggestions

1. Each workshop session must be carefully structured to insure maximum staff participation and interest.

2. Consultants should not be employed indiscriminately but only when a specific purpose is identified. For example, in a workshop on "The adolescent learner," a psychologist with considerable experience in adolescent behavior might be engaged to present current research findings on learning to the total secondary staff. He might then be used as a resource person in a small discussion group to follow.

3. Different programs should be planned for new and experienced teachers.

4. Imaginative supervisors can arrange after-school in-service programs on one of the local television stations. Educational channels are most often available for this purpose. The same careful planning is necessary, of course, and other interested districts should be involved.

5. Chief school officials in small districts can often pool their in-service resources by planning regional workshops, institutes, or cooperative projects through study councils. Administrative assistance is often available from the office of the county superintendent or the intermediate unit.

6. Principals, as the educational leaders of their schools, can plan periodic staff meetings on some phase of supervision. These can be scheduled within the district program planned by the administrative council. For example, an elementary staff might plan one or two sessions on techniques of teacher-parent conferencing. An outside consultant or the coordinator of elementary education in the district could direct this program. At the secondary level, the county reading supervisor might be asked to a faculty meeting to help all teachers become more aware of reading problems and their solution.

Examples of Successful In-Service Education Programs

1. One of the authors observed the operations of the Midwest Program on Airborne Television, Inc., based in Lafayette, Indiana. One of the problems in the administration of this ambitious program of instructional television is the number and variety of school districts served in the six-state area. Over 1,500 schools receive the airborne signal and use television in some way in their classrooms.

To meet the obvious problems of programming and scheduling, twenty advisory committees have been set up to keep MPATI headquarters informed of reactions from the field and to arrange in-service programs for teachers.

The Purdue Advisory Committee recommended that the broadcast day be extended by keeping the aircraft aloft one hour after the close of school so that teachers could receive in-service education in their school buildings. Other suggested times for in-service programming were early-morning and summer-vacation periods. In the latter case, college credit was recommended.

Special programs have been taped and broadcast to help teachers make more effective use of the MPATI programs for pupils. Suggestions on the proper use of the resource manuals were included. The coordinator of this advisory committee met with a number of teachers and administrators to plan these in-service programs. The television series was then followed by area workshops, which most teachers attended.

This has been a successful example of cooperative planning for an effective in-service program on television.

2. The following in-service project was successfully planned and carried out by the staff of an intermediate-size elementary district with approximately 3,500 pupils and 150 professional staff members.[15]

TREDYFFRIN-EASTTOWN ELEMENTARY SCHOOLS
IN-SERVICE EDUCATION PROGRAM FOR THE
1961-1962 SCHOOL YEAR

THEME: Contemporary Issues in Elementary Education

The 1961-1962 In-Service Education Program is designed to acquaint the staff of the Tredyffrin-Easttown Elementary Schools with the Contemporary Issues in Elementary Education and their implications as related to policy for elementary education.

The sound-color-slide presentation, *Guide Lines for Decision on Issues in Elementary Education,* produced by the Department of Elementary School Principals, NEA, will serve as the basic guide to the entire program.

This is a presentation dealing with realities of society and realities of learning which serve as guidelines for making decisions about contemporary issues in elementary education.

In general, the year's program will then deal with:

a. Realities of society
b. Realities of learning
c. The implication of the above two areas for making decisions such as: Homework, pupil placement, marking and reporting, school organization.

As educators, it is our responsibility and obligation to understand these realities and issues as we deal with instruction and curriculum development. "The elementary school continues to change today, for it must strive incessantly to take account of social change and to improve its effectiveness. In changing, it must pay due regard to the role which it alone can play, and to the growing body of knowledge about children and about learning." (Educational Policies Commission, *Contemporary Issues in Elementary Education*)

The Program

September 6, 1961—Paoli Elementary School Auditorium

First General Session—8:45 A.M.

A. Introduction to the staff of the year's program
B. The Role of the Professional Teacher in Today's Educational Pattern
   Dr. William Arnold
   Dean, School of Education
   University of Pennsylvania

[15] Used by permission of Weston C. Opdyke, Director of Elementary Education, Tredyffrin-Easttown Elementary Schools, Berwyn, Pennsylvania.

September 18, 1961—Valley Forge Elementary School

Second General Session—9:00 A.M.—Cafetorium

9:00 A.M. *Guidelines for Decision on Issues in Elementary Education.* A dramatic sound-color-slide presentation dealing with realities of society and realities of learning which serve as guidelines for decisions about contemporary issues in elementary education.

9:40 A.M. Free discussion period of filmstrip for all participants. Panel members will confer concerning their presentation which will follow. Coffee will be served.

10:00 A.M. Panel reaction to the 9:00 A.M. presentation. A panel comprised of a sociologist, economist, political scientist and a scientist will discuss the realities of society as presented in the filmstrip. Each speaker will discuss significant trends in his area of interest. Analysts will raise questions about their educational implications.

The realities of society to be considered include:

Rapid transportation and communication
Anxiety—tension—pressure
Economic disparity
Conformity—individuality
Atomic development
Population increases
Struggle between political ideologies

11:45 A.M. Lunch

1:00 P.M. Group Discussion Meetings

Twenty groups of eight each will discuss the realities of our society and their implications for elementary education. Five groups will discuss the realities from the viewpoint of the sociologist; five from the viewpoint of the economist; five from the viewpoint of the political scientist; and five from the viewpoint of the scientist.

2:20 P.M. Intermission

2:30 P.M. Re-showing of the filmstrip—*Guidelines for Decision*

2:30 P.M. Meeting of the recorders from the discussion group meetings to summarize reports.

3:00 P.M. General Meeting

Reports of recorders

a. Report of groups discussing viewpoint of sociologist.
b. Report of groups discussing viewpoint of economist.
c. Report of groups discussing viewpoint of political scientist.
d. Report of groups discussing viewpoint of scientist.

November 7, 1961—Hillside Elementary School

Third General Session

12:15 P.M. Luncheon

1:15 P.M. Realities of Learning

Panel reaction to the realities of learning based on filmstrip—*Guidelines for Decision.* A panel comprised of a psychologist, a physician, and a guidance person will discuss the realities of learning as presented in the filmstrip. Each speaker will discuss significant trends in his area of interest. Analysts will raise questions about their educational implications.

The realities of learning to be considered include:
Individual differences
Emotional climate
Environmental security
Self concepts
Rate of growth
Home environment
Cultural background

2:40 P.M. Group Discussion Meetings

Eighteen groups of nine each will discuss realities of learning and their implications for elementary education. Six groups will discuss the realities from the viewpoint of the psychologist; six from the viewpoint of the physician; and six from the viewpoint of the guidance person.

3:40 P.M. Meeting of recorders to summarize discussion of group meetings.

3:50 P.M. Intermission

4:00 P.M. General Meeting

Recorders will report on findings of group meetings.
Report of the recorders

a. Report of groups discussing viewpoint of the psychologist.
b. Report of groups discussing viewpoint of the physician.
c. Report of groups discussing viewpoint of the guidance person.

February 6, 1962—Devon Elementary School

Fourth General Session

12:15 P.M. Luncheon

1:15 P.M. General Meeting

A panel of staff members will review the findings concerning the realities of society and the realities of learning and their implications for elementary education.

1:30 P.M. Assemblies

Assemblies will be organized to give staff members an opportunity to discuss the areas of homework, pupil placement, and marking and reporting in relationship to the realities of society and learning.

The three assemblies involved will be:
a. Homework
b. Pupil placement
c. Marking and reporting
All staff members will spend an hour in each of the assemblies.
Organization of the assemblies will be as follows:
Panel reaction—20 minutes—panel to be comprised of a staff member, an outside educator, a parent.
Buzz groups—20 minutes
General discussion—20 minutes

May 8, 1962
Fifth General Session
12:15 P.M. Luncheon
1:15 P.M. General Meeting
"The implications of the realities of society and the realities of learning on the elementary school organization"
2:30 P.M. Assemblies
Four assemblies concerning organization at the various levels of the elementary school will be formed. Each teacher will attend one assembly.

SUMMARY

There are many ways of working with professional groups to improve the instructional program. Certain supervisory techniques can best be carried out through group interaction involving the sharing of experiences, ideas, and the findings of educational research. Dynamic, democratic leadership and effective human relations are essential to success in group supervisory activities.

The following have been identified as group techniques.

1. With the current large turnover of teachers in many school districts, it is essential that a comprehensive program be developed for the *orientation of new teachers.*

2. *Action research,* while subject to many definitions, is on-the-job practical research in the public school classroom. It is carefully planned and controlled, requiring definite steps in execution. Since the pupils, materials of instruction, and experienced teachers are available in the schools, more research should be conducted there.

3. An important supervisory technique is the *maintenance of professional libraries.* These should be established both in the school buildings and at the district level.

4. *Intervisitation* is one of the most promising group techniques for

improving instruction. All teachers can profit in some way from observing a master teacher at work, either inside or outside the district.

5. A good *student teaching* plan in a district can help to improve the entire instructional program and make a significant contribution to the profession at the same time. Teachers usually perform even better when they have interns in their classrooms.

6. Since achievement tests are one means of measuring the impact of classroom instruction on pupils, supervisors should evaluate their present *testing programs* to see if they are really measuring what is being taught. The achievement tests must be planned in relation to other tests, such as those in aptitude and ability.

7. The supervisor is concerned with any *new organizational plan*, such as team teaching, that might be introduced into the district. Indeed, the initial decision should be made on the basis of definite possibilities for improved instruction. It is important that supervisory personnel be involved in each planning step as new organizational patterns develop.

8. All administrators and supervisors need to be vitally concerned with *public relations* as an aspect of the improvement of instruction. The people of a community must feel that they have a part in the school program if curriculum advances and the funds to support them are to be forthcoming.

In-service education has been defined as any planned program involving supervisors and teachers in the improvement of classroom instruction. Included are staff conferences, workshops, study groups, and curriculum-development projects. The list of possible programs is almost infinite. Supervisors should work with teachers in planning, so that in-service activities will result in more real participation and lasting results.

SUGGESTED ACTIVITIES AND PROBLEMS

1. Develop a detailed plan for the orientation of new teachers in your school district.

2. Evaluate critically the steps in action research outlined in this chapter.

3. Prepare a proposal for an action research project in your district.

4. Differentiate between professional libraries at the building and district levels.

5. Interview a supervisor to determine the plan for teacher-intervisitation in his district. Criticize the program and make suggestions for improvement.

6. Develop a district policy for accepting and training student teachers.

7. Defend or refute this statement: "The testing program is a legitimate concern of the supervisor."

8. Discuss in detail the steps necessary to introduce a new plan of organization, such as team teaching.

9. Define in-service education, and outline the procedures to be followed in planning a program of in-service activities for a school year.

SELECTED READINGS

American Association of School Administrators, *The Superintendent as Instructional Leader,* Thirty-fifth Yearbook. Washington, D.C.: National Education Association, 1957.

Association for Supervision and Curriculum Development, *Research for Curriculum Improvement.* Washington, D.C.: National Education Association, 1957.

Burton, William H., and Leo J. Brueckner, *Supervision: A Social Process,* pp. 162-163 and 536-539. New York: Appleton-Century-Crofts, Inc., 1955.

Dreisbach, Dodson E., "A Survey of the Opinions of the Supervising Principals, Elementary Principals, and Elementary Teachers Concerning the In-Service Programs Conducted in the Joint School Systems of Berks County, Pennsylvania." Doctoral dissertation, Temple University, 1959.

Franseth, Jane, *Supervision as Leadership.* Evanston, Illinois: Row, Peterson and Company, 1961.

———, *Supervision in Rural Schools.* Washington, D.C.: U.S. Department of Health, Education, and Welfare, Office of Education, Bulletin 1955, No. 11, 1955.

Jantzen, John M., and James C. Stone, "More Effective Supervision of Beginning Teachers," *Journal of Teacher Education,* X, No. 2 (June, 1959), 246-248.

Kindred, Leslie W., *School Public Relations.* Englewood Cliffs, N.J.: Prentice-Hall, Inc., 1957.

———, and associates, *How to Tell the School Story.* Englewood Cliffs, N.J.: Prentice-Hall, Inc., 1960.

Lucio, William H., and John D. McNeil, *Supervision—A Synthesis of Thought and Action,* Chaps. 5 and 8. New York: McGraw-Hill Book Company, Inc., 1962.

McNally, Harold J., A. Harry Passow, and associates, *Improving the Quality of Public School Programs, Approaches to Curriculum Development.* New York: Bureau of Publications, Teachers College, Columbia University, 1960.

National Society for the Study of Education, *In-Service Education for Teachers, Supervisors and Administrators,* Fifty-sixth Yearbook, Part I. Chicago, Ill.: University of Chicago Press, 1957.

Research Division, N.E.A., *Orientation Programs for Teachers.* Washington, D.C.: National Education Association, October, 1957.

chapter eleven

How to Organize and Carry Out a Program of Curriculum Study and Development

It is difficult to exaggerate the importance of curriculum study when the sum total of man's knowledge is doubling each generation. Constant societal changes, shifts in man's cultural patterns, and the continuing explosion of knowledge all are interacting forces which increase the rate of obsolescence of school curricula. In an age of unprecedented change and tremendous challenges that threaten to rock the foundations of Western civilization, the nation's schools must direct their attention to a thorough evaluation of what they are teaching and how they are teaching it. No longer can the gap between research and classroom practice be tolerated. The newer trends in each subject field and discipline must be carefully examined for possible additions to the school program. At the same time, obsolete or less important topics must be dropped.

A massive effort is needed to redesign and repackage the entire course offering from kindergarten through high school. Existing educational programs are largely the result of piecemeal changes resulting from narrow pressures at different times. The most valiant efforts to preserve unity of purpose and sequential development of content, aimed directly at achieving the overall goals of a free society, have been insufficient to prevent proliferation and fragmentation. Refocusing is called for, and rearrangement of content into rational and workable schedules for teachers and students.[1]

According to a recent publication of the National Science Teachers Association, ". . . curriculum development is a dynamic process and must never be static . . . the curriculum should always be in process of revision leading to modernization, refinement, and enrichment."[2] Burton and Brueckner conclude: "A program of curriculum improvement is a, if not the, major concern of supervisory leadership. . . . A curriculum-improvement program is the vehicle for most of the general supervisory program."[3]

IS CURRICULUM DEVELOPMENT A NATIONAL, STATE, OR LOCAL FUNCTION?

There is overwhelming agreement that the control of public education should reside in the strong local school district. Since determination of the program of studies is one of the most basic decisions affecting the pupils, it follows that curriculum study and development should be primarily a matter of local initiative and concern. It will become apparent during the remainder of this chapter that the intermediate- or larger-size school system is better able to conduct an effective curriculum development program than is the small district. However, the chief administrator of the small unit should not wait for consolidation or reorganization of school districts. He has students to be educated today and he can initiate basic curriculum work, using some of the suggestions outlined below and in Chapter II.

The state has certain curriculum functions as required by law or by regulation of the department of public instruction. Legislatures often mandate courses of study and permit state councils or departments of

[1] *Education for Freedom and World Understanding* (Washington, D.C.: U.S. Department of Health, Education and Welfare, Office of Education, 1962), p. 13.

[2] National Science Teachers Association, *Planning for Excellence in High School Science* (Washington, D.C.: National Education Association, 1961), p. 49.

[3] William H. Burton and Leo J. Brueckner, *Supervision: A Social Process* (New York: Appleton-Century-Crofts, Inc., 1955), p. 570. Copyright © 1955, Appleton-Century-Crofts, Inc.

education to require or recommend others. For example, high schools in many states now must offer a course in earth and space science.

State department personnel usually can assist local curriculum studies in various ways:

1. Suggested subject area guides, based on current research and trends, are often prepared. These may cover one unit or an entire year's work.
2. Resource specialists are sometimes available as consultants to school districts.
3. Suggested daily schedules and time allotments for the various subject areas are often available.
4. Certain state departments have prepared excellent resource materials for the use of district curriculum committees. (A partial listing of these sources can be found in Appendix One, in the "General Curriculum Resource Materials" list, page 243.)

In summary, then, the state services should be chiefly advisory, with the main responsibility for curriculum decision resting on the local chief school administrator and his staff.

At the national level, a Commission for Curriculum Research and Development has been proposed. Proponents state that:

> Comparative education seems to support the position that democracy is best served if the control of curriculum is placed in the hands of people who are close to the sources of power—the school voters and parents in local and state communities. (However), for true unity the nation needs a better-unified system of schools—one suited to our new mobility and interdependence, more alert to our changing needs, more quickly responsive to the best leadership the country can produce. . . . (Therefore) we need a permanent nationwide commission on curriculum, nongovernmental, widely representative, and continuously at work on educational goals and balanced curriculum design. . . . (Such) a national commission would continuously: research, formulate, and reformulate the basic purposes of education for our national community in a world setting . . . research systematically all the expanding horizons of man's mind and spirit and abstract therefrom those values, generalizations, and competencies that are of vital interest to the survival of our national community . . . interpret these new ideas from all the academic disciplines and make the appropriate ones available to all concerned with curriculum development. . . . There is a growing awareness of the need to improve American education, particularly the common core of the curriculum. (Under this proposal) . . . the present educational structure (would be maintained) but . . . national leadership (would be provided) for guidance in making wise curriculum decisions.[4]

[4] Paul R. Hanna, "A National Commission for Curriculum Research and Development," *Phi Delta Kappan,* XLII, No. 8 (May, 1961), 333.

Such a national group could provide valuable resource help for local curriculum committees.

The final reports and recommendations of the National Education Association's comprehensive Project on Instruction should be required reading for all curriculum personnel. The project summary, entitled *Schools for the Sixties,* provides invaluable guidelines to help educators make decisions on curriculum content and organization for instruction. Also of considerable interest and value are the other project publications, which include: *Education in a Changing Society, Deciding What To Teach, Planning and Organizing for Teaching: The Scholars Look at the Schools, The Principals Look at the Schools: A Status Study of Selected Instructional Practices,* and *Current Curriculum Studies in Academic Subjects.*

Curriculum development, then, should be originated at the local level, with the staff seeking all possible help from state, national, and other sources.

BASIC CONSIDERATIONS AND PRINCIPLES IN CURRICULUM STUDY AND DEVELOPMENT

At least three plans of organization for curriculum improvement have been identified in the literature.

The Centralized Approach

The *centralized approach* is based upon the conviction that instructional improvement should be initiated, planned, managed, and conducted by persons in the central office of a school system. . . . Individuals in the central office determine the goals to be attained and prescribe the technics and methodology to attain these goals. . . . The centralized approach focuses on the common problems and concerns of the whole system rather than upon the problems and concerns peculiar to the personnel of an individual school. It is based on the premise that what constitutes successful practice in one situation will necessarily prove successful elsewhere.

The Decentralized Approach

The *decentralized approach* implies that instructional improvement is primarily the responsibility of the individual school or of the individual teacher. . . . The administrator may be advised or may know of the activity going on in the local school, but he assumes a minimum of responsibility for initiation, direction, and coordination of the program. . . . The decentralized position . . . seems reasonable to many persons because it appears to guarantee a maximum of teacher participation and a minimum of central office domination and interference.

The Centrally Coordinated Approach

The *centrally coordinated approach* to instructional improvement maintains that the efforts of individual schools, individual teachers, and the central office are significant. The teachers in individual schools are encouraged to improve the instructional process in order to serve *their* children better. At the same time, staff members of some or all schools, together with supervisors and others, may combine their efforts to attack a problem of instructional improvement common to all or several schools. . . . The centrally coordinated position implies that there is need for both general authority and individual responsibility. . . . Problems peculiar to an individual school and problems of general concern can be attacked at the same time. . . . The centrally coordinated approach to instructional improvement strives to secure some of the neatness and logical orderliness of centralization, yet it also seeks some of the permissiveness, freedom and democratic spirit of decentralization.[5]

The newer patterns of class and school organization definitely affect and possibly determine to some extent the shape of the curriculum. Should the school be graded or ungraded? Will team teaching improve instruction at the elementary and secondary levels? Should we individualize reading instruction or try cross grouping? Does research still support the self-contained classroom in the elementary grades? Is a core or common learnings program desirable in the junior high school? The answers to these and other similar questions could have a profound effect on any local program of curriculum study. While no organizational plan in itself will significantly improve instruction, some of the currently advocated schemes do show tentative potential for facilitating learning. The total staff may want to consider possible changes in their organization for teaching either before or during a curriculum development project.

Other basic considerations are the time and money that must be provided for an effective program of curriculum study. Time for full staff participation and money for resource persons, research materials, summer curriculum staff, and additional teachers to reduce instructional loads are all essential to the success of such a study.

Teachers cannot be expected to work productively for several hours in the late afternoon after a full day of teaching. Consequently, released time or extra calendar days should be provided for curriculum work. At the very minimum, five or six full days or their equivalent per school

[5] American Association of School Administrators, *The Superintendent as Instructional Leader*, Thirty-fifth Yearbook (Washington, D.C.: National Education Association, 1957), pp. 170-173.

year are needed to carry out any significant project. At least ten days per year or weekly released time is recommended. Also, if teachers are to have time for needed reading and research between regularly scheduled curriculum days, teacher-pupil ratios and class loads must be reasonable.

School districts with experience in curriculum study have found that it is most important to hire administrators and teachers during the summer months to collate, edit, and further develop material which has been prepared by staff committees during the school term. In this way, no time is lost, continuity is established, and teacher interest can be maintained from year to year. Summer regression in curriculum work can be as disastrous as pupil regression in some areas.

A substantial sum should be provided in the budget for initial resource persons and curriculum study materials. This amount should be increased for each additional subject area to be studied. The need for funds will vary according to the amount of current curriculum materials already on hand and the availability of resource persons from the county superintendent's office, the state department, or local colleges and universities.

It should be evident from the foregoing discussion that time and money are indeed vital ingredients in any program of curriculum development. If they cannot be provided as indicated, then the outcomes will be limited accordingly.

Basic principles of curriculum development have been evolved through research and are summarized here as a foundation for local district study. (For detailed discussions, see selected readings at the end of this chapter.)

1. Dynamic leadership from the chief school administrator and his assistants is essential.

2. All professional staff members should be involved to some extent in curriculum development. Therefore, projects should be sensible in scope and not too burdensome to staff members.

3. The values, attitudes, and prevailing opinions of the citizens of the community must be ascertained through lay advisory committees or similar groups.

4. All effective curriculum work will evolve from actual teaching situations and problems, and will continually be related to classroom experiences. Any study should begin with the existing curriculum of the district.

5. Curriculum development must be continuous; the job is never finished. Proceeding from year to year, modern curriculum revision is no "one shot" effort.

6. The "bandwagon" philosophy is shunned. New programs are con-

sidered only when they can be justified in terms of the needs of the community and society and have been proven valuable through sound educational research and experimentation.

7. Time and money in sufficient quantities must be available. (See discussion above.)
8. The program must be well-planned, logically organized, and crisply launched.
9. District-wide coordination of the curriculum is essential.
10. Evaluation must be continuous and comprehensive.

The remainder of this chapter is a step-by-step program designed to assist the school administrator or supervisor who wants to initiate curriculum study and development with his staff. There is no magic in the outline which follows. Many variations of the steps are possible and desirable in certain situations, according to the needs, facilities, staff talents, and resources of particular districts. If curriculum work has been inaugurated before, some of the preliminary steps may be omitted or modified. The format and suggested procedures are designed to be helpful at any stage of curriculum study. The best time for beginning Step 1 is the spring of the year, when the initial phases of the district program can be organized. In this way the first four steps can be completed before the close of school and the calendar can be set for the following year.

Many definitions of *curriculum* are available to the reader. Each district will have to agree on the scope of the term for its own purposes. The authors believe that the curriculum is the sum total of learning experiences which are introduced, structured, or used purposefully by the school to achieve its philosophy and objectives. The experiences over which the school has some direct measure of control are those which can be identified, evaluated, and developed into a meaningful curriculum.

OUTLINE FOR ACTION IN CURRICULUM DEVELOPMENT

Step 1

At a meeting of the administrative and supervisory staff, or district administrative council, curriculum needs and problems are explored. The state of the existing program of studies is discussed, as well as possible starting points in identification of subject areas that need evaluation.

If the district is just beginning a planned curriculum study, a good speaker could be invited at this point to address the total staff on such a topic as "A Dynamic Curriculum for a Changing Society."

Step 2

Through classroom observation, informal supervisor-teacher conferences, and building meetings held by the various principals, problem areas in the curriculum begin to be revealed. Gradually priorities emerge as the total elementary and secondary staff takes a problem census and begins to think seriously about curricular needs in terms of the district philosophy of education.

During this stage, the chief school administrator should make available the current thinking of his citizens' advisory committee or other interested lay groups, if any, regarding the adequacy of the present curriculum and course offerings.

Important leadership note: If little or no initial interest or need is felt by the teachers, it is the responsibility of the chief school official and the supervisory staff to create a climate in which proper attitudes toward curriculum development have a chance to flourish. Teachers are stimulated most by supervisors who are vitally interested in current curriculum trends, materials, and techniques. The reader is referred again to the characteristics of modern supervision in Chapter I, which must be somewhat in evidence if a staff expects to work cooperatively in the improvement of the instructional program.

Step 3

A curriculum steering committee is organized. Districts with a functioning administrative council may decide to expand this group into the steering committee. In any event, membership includes the chief school official; assistant superintendent in charge of instruction and all general supervisors or coordinators, if any; building principals; and classroom teachers as follows: one or two teachers each from the primary and intermediate levels, selected by the elementary teaching staff; department heads (if any) at the high school level, or representatives from the subject areas, selected by the secondary staff. The junior and senior high school levels each should be represented. In addition, a resource person or consultant from the county, state, or a nearby university might be secured.

It may be desirable to establish minimum requirements for the teacher representatives on the steering committee. These might include a Master's degree, at least three years' teaching experience, and the demonstration of some leadership qualities.

The chairmanship of the steering committee may be rotated periodically. The most likely initial chairman would be the chief school official or assistant superintendent in charge of instruction. However, any other qualified administrator or classroom teacher could be elected chairman by the group.

Step 4

The curriculum steering committee meets and accomplishes the following:

1. Curriculum areas that seem to exhibit the most crucial need for study, kindergarten through high school, are tentatively selected. It is, of course, impossible to study all or most of the major areas simultaneously, except possibly in very large districts where permanent committees are established for each main curriculum area. An effective working committee should number from four to eight classroom teachers plus a leader or resource person from the administrative level. Therefore, the size of the total teaching and supervisory staff will be one factor in determining the number of subject areas that it is feasible to study at one time. A district just beginning curriculum development will want to limit the study to one or two subjects the first year. If this is the case, other concurrent in-service training programs can be planned for staff members not involved in curriculum work the first year.

2. The time schedule for a year's program is set up and recommended to the school calendar committee. Five to ten full days or more should be planned for curriculum study throughout the year. Some districts plan for two or three days before school opens, and then block out the other days during the term. If full days are not always available, then a number of partial days could be provided.

Important leadership note: There must be enough time between full curriculum work days to permit necessary committee research and consultation. Teachers are very busy, and some of the tasks suggested in this chapter will require out-of-school time. In this connection, many districts are defining the teacher-day in their professional contracts to include time before and after the pupil-day for planning, conferences, and curriculum research.

3. Several resource persons are suggested for each of the subject areas considered. Such consultants are most likely to be found in the state department of education, college and university education departments, offices of county school superintendents, or the curriculum offices of larger school districts.

4. A budget for the entire program must be prepared. Items such as the following should be included:

A. Fees for curriculum consultants.

B. Funds for developing the district curriculum center. (See Step 6.)
C. Summer salaries for selected staff members. (See page 212.)
D. Clerical and postal costs.

5. *Curriculum Bulletin No. 1* should be issued to each professional staff member announcing the date of the first general meeting in Step 5 and outlining the tentative conclusions reached in Step 4. This is the first of a series of bulletins to be issued by the steering committee to keep the staff fully informed during the curriculum study.

Step 5

A general staff meeting is convened for the purpose of discussing progress to date; reporting in detail the tentative plans made by the steering committee; reaching agreement on the over-all structure of the curriculum project; and obtaining staff preferences for their participation in the year's work. The chief school official or the chairman of the steering committee presides, and his agenda could include the following:

1. Outline the scope of the proposed curriculum study as planned by the steering committee. This would include a general overview of district curriculum development to date and a presentation of the areas proposed for study at this time.

2. In small or intermediate-size districts, a general discussion of plans would be in order. Consensus could be reached on curriculum areas to be studied and teachers then asked to list their preferences for the year's project.

In larger districts, general discussion would not be possible because of the total staff size. Decisions on the subject areas to be examined could be made in building meetings and the conclusions sent to the assistant superintendent in charge of instruction. Or mimeographed sheets such as the following could be distributed, on which teachers could indicate their choices for the year's work.

UNION SCHOOL DISTRICT #1

Please check two.

Of the curriculum areas presented by the steering committee, I believe that these two are most important for district study this year, kindergarten through twelfth grade.

_____________ Social Studies
_____________ Science
_____________ Foreign Languages
(Including consideration of instruction at primary and intermediate grade levels.)

Please indicate first, second, and third choices by numerals 1, 2, and 3.
This year I would like to take part in the following program:

Curriculum development

__________ Social Studies
__________ Science
__________ Foreign Languages

Other in-service programs

__________ Research on team teaching
__________ The psychology of learning
__________ Trends in reporting pupil progress

Note: All first-year teachers will participate in a special workshop series.

3. This general staff meeting might be concluded with these announcements and information items:

A. First choices for curriculum or other in-service participation will be granted wherever possible, but second and third choices will be used to balance the committees. Also, two of the three subject areas will be finally selected from the tabulation of staff responses above.
B. The completed sheets should be handed to building principals in two or three days. [Give the due date.]
C. [The time schedule for the year's curriculum and in-service work is reviewed.]
D. The next curriculum bulletin will list the subject areas to be studied and the final committee assignments.

Step 6

After the staff responses are tabulated, a district curriculum center or laboratory is established or expanded. It is imperative that a qualified teacher or supervisor be given responsibility and time to organize or upgrade this materials center. This is one of the most important steps in curriculum development. Effective progress cannot be made without resources and research findings. According to Wiles,

> Any faculty needs to be sure that in its work procedures time is provided for the collection of evidence on which to base decisions. A decision made on the spur of the moment without taking the time or making the effort to collect sufficient data to make an intelligent decision may result in a deterioration rather than an improvement in the school program.[6]

---

[6] Kimball Wiles, "Does Faculty Participation Produce Curriculum Improvement?" *Educational Leadership,* XV, No. 6 (March, 1958), 349.

It should be apparent that an abundance of material is needed for the various committees to maintain staff interest and to insure profitable results.

The steering committee and the designated person in charge of the curriculum center will have to locate an accessible room in the district and see that shelves are available. Then the following sources should prove helpful in stocking the laboratory.

1. The personal files of the chief school official, assistant superintendent in charge of instruction, the coordinators or supervisors, and principals should contain a wealth of material that can be catalogued and filed in the curriculum lab.
2. Current written courses of study can be obtained from state departments of education, county offices, college and university curriculum libraries, and from other school districts. The resource consultants suggested in Step 4 will often have many guides and courses of study available or will know where they can be procured.
3. General reference works and bibliographies should be studied to identify the latest research findings in the subject areas on the agenda for the year. Such sources include *Education Index, Encyclopedia of Educational Research, Readers' Guide to Periodical Literature, Vertical File Index,* and *Doctoral Dissertations: Index to American Doctoral Dissertations.* Copies of pertinent studies should then be ordered.
4. The United States Office of Education publishes numerous pamphlets, booklets, and research studies in all of the subject areas and in general curriculum development. A complete bibliography is available on request.
5. The National Education Association *Publication Index* lists a wide variety of printed materials from the Association for Supervision and Curriculum Development and the other departments and commissions of the N. E. A.
6. Current issues of educational periodicals can be checked for appropriate articles. The subject-area magazines are very helpful, as well as journals like *Review of Educational Research* and *Educational Leadership.*
7. State departments of education will often be able to send bibliographies of curriculum research publications and suggested state curriculum guides in the various areas.
8. There are a number of school study councils throughout the country. Some of these make significant contributions to local curricu-

lum development. A list of recent publications should be available from nearby study councils.

9. All companies publishing textbooks, supplemental books, or workbooks in the fields to be studied should be asked to send samples for the use of the curriculum committees. For complete coverage, *Textbooks in Print*, published annually by R. R. Bowker Company, lists all current schoolbooks by subject area, title, and author. Professional texts are included also.
10. Sources of free and inexpensive materials for classroom use are published by Field Enterprises; Educators Progress Service; and the Division of Surveys and Field Services, George Peabody College for Teachers. These can be helpful near the end of the study when classroom instructional materials are selected.

Important leadership note: One of the authors has prepared detailed curriculum resource materials lists, examples of which may be found in the Appendix, pages 241 to 253. The general list includes the sources mentioned above and many others that have proven valuable. Letters should be written to all of the districts, organizations, and groups, requesting their current bibliographies in the areas to be studied. Then materials for the new curriculum center can be ordered.

In the Appendix also are suggested resource lists for language arts and science. Such guides must be prepared by the district supervisory staff for each of the subject or problem areas to be evaluated, as decided by the staff in Step 5.

The building of a curriculum center or laboratory requires careful planning. Resource materials lists such as those described and illustrated can be invaluable in launching this step. They should be continually revised and brought up to date.

Step 7

The steering committee sets up work committees based on staff interest as indicated by the questionnaires. Depending on the number of curriculum areas to be studied at one time, teachers are assigned to subject-area or in-service groups, using first choices where possible. Curriculum development committees should be limited to about eight teachers in order to allow maximum participation. These may be organized K-12, with equal representation from the primary, intermediate, and junior- and senior-high levels. Or the committees may be basically elementary or secondary, with teacher representatives from the other area.

Here are several possible plans for organizing a staff of 100 in a typical intermediate-size district. There are many options, depending on variables in any given district.

Plan A—Two subject areas, social studies and science, have been selected for K-12 review and development of curriculum guides. Five work days have been placed in the calendar; school will be closed and all staff members have expressed preferences for committee assignments.

Social studies—2 primary-level teachers
- 2 intermediate-level teachers
- 2 junior high school teachers
- 2 senior high school teachers, including the head of the social studies department
- 1 elementary principal

Science—1 primary-level teacher
- 2 intermediate-level teachers
- 2 junior high school teachers, including the head of the science department
- 3 senior high school teachers, 1 each in biology, chemistry, and physics
- 1 secondary principal

Other in-service programs (Groups include elementary and secondary teachers and administrators)

Workshop for first-year teachers	—	16
Psychology of learning	—	37
Trends in reporting pupil progress	—	27

Note: The superintendent and the assistant superintendent are not assigned.

Important leadership note: As the year's work progresses, the science and social studies committees may decide to set up subcommittees to pursue specific subjects after general objectives, scope, and sequence have been identified. For example, it might be desirable to organize work groups in biology, chemistry, and physics. This means that staff members taking part in the initial in-service programs would have a later opportunity to participate in the curriculum study or to take another in-service unit. To permit this flexibility, the first two or three curriculum days in the calendar should be used to complete the first in-service series. Then new programs could be set up for those staff members not ultimately involved in the expanded curriculum study.

Plan B—Assume that two subject areas, arithmetic and reading, have been identified for study at the elementary level and three, English, social studies, and foreign languages, at the secondary level. School will be closed for five curriculum days. Committee assignments might be broken down as follows.

Elementary arithmetic—6 primary-level teachers
6 intermediate-level teachers
2 junior high school teachers
2 senior high school teachers
1 elementary principal
1 coordinator of elementary education
All buildings and grade levels should be represented if possible. There would be two committees, one operating at the primary and one at the intermediate level. There would be some joint meetings during the year. These comments also apply to:

Elementary reading—6 primary-level teachers
6 intermediate-level teachers
3 junior high school teachers
1 senior high school teacher
2 elementary principals
1 secondary principal (junior high)

Secondary English—4 senior high school teachers, including the head of the English department
4 junior high school teachers, including the head of the English department
2 intermediate-level teachers
2 primary-level teachers
1 secondary principal (senior high)

Practically all secondary English and reading teachers are on this committee. Exceptions are those who chose other assignments at the elementary level or in another field. While this group would meet together initially, it would divide into two subcommittees at the junior high and senior high school levels.

Secondary social studies—5 senior high school teachers, including the head of the social studies department
4 junior high school teachers, including the head of the social studies department
3 intermediate-level teachers
2 primary-level teachers
1 elementary principal

Virtually the entire membership of the secondary social studies departments is included on this committee, which undoubtedly will break up into three subcommittees, perhaps on American history, world cultures, and government. Each of the smaller groups would consider the coordinated program from Grades 7 through 12, with attention to the foundations provided by the elementary-school social studies. The elementary teachers would provide valuable help in articulation.

Secondary foreign languages—4 senior high school teachers, including the head of the modern foreign language department
3 junior high school teachers
1 primary-level teacher
2 intermediate-level teachers
1 elementary principal
1 elementary French teacher

After initial work on the scope of the new foreign language program, possible new languages to be offered, and establishment of elementary grade levels for introduction of a foreign tongue, this group would probably divide into French, Spanish, and German subcommittees.

Additional in-service program. The 16 first-year teachers will be involved in a special workshop.

Note: The superintendent and assistant superintendent will provide the general supervision of all committees. The five district specialists in art, music, and physical education are not assigned above, and, of course, should be included in one of the scheduled programs. At other times, curriculum work in the special fields would proceed as outlined above.

Important leadership note: If curriculum days are scheduled in the school calendar, then provision must be made for all members of the staff. An infinite number of organizational patterns are available to the steering committee. Those outlined immediately above serve only as examples. It is obvious, however, that all personnel must have a meaningful assignment on each work day. This will often mean an additional in-service program running concurrently with curriculum development. A district experienced in curriculum study can involve all or most of the professional staff on curriculum committees because teacher and supervisory leadership have been developed.

The alternative to full staff involvement on a given day is the provision of substitute teachers at staggered times throughout the year so that committees can meet during the school day. If there is a lack of sufficient administrative and supervisory personnel for committee assignments, this plan enables the chief school official or the assistant superintendent to meet with each curriculum study group.

Step 8

The steering committee takes care of these administrative matters:

1. A curriculum bulletin is issued, listing all committee assignments for the first work day and including a reminder of the date. Teachers are urged to bring all available course outlines (if any), state guides, and lists of instructional materials presently used in the district in the subject area and grade levels assigned. (See Step 9.)
2. Considering individual talents, at least one administrator or supervisor is appointed to each curriculum committee and in-service program.
3. Outside resource persons are secured immediately, if any are needed at this time.
4. A format for the first day's work is developed, and a copy is sent to all staff members. In addition, a number of these sheets are duplicated for use during Step 9. (See Appendix, page 254, for a suggested outline.)

Step 9

The first full-day session convenes for the purpose of examining the present state of the district curriculum in the areas that have been selected for study. These procedures might be followed.

1. In a brief general meeting, review the scope of the day's work. Using the suggested format, discuss the main objective for the day: to outline in some detail the existing curriculum for each subject area under study. In other words, "What are we teaching now?" The following should be listed on the outline sheets provided to each committee:
   A. Subject-matter units or topics with specific objectives.
   B. Concepts, generalizations, attitudes, and skills to be developed.
   C. Suggested teaching techniques and pupil experiences.
   D. Teacher-pupil resources and instructional materials.
2. The staff divides into the various committees, which proceed as follows:
   A. If group process has been developed in the district, a chairman and a recorder are elected. Otherwise, the administrator might lead the committee initially, with the chairmanship changing as the leadership role emerges from the group.
   B. Following the format, the existing curriculum for the subject area is summarized.

The subcommittees may be formed at this time. Staff members will be working individually or in two's and three's. The chairman makes sure that everyone understands his assignment and that all grade or instructional levels are covered. For example, if Miss Jones and Miss Smith are the two primary-level representatives on the social studies committee, it is their responsibility to list the existing curriculum in that area from grades kindergarten through third.

Note: All units or topics that are taught by at least one teacher are a part of the current course of study and should be included.

3. At the close of the day's work, the steering-committee members collect the curriculum outlines from the various chairmen.

Important leadership note: Some individuals will need more time to complete this project. The chairman of the steering committee should ask for all outlines to be completed by a reasonable date—for example, two weeks later.

Step 10

The steering committee compiles and duplicates the summaries of the existing curriculum in the areas under study. Copies are sent to all staff members with a request that they examine the outlines for omissions, overlapping, and inconsistencies. Reactions should feed back to the steering committee through its members, through the chairmen of all committees, and through the principals in particular. One or two building-staff meetings might be devoted to this purpose.

The next steering-committee meeting includes all curriculum-committee chairmen. The suggested agenda would include the following:

1. An evaluation of the first day's work and the present state of the district's curricular offerings would be the first item. "Where are the gaps?" "How much overlapping and repetition do we have?"
2. A final check is made on research and resource materials in the district curriculum center to be sure that all groups have adequate supplies for the next work day. The person in charge of the center will arrange these materials by subject areas and have them ready for the committees. It may be necessary at this point to send for additional books, pamphlets, or research reports.
3. The purpose of the next full-day session (Step 11) is clearly stated: To begin to examine current philosophy, theory, research, and trends in each area, and to compare the findings with present practice in the district.
4. The general staff meeting for Step 11 is planned.

Step 11

The next curriculum day begins with a general staff session in which the total project to date is summarized. The chief school official or the chairman of the steering committee presides, and each committee chairman gives a brief report on staff reactions to the existing curriculum as outlined. Any problem areas that have been identified are presented at this time. Vertical overlapping is stressed particularly, along with any obvious gaps in the program. In some subject areas, a shortage of up-to-date instructional materials might be noted.

The remainder of the day is allotted for curriculum committee meetings. In these sessions, readings can be assigned to each member from the resources that have been compiled. Lively, open discussions should then enable all participants to begin to share the current theory, research, and practices in the area under study. Broad cultural and societal goals can be tentatively identified in relation to the needs of pupils and the present curriculum. Committee members are encouraged to borrow books, research materials, and other available items at the end of this day so that they can continue to develop ideas on objectives and general philosophy.

Important leadership note: This day should not be spent in examining sample textbooks or courses of study in detail, although these are on hand for future reference. The temptation is great at this point, especially with the inexperienced curriculum worker, to select a particularly attractive text and to suggest that this might form a good basis for the revised course. Equally dangerous is the common practice of "borrowing" a course of study from another district. Some committee members will be ready to accept almost word for word a well-bound and impressive curriculum outline already prepared by another school staff. Since much of the value of curriculum work is found in the process, the two quick solutions suggested above should be rejected. Textbooks as instructional aids will be selected near the end of the study when objectives, units, concepts, generalizations, attitudes, and skills have been developed. Then, and only then, will it be possible to determine intelligently the necessary materials of instruction for the course.

Obviously, work should not be duplicated unnecessarily, and committees may want to use or adapt portions of several courses of study from other districts. However, this is not the time to narrow the method in this manner. Rather, the chairman must make sure that the study proceeds in depth through all the research and resource materials that are available.

Step 12

The steering committee convenes immediately after the work session to check the progress of all groups. Some committees may require a resource person or additional research materials. Generally, good working relationships should be established by now.

From this date, the steering committee will meet at the discretion of its chairman and always at the end of each curriculum day. Continuing functions are to guide, support, and coordinate the various studies.

Step 13

On the next work day, the committees continue to discuss and investigate further the research findings, courses of study from outside districts, and other pertinent materials. Basic questions must be raised and answered:

1. What are we now teaching that is outmoded or that does not agree with our philosophy and objectives?
2. In what ways should our course objectives be changed, if any?
3. What are the big ideas in this field today?
4. What does educational research say about scope and sequence for today's curriculum?
5. What are the current trends in this subject area, and why? Are they valid?
6. In terms of the needs of our boys and girls in this community, nation, and world, what are the concepts, generalizations, attitudes, and skills that should be stressed in this subject field?

According to Goodlad,

> In curriculum planning, disciplined choice must replace the leisurely, often whimsical, cumulative processes of the past. The selection of most significant bits of content no longer is difficult; it is impossible. Consequently, teachers and pupils must seek out those fundamental concepts, principles, and methods that appear to be most useful for ordering and interpreting man's inquiries.[7]

Step 14

The next curriculum day is a continuation of the last, as all committees continue to plumb their research materials under the direction of the

---

[7] John I. Goodlad, *Some Propositions in Search of Schools* (Washington, D.C.: Department of Elementary School Principals, National Education Association, 1962), p. 29.

chairmen or outside resource consultants. After the questions in Step 13 have been reasonably answered and tentative objectives identified for the broad subject areas, the task of curriculum construction or revision begins. This work will continue for the remainder of the school year. Depending on their over-all teaching loads, committee members will assume certain responsibilities between work days, as decided by their group and chairman.

At this stage, the N.E.A. Project on Instruction reports should be most helpful in deciding what content to include and which methods to use.

All committees will use the same format for their emerging courses of study; it is desirable that the curriculum guide of a district follow the same physical pattern. This gives evidence of coordination of effort and makes the resulting guide much more understandable.

It is recommended that an outline similar to the sample on page 254 of the Appendix be used by districts during the early stages of formal curriculum development. More experienced staffs may want to add additional headings or detail.

In any event, the immediate task is identification of subject-matter units or topics for the course under consideration. Following the sample outline, the suggested units with specific objectives are written in some detail in the first column. Then decisions are reached on concepts, generalizations, attitudes, and skills to be developed for each unit, and these are detailed in the second column. Goodlad has made some positive suggestions for this phase of the project:

> The school curriculum should be planned to reveal continuing threads—ideas, generalizations, principles, concepts, methods—by means of which specific learnings might be related effectively one to another. These threads are derived from at least three sources: the developing characteristics of children, the subject-matter disciplines, and the nature of society. . . . However, schools have tended to stress specific bits and pieces of knowledge, in part because these can be packaged attractively for instructional occasions and in part because more basic methods and principles were thought to be beyond the grasp of the young. Research into the alarming rate at which youngsters forget information they have not organized or related and recent experimentation with children's ability to comprehend fundamental methods and principles force a new look at the variables and constants of the . . . curriculum. In the past, specific content has tended to be the constant. Teachers and pupils alike have been left to find unifying principles where and when they could. . . . In the future, specific content must be recognized as dispensable data in the effort to understand things more fundamental and constant.[8]

---

[8] Goodlad, *Some Propositions in Search of Schools, op. cit.*, pp. 23-24.

Concepts, principles, and generalizations, then, are most important. In a world where man's knowledge is doubling each generation, a curriculum based on factual content alone is obsolete before it is published.

As curriculum construction proceeds, all members need to think of learning experiences continuing from level to level. There is no room in the modern curriculum guide for rigid grade content. Rather, units are introduced at recommended levels to avoid overlapping, but pupils are encouraged to progress as rapidly as they can. A good outline will enable a teacher to review when necessary—to know which concepts have been introduced and which are yet to come.

Continuing with the suggested format, the third column is used for teaching techniques or methods and pupil experiences recommended to achieve the objectives. In the last column, teacher-pupil resources and instructional materials are listed. (See Step 15.)

Important leadership notes:

1. The evolving written courses of study should not be overemphasized. While these are important, since they reflect the over-all framework of the district curriculum, important values of curriculum revision are to be found in the actual participation by staff members. This cannot be emphasized too strongly. Throughout the study, research is evaluated, goals are examined, and attitudes are challenged and sometimes modified or changed; a healthy group interaction takes place. In other words, changes emerge in people and in their classrooms which cannot be measured merely by the final written course of study.
2. It is imperative that all staff members be informed by curriculum bulletin and in meetings of the deliberations of the study committees. Constant intercommunication must take place if, for example, fifty elementary teachers are to accept and begin to teach a new curriculum in social studies prepared by eight of their colleagues.

   Building meetings must be held throughout the year to discuss the curriculum work. Administrators and supervisors should take advantage of every opportunity to talk about philosophy, objectives, or contemplated changes at the various levels. Informal discussions between teachers and administrators will reveal any areas in need of clarification, further study, or integration.

   It is the responsibility of the committee chairmen and the steering committee to make sure that sufficient communication takes place among all concerned groups. On a given curriculum day, for example, the elementary reading and the secondary English committees might profitably plan a joint session to share findings to date and to discuss correlation of their work. Of particular interest would be the programs in the sixth and seventh grades, if the elementary-junior high break occurs here.

At the secondary level, several departments will meet together on occasion to coordinate efforts. For example, groups working in mathematics and science will have reason to discuss common areas.

Step 15

The selection of instructional materials—an important step in curriculum development—is discussed in Chapter IX. Only after the units, concepts, generalizations, attitudes, and skills have been structured are the committee members ready to assemble suggested techniques and aids to instruction. This is a continuous process that is never complete. Many good sources of materials are available; some of the following list should be included for each unit. The "Resources" column on the curriculum outline should be as complete as possible—including, for example, titles of films, tapes, and programmed learning devices.

List of teacher-pupil resources and instructional materials

Textbooks (Basic and supplementary)
Trade and library books
16mm motion picture films
Filmstrips
Commercial and teacher-made slides
Educational television programs (UHF, VHF, and closed circuit)
Programmed learning materials, including teaching machines and programmed textbooks
Tape recordings and transcriptions
Phonograph records
Picture collections (for bulletin board and opaque projector)
Exhibits
Charts
Displays
Community resource persons
Field trips
Projects
Dramatization
Maps and Globes
Flannelboards
Free and inexpensive materials (See "General Curriculum Resource Materials," Appendix One, page 244, for sources.)

Note: An excellent booklet from the Pennsylvania Department of Public Instruction, entitled "The School Instructional Materials Center and the Curriculum," describes ways to set up a center for many of the instructional materials listed above.[9]

Step 16

The steering committee makes a final editing of the year's work as written courses of study and progress reports are submitted. Any completed courses are duplicated to be presented for full staff approval or modification early in the fall. Loose-leaf binding is best for this purpose so that the curriculum guides can be kept current. The chairman of the steering committee makes sure that all completed materials are collected from the various chairmen before school closes for the summer.

Important leadership note: Many districts are hiring interested and qualified teachers, administrators, and supervisors to work during the summer in compiling and editing the work of curriculum committees. Indeed, this is often the only feasible way to complete the work in a reasonable time. The persons assigned to this work should be good writers and experts in the techniques described in this chapter. The summer teams work hand in hand with the regular staff committees. Total involvement in curriculum is desirable, but it is most difficult to complete the entire job during the school year. Thus, a combination of summer work and the regular procedures described herein is best.

Step 17

The first general staff meeting in the fall should provide opportunity for a review of curriculum development to date, including any work done over the summer. Copies of completed or tentative course outlines should be distributed. In the small or intermediate-size district, discussion can be invited.

Step 18—Continuing Curriculum Study

Continuous evaluation of the ongoing curriculum work is essential. The steering committee will make sure that a reasonable amount of curriculum development is proceeding at all times. Classroom teachers are usually involved in no more than one committee assignment at a time. Administrators and supervisors often will have multiple responsibilities and assignments as resource persons and group leaders.

---

[9] Commonwealth of Pennsylvania, *The School Instructional Materials Center and the Curriculum,* Curriculum Development Series No. 5 (Harrisburg, Pa.: Department of Public Instruction, 1962).

The chief school official and the chairman of the steering committee must always be aware of the total program so that current needs and problems can be assessed.

Each year the cycle of curriculum study will lead the steering committee back to Step 4. The personnel of this group can change as more staff members develop interest and ability in curriculum development. In this way there will be a widening circle of staff leadership in this vital area.

Important leadership notes: As a district gains experience in curriculum work, additional procedures such as the following may be used:

1. Curriculum guides will contain blank spaces or pages on which classroom teachers may make suggestions for changes, additions to the curriculum materials list, and other comments.
2. Separate tracks may be prepared for the slow, average, and academically talented learners in all subject areas and at all grade or unit levels. Appropriate instructional materials and techniques can be suggested for the varying learning abilities of the pupils. Thus, well-developed courses and units will list experiences geared to the potential of a wide variety of students.

Curriculum development, then, is seen as a continuous process which is never completed. In an ever-changing society, the curriculum cannot be static. It is always in process, and this means continual staff evaluation. A written course of study in earth and space science, for example, may represent the best staff thinking at the moment of its completion. However, under classroom use and evaluation, it may prove defective or incomplete, in some respects, within a year. Or it may prove to be basically sound for several years. Only constant evaluation will indicate the appropriate time for complete revision of a course.

A staff trained in curriculum study is always alert to the changing needs of the school and community. Curriculum development is one of the most vital supervisory functions. It must be done thoroughly if subject matter is to come alive in the classroom. Teachers who have a role in democratic curriculum work are more apt to know what they are teaching and why they are teaching it.

SUMMARY

Curriculum study is one of the most significant tasks facing the supervisor today. In an age of unprecedented change and challenge, the nation's schools must direct their attention to a thorough evaluation of what they are teaching and how they are teaching it. Newer trends and research findings in each subject field and discipline must be carefully examined.

Curriculum development should originate at the local level, with the supervisory staff seeking resource help from state, national, and other agencies. An effective program of curriculum study assumes certain basic principles, including time and money for the project, dynamic leadership, total professional involvement, continuity, sound research procedures, coordination, and evaluation.

Curriculum is the sum total of learning experiences which are introduced, structured, or used purposefully by the school to achieve its philosophy and objectives. Those experiences over which the school has some direct measure of control are those which can be identified, evaluated, and developed into a meaningful curriculum.

A comprehensive, step-by-step program must be used to initiate and successfully carry out a curriculum development project.

In an ever-changing society, the school's instructional program cannot be static. It is always in process, with some areas under careful study at all times. Curriculum development is a continuous function which is never completed.

SUGGESTED ACTIVITIES AND PROBLEMS

1. To what extent is curriculum development a state function?

2. Defend or refute the following statement: "A basic, national curriculum should be established."

3. Discuss in some detail the fundamental principles of curriculum development.

4. Interview a chief school official with the purpose of determining the status of the curriculum development program in the district. At which step should this staff begin or continue working?

5. Outline clearly the functions of a curriculum steering committee.

6. Set up an appropriate time schedule for one year of curriculum study in a district of your choice. Include a brief agenda for each day's work and a description of summer plans.

7. How would you organize a curriculum center or laboratory?

8. Assess the importance of written courses of study as a final outcome in curriculum development.

9. Discuss the selection of instructional materials as a step in curriculum study.

SELECTED READINGS

American Educational Research Association, *Review of Educational Research: Curriculum Planning and Development,* Vol. XXX, No. 3. Washington, D.C.: National Education Association, June, 1960.

Association for Supervision and Curriculum Development, *Leadership for Improving Instruction,* 1960 Yearbook, pp. 93-126. Washington, D.C.: National Education Association, 1960.

Association for Supervision and Curriculum Development, *What Are the Sources of the Curriculum? A Symposium.* Washington, D.C.: National Education Association, 1962.

Burton, William H., and Leo J. Brueckner, *Supervision: A Social Process,* Chap. 16. New York: Appleton-Century-Crofts, Inc., 1955.

Commonwealth of Pennsylvania, *The School Instructional Materials Center and the Curriculum,* Curriculum Development Series No. 5. Harrisburg, Pa.: Department of Public Instruction, 1962.

Eash, Maurice J., and Robert E. Chasnoff, "Framework for Effective Curriculum Improvement," *Overview,* I, No. 3 (March, 1960), 64-65.

Fleming, Robert S. (ed.), *Curriculum for Today's Boys and Girls.* Columbus, Ohio: Charles E. Merrill Books, Inc., 1962.

Fliegler, Louis A., *Curriculum Planning For the Gifted.* Englewood Cliffs, N.J.: Prentice-Hall, Inc., 1961.

Goodlad, John I., *Some Propositions in Search of Schools.* Washington, D.C.: Department of Elementary School Principals, National Education Association, 1962.

Lucio, William H., and John D. McNeil, *Supervision–A Synthesis of Thought and Action,* Chaps. 5 and 8. New York: McGraw-Hill Book Company, Inc., 1962.

McNally, Harold J., A. Harry Passow, and associates, *Improving the Quality of Public School Programs, Approaches to Curriculum Development,* Chap. 2. New York: Bureau of Publications, Teachers College, Columbia University, 1960.

Project on Instruction, N.E.A., *Schools for the Sixties* and other final Project publications. Washington, D.C.: National Education Association, 1962 and 1963.

Spears, Harold, *Curriculum Planning Through In-Service Programs,* pp. 51-54. Englewood Cliffs, N.J.: Prentice-Hall, Inc., 1957.

"Staff Participation in Curriculum Development–A Searching Look," *Educational Leadership,* XV, No. 6 (March, 1958).

"Who Should Plan the Curriculum?" *Educational Leadership,* XIX, No. 1 (October, 1961).

Wiles, Kimball, *The Changing Curriculum of the American High School,* Chaps. 11, 12, 13, and 14. Englewood Cliffs, N.J.: Prentice-Hall, Inc., 1963.

chapter twelve

The Evaluation of Supervisory Programs

Although a number of research studies have conclusively indicated the need for supervision of instruction in the public schools,[1] there have been comparatively few attempts to outline a comprehensive program for the evaluation of supervisory activities in a district. It is evident, however, that the effectiveness of supervision should be measured by the best means available.

[1] Johnnye V. Cox, *Research Findings on the Education of Supervisors,* Bulletin (Athens, Ga.: Cooperative Program in Elementary Education, College of Education, University of Georgia, 1956), pp. 8-10; Evans, "The Status and Function of the Public Elementary School Supervisor in the Third and Fourth Class Districts of the Pennsylvania Counties of Chester, Delaware, and Montgomery," pp. 20-22.

To date, various check lists have been devised, some for self-evaluation by the supervisor, and others for the rating of supervisory personnel by their superiors or by the teachers they serve. Harman stressed the program rather than the individual by asking teachers to indicate the most and least effective supervisory procedures used in their school.[2]

Actually, in many school districts today, supervision is evaluated very informally and grossly, if at all. It is apparently assumed that all persons engaged in coordinating or directing the improvement of instruction must be making a contribution to the education of pupils. The very existence of the supervisory positions and the increased activity in curriculum work and other in-service programs, for example, are often taken as evidence of real progress.

We need a total or comprehensive approach to the difficult and involved problem of evaluating supervisory programs. Just as the entire teaching-learning situation is evaluated today, and not the teacher alone, so must we seek to appraise not only the supervisor but also the whole school program of which he is an integral part. Since all evaluation involves human relationships and personalities to a great extent, subjective judgment will always play an important role. For this reason some say it is impossible to assess the contributions of teachers, administrators, and supervisors fairly. However, competent, well-trained, and experienced professional educators have repeatedly demonstrated that they can work together cooperatively in the development and evaluation of educational experiences for pupils. Again we refer the reader to Chapter I and a consideration of the characteristics of modern supervision. If these are valid for the development of a supervisory program, they are no less so for the evaluation of it. In fact, fundamental human relations and real democracy in administrative functions are prerequisites to the suggestions outlined below.

METHODS OF EVALUATING SUPERVISION

Two approaches are indicated for comprehensive evaluation of supervision in a district. First, the total instructional program must be appraised, considering all of the factors which affect pupil experiences in the classroom. Second, the supervisory personnel need to be evaluated, considering the role that each is supposed to play in the improvement of instruction.

---

[2] Allen C. Harman, "Supervision in Selected Secondary Schools" (Doctoral dissertation, University of Pennsylvania, 1947), pp. 102-108.

Evaluation of the Total Program

In considering the various aspects of the instructional program listed below, the following basic questions should be constantly raised as an aid to evaluation.

1. What is most effective in this situation?
2. What is least effective in light of our goals?
3. Where problems are evident, what are we doing about them?
4. Who is responsible for the present situation?
5. Who should be stimulating action for improvement?
6. Is the latest educational research being considered?
7. Are we good enough in this area? Can we be satisfied with what we are doing?
8. Where are our pupils encountering difficulties? Why?

These and other important questions can be discussed in the district administrative council, in staff meetings, and in supervisory conferences. By continuous probing in this manner, weak areas in the program of instruction are bound to be identified. Some specific facets are detailed below, with suggested questions. It is essential that evaluation check lists using these and other questions be prepared cooperatively by teachers, administrators, and supervisors.

Pupil progress and achievement. If measured by the best instruments available against the goals of the curriculum, then real pupil achievement should give an important clue to the quality of the educational program.

1. How clearly are the philosophy and goals defined? Do all teachers know what they are?
2. Have teacher-made and standardized tests been carefully selected? When was the testing program last revised?
3. In terms of their abilities, home and cultural backgrounds, and other limiting factors, how are our pupils achieving? Do principals and teachers recognize each child and his profile—not merely the median test scores of a group?
4. Are the limitations of all tests—intelligence, achievement, and aptitude—recognized by staff members?
5. Are national medians considered in their proper perspective in interpreting the performance of local pupils?
6. Do teachers and supervisors have many opportunities to discuss pupil progress, from one group to another, and from one grade or level to the next?

7. Is the teacher's professional judgment given adequate weight in the measurement of pupil progress?

Curriculum study and development. The status of the curriculum in a district must weigh heavily in any assessment of the effectiveness of supervision.

1. Is there evidence of curriculum coordination, kindergarten through high school? Or are there great gaps, say, between the elementary and junior high school grades?
2. Is a comprehensive program of curriculum development (such as that outlined in Chapter XI) carried out in the district? If not, why not? Who is responsible for instruction?
3. Have all subject areas been studied in the last five years?
4. Are courses of study available to all staff members?
5. Are teaching materials up-to-date or obsolete?

Pupil needs and the curriculum. To be truly successful, the instructional program must meet the needs of *all* pupils in the district.

1. What percentage of those taking the academic curriculum actually enter institutions of higher learning? How many of the others elect this course because there is none to really satisfy their needs?
2. What happens to non-college-bound graduates? Have they been prepared for the fields they enter? Is there a lack of high-level technical education in the secondary school?
3. What is the drop-out rate? How many of these pupils quit because there is little to hold them in the existing curriculum? Is there a sufficient variety of courses in the high school?
4. Are adequate provisions made for the slow learner, the child with creative talent, and the gifted pupil in both elementary and high school?

Supervisory techniques employed in the district. Evaluation of the various techniques used to improve instruction will help to indicate their effectiveness. Chapters IX and X discuss a number of widely used individual and group procedures.

1. Do teachers feel that the in-service programs are helping them to improve classroom instruction? Do they have a part in planning them?
2. How often do principals and supervisors visit classrooms? Are follow-up conferences held, and do teachers feel that the visits are valuable?
3. What procedures have been established for the selection and orientation of new staff members? Is the district securing and keeping good teachers?

4. Is there a carefully developed plan for teacher intervisitation? Do benefits accrue from this program?

Important leadership note: Check-list questions like the above can be made up from the main sections of Chapters IX, X, and XI. These should be structured according to the organizational and supervisory patterns of the district. The main aims are: (1) to determine the most successful supervisory techniques as an aid to the over-all evaluation of the instructional program; (2) to identify those practices which should be eliminated.

Evaluation through outside committees. Such evaluation should be welcomed by all schools. Some good criteria have been developed by commissions, state departments of education, and other groups at both the elementary and secondary levels. Many secondary schools are now evaluated by a visiting team at least every ten years. There is a growing movement for similar evaluation of elementary schools. Any district can profitably engage in a self-evaluation, using one of the available criteria. Then a team of administrators, supervisors, and teachers can be invited to the district for a detailed appraisal. The result should be a better understanding of the strengths and weaknesses of the current instructional program, if the evaluators are objective and decisive.

Moorer has developed an instrument that should be valuable for self-analysis of the supervisory program.[3] (See Appendix Five, pages 255-266.)

Evaluation of the Supervisory Personnel

The second approach to comprehensive assessment of the value of supervision in a district involves complete evaluation of the work of each supervisor, both by himself and by other professional personnel. Again, the difficulties that will be encountered should not be allowed to scuttle this effort.

Self-evaluation. This is the real key to effective analysis of one's contribution to the improvement of instruction. It cannot be assumed that individuals will regularly engage in this practice unless the administrative council develops some criteria and check lists. The superintendent must set the example by helping to develop an instrument for his own self-appraisal.

Wiles has prepared a "Self-Evaluation Check List" which should assist all supervisory personnel in the preparation of their own.

---

[3] Sam H. Moorer, "How Good Is Your Supervisory Program?" (An Instrument for Self-Analysis, Florida State Department of Education, 1950)

Do I:

1. Set up a schedule of activities for each week?
2. Make changes easily?
3. Use criticism to improve my procedures?
4. Get more teachers to experiment?
5. Stimulate action research?
6. Get parents involved in the work of the school?
7. Secure an increase in the reading of professional books and participation in professional organizations?
8. Succeed in increasing the amount of cooperative planning?
9. Get teachers to be more self-directing?
10. Increase the use of a wider variety of instructional materials?
11. Promote increased pupil achievement?
12. Obtain a full description of the school's program on a given date to serve as a base line in determining the amount of progress that is being made in program development?
13. Bring teachers, pupils, parents, and community members into the judgments concerning the progress that has been made?
14. Encourage revision of goals or procedures in areas in which the group decides progress is unsatisfactory?
15. Judge my success by the progress of the school program toward goals accepted by the group? [4]

Such check lists can be developed for each position according to the job descriptions and the working relationships and responsibilities existent in the district. This suggestion, of course, assumes that line and staff functions have been defined according to the modern democratic principles of supervision outlined in Chapter I. The check list items would vary somewhat from one position to another. It is essential, however, that all supervisors participate: the superintendent, assistant superintendent in charge of instruction, coordinators of elementary and secondary education, principals, and special supervisors or coordinators.

Ayer and Peckham have prepared a comprehensive "Check List For Planning and Appraising Supervision." Stated purposes of this form are: to help supervisors in self-evaluation; to help plan supervisory programs; and to provide a basis for the evaluation of supervision.[5]

The experience of the authors indicates that many persons with supervisory roles are quite willing to face squarely their shortcomings as well as their strengths so that all may work together for the improvement of instruction. Those who refuse to acknowledge deficiencies, either per-

---

[4] Kimball Wiles, *Supervision for Better Schools: The Role of the Official Leader in Program Development* (Englewood Cliffs, N.J.: Prentice-Hall, Inc., 1955), 2nd ed., pp. 328-329. By permission of the publisher.

[5] Fred C. Ayer and Dorothy Reed Peckham, "Check List For Planning and Appraising Supervision" (Austin, Texas: The Steck Company, Publishers, 1948).

sonal or professional, are probably most aware of them. Fellow supervisors will have to help these individuals to accept evaluation and then to move on toward the commonly identified goals.

Evaluation by others. It has been truly stated that this type of rating goes on daily among teachers and supervisors. It is difficult to find, however, carefully planned procedures for the evaluation of supervisory personnel. The literature again suggests the use of check lists. Some of those developed for self-evaluation can be used by other persons. For example, the list prepared by the assistant superintendent for his self-appraisal could be given to principals and supervisors also, for their evaluation of him. Wiles's question, "Do I use criticism to improve my procedures?" would be changed simply to "Does *he* . . . ?"

Here is a simple check list developed by an elementary principal. The form was distributed to all teachers, and their anonymous reactions were sought. Following the check list is a description of the procedures followed in this evaluation and the subsequent steps taken by the principal to improve his effectiveness with the staff.

TEACHER EVALUATION OF PRINCIPAL

(Please number according to principal's areas of best performance: #1 best, #2 next, etc., with weakest area indicated as #4.)

( ) Supervision and Improvement of Instruction
( ) Leadership in Personnel Relations
( ) Development of Community and Public Relations
( ) Maintenance of School Plant

Please use this scale in evaluating the following characteristics:
5—Superior
4—Very Good
3—Average
2—Below Average
1—Unsatisfactory

Personal
( ) Personal appearance.
( ) Resourcefulness.
( ) Initiative; drive.
( ) Dependability.
( ) Enthusiasm.

Supervision and Improvement of Instruction
( ) Curriculum guidance.
( ) Help in getting the professional and classroom materials needed.
( ) Classroom visitation.

Personnel Relations
Relationships with:
( ) Teachers.

( ) Pupils.
( ) Parents.
( ) Custodians.
( ) Secretary.

( ) Ability to deal with individual staff problems.
( ) Cooperation with staff members; group participation in school policy-making encouraged.
( ) Democracy in philosophy and procedures.
( ) Conduct of staff meetings.
( ) Administration of routine duties, such as administrative procedures, handling of materials and supplies, and keeping of school records.

Please use back of sheet to complete the following: (Be specific.)

Areas of greatest strength.
Needs for improvement.
How can the new teacher be helped more effectively? (First-year teachers please complete this item.)

How teachers helped a principal to evaluate his effectiveness. An important phase in the evaluation of the elementary school is the assessment of the effectiveness of the principal. Teachers can and should play a role in helping the elementary principal to evaluate his work and relationships with the staff.

The value of such total staff involvement in evaluation of the administrative and supervisory functions can be found in experiments like the one conducted by the writer with his 14-teacher staff at the close of the school year.

First of all, the form printed above was developed from research on the role of the principal. Copies were distributed to members of the teaching staff, and they were urged to complete the items according to the indicated scale and to make further subjective comments on the sheet. The purpose was explained as one of attempting to improve the role of the principal in instruction and in dealing with his staff. Personal as well as professional relationships are explored on the evaluation sheet.

The results were quite interesting and helpful. It was possible to identify the areas that were in need of improvement, both from the point scores and from the subjective comments. The main areas of weakness may be summarized as follows:

1. Classroom visitation was felt to be inadequate, both in the number of visits and in the constructive help offered to the teachers. It was

suggested that more specific curriculum aids be provided after the visitations and follow-up conferences.

2. It was proposed that the principal develop a more thorough knowledge of the primary-grade children and their needs, as well as more extensive understanding of the techniques of instruction in the lower grades.

3. The staff felt that there was good group participation in policy formation. However, it was made clear that the principal should be more firm in carrying out and administering group decisions. It is his major responsibility to see that staff members cooperate within the framework of the school policies. In this connection it was pointed out that some teachers who do not see their responsibility as part of the staff should receive firmer guidance from the principal.

4. Many excellent suggestions were made by the first-year teachers regarding items to be included in the new-teacher orientation at the start of the fall term. There apparently had been some deficiencies in this area.

It is not enough to make such an evaluation. The principal must combine the results with his own self-evaluation and that of his superiors. Then he should be in a position to constructively improve his staff leadership.

Acting on the above conclusions, reported by his staff and verified in his own thinking, the writer took the following steps toward improvement, and noted the indicated progress.

1. Schedule-wise, more time was set aside for classroom visitation and conferencing with teachers. The curriculum and professional libraries were expanded and more of the principal's time was spent in bringing techniques and materials of instruction to the classroom situation.

2. The principal, whose teaching experience extended down to fifth grade only, began to do some substitute teaching from first grade on up. This, of course, required extensive study and preparation in the principles of primary-grade education. Much was learned through classroom observation. Much more was learned through the exciting experience of teaching. As a result, the principal has a much greater understanding of the growth patterns of six-, seven-, and eight-year-olds, and should be in a better position to help primary teachers in the classroom situation.

3. Steps have been taken to see that policies decided by group decision are properly administered.

4. The orientation program for new teachers has been improved through the suggestions of the first-year teachers.

The elementary principal who is seriously interested in improving his effectiveness will find an instrument such as this a valuable aid in the total program of evaluation.

* * * * * *

It is imperative that all persons with supervisory roles be evaluated by each other and by the classroom teachers. The check lists may be used annually, but evaluation can and should take place at any time, as indicated above. If the proper climate of personal relationships and group interaction exists, staff members learn to share successes as well as failures. Each person, as he matures in this type of environment, faces up to his own problems and does not blame someone else. On the other hand, credit is given where it is due. Evaluation then becomes an honest and fair assessment of the contribution of each individual to the instructional goals. With a number of persons involved, the total result should be helpful to the teachers and supervisors and to the program of instruction.

Much research is needed in the development of more precise methods of evaluation. Probably, there will never be perfection in the measurement of relationships among human beings, but we should be able to discover more effective ways of assessing the contribution of each to the goal of better pupil learning experiences.

SUMMARY

While some check lists have been devised for the evaluation of supervisors and their work, in many school districts today the process of supervision is evaluated very informally and grossly, if at all.

Two approaches are indicated for comprehensive appraisal of the supervisory function in a district. First, the total instructional program should be evaluated, including the areas of pupil progress and achievement, curriculum study and development, provision for pupil needs, and the supervisory techniques employed. Second, each supervisor must be evaluated, both by himself and by other professional personnel.

Additional research is needed to develop more exact methods of evaluation.

SUGGESTED ACTIVITIES AND PROBLEMS

1. In what ways can self-evaluation help a supervisor assess his contributions to the total program?

2. Select a supervisory position and devise a simple check list for the evaluation of a person in that situation.

3. Defend or refute this statement: "Because of the subjective judgment involved, it is impossible to evaluate the work of a supervisor."

4. Interview a high school principal to find out how well the curriculum meets the needs of all pupils. (As a guide, use the questions under "Pupil needs and the curriculum" in this chapter.)

5. Discuss the possible outcomes of school evaluation by outside committees.

SELECTED READINGS

American Association of School Administrators, *The Superintendent as Instructional Leader,* Thirty-fifth Yearbook. Washington, D.C.: National Education Association, 1957.

Ayer, Fred C., and Dorothy Reed Peckham, "Check List For Planning and Appraising Supervision." Austin, Texas: The Steck Company, Publishers, 1948.

Burnham, Reba M., and Martha L. King, *Supervision in Action.* Washington, D.C.: Association for Supervision and Curriculum Development, National Education Association, 1961.

Duff, Lloyd W., "Criteria For Evaluating the Supervision Program in School Systems." Doctoral dissertation, The Ohio State University, 1961.

Franseth, Jane, *Supervision as Leadership,* Chaps. 16 and 17. Evanston, Illinois: Row, Peterson and Company, 1961.

———, *Supervision in Rural Schools,* Chap. 3. Washington, D.C.: U.S. Department of Health, Education, and Welfare, Office of Education, Bulletin 1955, No. 11, 1955.

Moorer, Sam H., "How Good Is Your Supervisory Program?" Tallahassee, Florida: Florida State Department of Education, 1950.

chapter thirteen

A Look Ahead

How will supervision change in the next decade or so? Why will it change, and what are some of the contributing factors?

Although no one can foretell accurately the future in this rapidly changing world, certain trends are discernible that may give us some hints concerning the directions in which education and, consequently, supervision might move.

This chapter will be concerned with some of the factors that are producing changes in education, a description of some of the probable changes, and a few of the implications for supervision.

FACTORS THAT ARE PRODUCING CHANGES

It would be impossible to enumerate here all the factors that will likely affect education in the future. Some are so subtle in their influence that relationships are difficult to establish. Others, as yet, have not made their appearance upon the scene. The following list, though far from complete, will be discussed in this chapter: population explosion and urban renewal, automation, scientific discovery and invention, rediscovery of liberal education, increased leisure time, the cold war, earlier maturity of children, and child development and learning.

Population Explosion and Urban Renewal

Some years ago, population forecasters warned us that our population would level off soon and that we would become a nation of old people. Instead, our population has been growing in leaps and bounds. Providing for this population explosion has become one of the major problems in this country, as well as in many other parts of the world.

As our population has expanded, people who could afford to leave the city moved into the suburbs. Overproduction on the farm resulting from the use of machinery and improved agricultural procedures has made it necessary for the younger generation to leave the farm and move to the city and suburbs to seek other employment. The time is rapidly approaching in many areas, and has arrived on the East Coast, where the suburbs of one city have reached those of another to form one gigantic sprawling metropolis.

When the economically more fortunate families moved out of the cities, slums developed as the less economically and socially favored families moved into the city. Although these slums have been tolerated for many years, our great cities are at last awakening, and urban renewal is on the way.

Probable effects on education and supervision. The population explosion has created and will continue to create problems in the areas of staffing and school buildings. These factors, in turn, will affect class size. Hand in hand with population explosion comes the resulting mobility of population, which usually means a high rate of teacher and pupil turnover.

With urban renewal proceeding at a rapid pace, providing decent new housing for the culturally deprived masses is not enough. Adults must be re-educated to a new way of life, and their children must receive a kind of education different from that given to those who have been raised in more favorable home environments.

These, together with other factors to be mentioned later, will make it desirable to place greater emphasis on learning than on teaching. Supervisory programs must be geared to assist teachers to acquire know-how in helping children to become independent learners. The superior teacher of the future will be the one who enables the child to become a self-dependent, self-motivated learner. This new breed of teacher works himself out of a job. Chase agrees with this prediction as follows:

> A new image of the school is emerging, one in which the focus will be on learning rather than teaching, and in which teaching will be not so much a means of imparting knowledge as a way of managing a great variety of resources for learning and of creating situations through which learning progress may be motivated, systematized, and appraised.[1]

Prudent and expeditious use of audio-visual aids, programmed instruction, teacher aides, interns, clerks, and large-group instruction will enable master teachers to have a much wider sphere of influence.

As more and more individuals with little or no professional preparation and teachers who have been absent from the profession to raise a family join or return to the ranks, many new problems face the supervisor. The spread in professional know-how on some faculties will be so great that several levels of in-service education will have to be operating simultaneously. Ingenious techniques and procedures must be developed to prepare teachers on the job and new types of relationships must be formed with colleges having teacher-education programs.

Not only will the shortage of professionally prepared teachers persist, but space for teaching and learning will continue to be at a premium. The school of the future will have to become a learning center for six days a week and twelve months a year. More and more secondary-school buildings will need to be used during the evening hours. The twelve-hours-a-day, six-days-a-week, twelve-months-a-year schedule will create numerous supervisory problems. Supervisory personnel may find themselves working in shifts or even in an "on call" status. Unless supervisors are assigned to teaching platoons, they may be working with a larger number of individuals. The use of the same physical facilities and instructional materials by several different groups of teachers also may present some morale problems for the supervisor.

Finally, supervisors must become much more creative and imaginative in developing instructional materials and procedures for the thousands of culturally deprived youngsters found in our large cities. It is unrealistic to expect to meet their needs by subjecting them to the same middle-class educational fare served today in the majority of the classrooms throughout our land.

---

[1] Francis S. Chase, "University Versus Excellence in Education," in *Education Looks Ahead* (Chicago: Scott, Foresman and Company, 1960), p. 37.

Automation

Research in the field of automation is progressing so rapidly that a machine can scarcely be built and put into use before it is obsolete. In every line of work we find machines taking over the tasks formerly done by human beings. What American was not thrilled as he viewed on television the intricate computers and numerous gadgets located in the control room at Cape Canaveral? Who doesn't enjoy listening to election returns with increased interest because of the predictions of results by electronic computers? Will automation be a boon and a blessing to our society, or will it prove to be a woe and a calamity? Only time will tell; but, if schools will accept the challenge, the machine can be made to serve man—otherwise, man may succumb to his own creation.

Probable effects on education and supervision. It is safe to predict that advancing technology and automation will affect education in a number of ways. Not only will the content of the curriculum be changed, but the purposes, program, techniques, procedures, and the entire scope of education will be affected. The day is fast arriving when adult education at public expense will become a big business.

This prediction was highlighted recently when a group of educators and laymen met in Washington to discuss the educational implications of automated manufacturing techniques. Although the group could not concur on specific recommendations, they seemed to be in general agreement on certain observations which would result in radical changes in education as automation becomes more commonplace. Some of these observations are as follows:

1. Learning must become a lifelong activity; the pace of change is such that most workers now entering on careers must look forward to being trained for three or four different jobs requiring different skills and knowledge in the course of their lives.
2. Automation will lead inevitably to a reduction in the work week, perhaps to the 3- to 4-day week, and this indicates need for the proper use of leisure time or for secondary "noneconomic" career activity.
3. Vocational education, as it is now known, often lags seriously behind the pace of change in business and industry. It must, because the pace of change is so fast, seek to develop transferable skills.
4. Adult education must abandon many of its traditional values and assume a much greater role in updating skills and promoting continued learning. Refresher or extension courses will become routine for workers on the lowest as well as the highest echelons.[2]

---

[2] National School Public Relations Association, *The Shape of Education For 1962-63* (Washington, D.C.: National Education Association, 1962), p. 20.

Several direct effects of this move toward automation are being felt in the public schools. One important result will be a great reduction in the amount of clerical work that needs to be done by teachers and administrators. Among other things, data-processing machines are now handling pupil schedules, conflict sheets (schedule errors), attendance lists, athletic lists, class lists, book and equipment inventories, report cards, payroll checks, payroll registers, transportation assignments, and testing programs.[3]

The implications here for supervision are quite apparent. As teachers and supervisors are freed from routine clerical duties, they will have more time to improve the curriculum and perfect their teaching and supervisory techniques.

In the not too distant future, data-processing equipment may become a valuable aid in curriculum revision and in the learning process itself. In addition, the entire process of educational research can be speeded up through the use of these new tools.

Extensive use of automated teaching or programmed learning can, from present trends, also be safely predicted.[4] This alone could change radically the role of the supervisor. How can the supervisor assist teachers to choose and develop adequate programs for programmed learning? Will it be necessary to alter the basic theory of curriculum? How can children who experience repeated success through programmed instruction be encouraged to face possible failure in group competition? Answers to these and other questions must be sought as a result of automation.

Scientific Discovery and Invention

Man has discovered many of the secrets of nature, and daily he is creating and producing new foodstuffs, household appliances and products, building materials, fuels, wearing apparel, and drugs. He has invented machines and gadgets to amuse himself and to perform many onerous tasks. He has harnessed the atom, and he is now fathoming the mysteries of the universe. He has conquered the earth and is now

---

[3] For example, see Roger Dombrow, "A Study of Manual and Machine Techniques for Processing Clerical Data in Secondary Schools of 1000" (Doctoral dissertation, Temple University, 1960).

[4] For an excellent reference, see A. A. Lumsdaine and Robert Glaser, eds., *Teaching Machines and Programmed Learning, A Source Book* (Washington, D.C.: Department of Audio-Visual Instruction, National Education Association, 1960).

reaching for the stars. Yesterday's dreams are today's realities; today's visions will become tomorrow's actualities.

Man has also turned the x-ray and the microscope on himself. The use of miracle drugs, the transplanting of human tissues and organs, and the substitution of man-made materials for human tissues have prolonged the life of man appreciably and wiped out many dreaded diseases.

Psychiatry, psychology, and surgery are slowly revealing to man some of the mysteries of the human mind. Sociology, social psychology, and group dynamics are assisting us to understand better group interaction and behavior.

Probable effect on education and supervision. Just as the marvelous discoveries of science are revolutionizing other areas of living, they will continue to affect education. Through the use of new building materials, improved lighting, air-conditioning, and acoustical treatment, the learning environment of students will be greatly improved.

New gadgets in the field of audio-visual education will greatly increase the repertoire of teaching and learning aids. Telstar and its successors will bring to the classroom history as it is being made any place on the earth, and from outer space as well.

New drugs will be discovered that will assist in the learning process, subliminal learning will be employed, and auto-conditioning and hypnosis may some day be utilized as aids to learning.

As transportation becomes swifter and cheaper, field trips to any point in our nation and to other continents as well will become as common as the class excursion by bus is today.

With this brief look at the probable effects of scientific discovery and invention on instruction and learning, let us hypothesize what they will be on the curriculum. Certainly, more and more science will be taught and current events will play an increasingly more important role in the social studies program. However, the language arts and foreign languages may be in for a surprise treatment. Because of inventions now being perfected, the English language will have to become completely phonetic in structure.[5] Electric typewriters which automatically type out dictated material will place greater emphasis on the learning of correct oral English. Other gadgets, as yet unnamed, will translate any spoken language into any other language by the flick of a switch. What will happen to shorthand classes and foreign language laboratories when these things come to pass?

If TV dinners, frozen soups, pies, cakes, and what have you continue

---

[5] For example, see John R. Malone, "The Larger Aspects of Spelling Reform," *Elementary English*, XXXIX, No. 5 (1962), 435.

to increase in popularity, and ready-made clothes (including disposable paper garments) are available at prices that are competitive with home-made garments, the content of the home economics courses will have to change drastically.

Finally, how will the widespread use of computers and data-processing machines affect the mathematics and commercial education curriculum? Will we continue to teach to human beings skills that have been made obsolete by machines?

If and when these predictions become a reality, the implications for supervision will be tremendous. In fact, an entire new pattern of action will be required. However, experimentation and research in group behavior and the development of supervisory theory will also present a challenge to the supervisor.

The other factors producing changes in education are less dramatic but nevertheless have significant implications for supervision. Because they are more familiar to the reader, they will be discussed in less detail.

Rediscovery of Liberal Education

The voices that clamor for more book learning have always been present, but they have grown increasingly louder in the past decade and, doubtless, will continue to increase in volume. Here in the United States we have always admired the well-read individual, and many of us have been awed by the encyclopedic minds of our most eminent scholars. In recent years, frequent comparisons have been made between the difficult educational fare of European children and the less exacting menu of American children.[6] The "heat is on," and it is affecting education from kindergarten to the university.

It also is safe to predict that there will be a rebirth of the arts in the public schools. A liberally educated individual must be a patron of the arts. Movements throughout the world for cultural exchange programs and the presence of the National Cultural Center in Washington, D.C., will supply needed stimulation.

Increased Use of Leisure Time

The trade unions are already predicting a five-hour work day and a twenty-hour work week. As man finds more and more free time on his hands, he must be equipped to engage in a variety of worthwhile leisure-

---

[6] For example, see Hyman G. Rickover, *Swiss Schools and Ours* (Boston: Little, Brown and Company, 1962).

time activities. Boredom will become one of the greatest enemies of mankind unless individuals are prepared adequately to participate actively in stimulating experiences during their free time.

The Cold War

World leaders inform us that the threat of war will hang over our heads for many generations to come. At the time of this writing, the newspaper carries an article on "doomsday machines." What effect is this threat having and will it continue to have on education? Recently an elementary school in New Mexico has been constructed completely underground. Many states, as well as the federal government, are recommending that school basements be utilized as fallout shelters. Russian is being taught, and units on Russia, China, and other communistic countries are becoming part of the social studies program, so that each generation will be better equipped to deal with the problems brought on by the cold war. The competition between the free world and the communistic world to conquer space and to gain superiority in military power has been felt by all. This has led to much of the scientific discovery previously discussed as a factor, with the resultant emphasis on science and mathematics in the educational program.

Earlier Maturity of Children

Whether imagined or real, the common belief held by many persons today is that children now mature sooner than they did formerly. This, of course, is a relative judgment. Certainly no one would claim that the twelve-year-old should earn his living as his great-grandfather did in the days when "sweatshops" existed before adequate child labor laws were passed. On the other hand, it would be foolish to deny that children of today are healthier, better informed, and socially more mature than their counterparts of the late nineteenth and early twentieth centuries. This has resulted in a stiffening of the elementary-school curriculum, modification of elementary-school organization, and much earlier socialization between the sexes.

The school of tomorrow will give due recognition to the fact that the maturation of girls is more rapid than that of boys. Perhaps we will eventually develop achievement norms based on sex as well as grade level.

Child Development and Learning

When some of the mass-education procedures being advocated at present, such as large-group instruction and television teaching, are examined, one may get the impression that the vast amount of knowledge accumulated about children and how they learn is being wasted. However, on the other hand, when one reads about the strides being made in individualized reading, programmed instruction, ungraded primary units, and programs for the gifted, one finds ample evidence that individual differences in learning are not being neglected. The authors do not believe that research in this field will stop or be ignored. They feel optimistic about the future.

Two rather recent developments that give some cause for optimism are the investigations in the field of creativity (briefly reported in Chapter IX) and studies of sex differences in learning.[7] The school of the future will recognize and foster creativity in pupils. It also will make provisions in the curriculum and in grouping, marking, and promotion policies to assure that these sex differences in learning and maturation are taken into account.

CURRICULUM REVISION AND THE FUTURE

In addition to the factors previously discussed, the following developments may affect drastically the procedures used in curriculum revision in the schools of the future: (1) large school districts, (2) more state control of education, (3) greater influence of the federal government, and (4) accelerated research in the various areas of the curriculum. Although schools that are assuming a leadership role will be searching for original solutions to problems, curriculum revision in most schools no longer will be a "start from scratch" procedure. Instead, it will be a matter of selection and adaptation from the giant smorgasbord which is adding "new dishes" of educational fare almost daily.

The curriculum leader of the future must know how to work with staff members so that they improve in their ability to pick and choose wisely from the large selection that will be available. After the selection has been made, they must develop skill in adopting and adapting their choices so that the local school curriculum becomes a meaningful whole. Otherwise, hodgepodge learning will result.

Opportunities must be provided for teachers to travel, so that they may observe at first hand the new programs that later may be adopted *in toto* or in part. Teachers and supervisors also must acquire greater skill in evaluation, with particular emphasis on outcomes.

---

[7] For example, see E. Paul Torrance, *Guiding Creative Talent* (Englewood Cliffs, N.J.: Prentice-Hall, Inc., 1962), and Walter B. Waetjen, "Is Learning Sexless?," *NEA Journal,* 51, No. 5 (1962), 12.

The curriculum maker of the future also must be prepared to push back the frontiers of learning by participating in research and by sharing his findings with others.

SUMMARY

Civilization is on the move and society is ever changing. Many of the factors producing change affect education and in turn are influenced by it. Population explosion and urban renewal, automation, and scientific discovery and invention have all left deep imprints on education and may be expected to continue to do so. The rediscovery of liberal education, increased leisure time, the cold war, earlier maturity of children, and the findings of research in child development and learning will each continue to play an influential role in shaping our educational program.

As education changes, supervision also will change. Individuals serving in supervisory roles in the schools of the future will have at their command many new instructional techniques and procedures. Continuous curriculum development will be one of the most important supervisory tasks, as patterns of cultural change evolve in the world community.

SUGGESTED ACTIVITIES AND PROBLEMS

1. Write a brief case study (hypothetical or real) of a school district that has experienced a sudden population explosion. In your case study indicate the supervisory problems that the district faced as a result of the rapid increase in population.

2. Discuss the instructional problems faced by an elementary-school staff in a culturally deprived area. If you were serving in a supervisory position in this school, how would you proceed in the solution of these problems?

3. Describe a school in the year 2000 that has an instructional program and curriculum based on several of the predictions made in this chapter. Depict what you believe the job of the supervisor would be like in this fictitious school.

4. Locate and read some recent research on sex differences in maturation, motivation, and learning. Outline an educational program that takes these differences into account.

5. What implications for the instructional program are there in recent research on creativity?

SELECTED READINGS

Burr, James B., William Coffield, T. J. Jenson, and Ross L. Neagley, *Elementary School Administration,* Chap. 15. Boston: Allyn and Bacon, Inc., 1963.

Goodlad, John I., *Some Propositions in Search of Schools.* Washington, D.C.: Department of Elementary School Principals, National Education Asociation, 1962.

Gwynn, J. Minor, *Theory and Practice of Supervison,* Chap. 21. New York: Dodd, Mead, and Company, 1961.

Morse, Arthur D., *Schools of Tomorrow Today.* Garden City, N.Y.: Doubleday and Company, Inc., 1960.

Swearigen, Mildred E., *Supervision of Instruction: Foundations and Dimensions,* Chap. 12. Boston: Allyn and Bacon, Inc., 1962.

Trump, J. Lloyd, and Dorsey Baynham, *Guide to Better Schools.* Chicago: Rand McNally and Company, 1961.

Wiles, Kimball, *The Changing Curriculum of the American High School,* Chaps. 11, 13, and 15. Englewood Cliffs, N.J.: Prentice-Hall, Inc., 1963.

APPENDICES

appendix one

Curriculum Resource Materials—General

1. United States Office of Education, Washington 25, D.C.

   A variety of pamphlets, booklets, and research studies on all subject areas and general curriculum development. Free copies are available at the U.S. Office Library in Washington. Complete bibliography of publications available on request.

   A. *Principles and Procedures of Curriculum Development.*
   B. OE-32005 (Revised) *Curriculum Guides Dealing With Early Elementary Education.*
   C. *Issues in Curriculum Development.*
   D. *Curriculum Planning to Meet Tomorrow's Needs.*
   E. *Where Children Live Affects Curriculum.*

2. The National Education Association, 1201–16th Street NW, Washington 6, D.C.

   A. All departments, subject-area and special. Send for *Publications List.*
   B. Association for Supervision and Curriculum Development.
      (1) Yearbooks, research booklets, exhibit guides.
         a. *Selected Bibliography for Curriculum Workers.*
         b. *Research for Curriculum Improvement,* 1957 Yearbook.
   C. *What Research Says to the Teacher* series.
   D. Research Division. Send for *References on the Curriculum.*
   E. *N.E.A. Journal* articles on curriculum and subject areas.
   F. Department of Elementary School Principals. Yearbooks and periodical, *National Elementary Principal.*
      (1) "Techniques for Curriculum Improvement," Parts I and II, *National Elementary Principal,* Oct. and Dec., 1957.
   G. National Association of Secondary-School Principals. *Bulletin,* manuals, pamphlets.
      From NASSP *Bulletin:*
      (1) "Curriculum Practices," Oct., 1960.
      (2) "Patterns of Curriculum Practices," Feb., 1960.
      (3) "The Principal's Role in Improving the Curriculum," Feb., 1959.
      (4) "The Advance Curriculum," Dec., 1958.
      (5) "Changing to a Core Curriculum," March, 1957.
      (6) Five articles on curriculum improvement, Feb., 1960.
      (7) "Curriculum Design—Strengths and Weaknesses," April, 1961.

(8) "How to Modify the Curriculum to Benefit Academically-Talented Students," 1961.

H. Project on Instruction—a comprehensive study to define and state the views of the organized profession on the directions, tasks, and quality of the instructional program in the 1960's.

(1) The following summaries and final reports should provide valuable aid to districts in developing or revising their curricular programs: *Schools for the Sixties; Education in a Changing Society; Deciding What to Teach: Planning and Organizing for Teaching; The Scholars Look at the Schools; The Principals Look at the Schools; A Status Study of Selected Instructional Practices;* and *Current Curriculum Studies in Academic Subjects.*

3. Association for Childhood Education International, 3615 Wisconsin Avenue, N.W., Washington 16, D.C.

   Excellent bulletins and portfolios on the curriculum from pre-school through junior high.

4. General reference works and bibliographies.
   - A. *Cumulative Book Index.*
   - B. *Doctoral Dissertations: Index to American Doctoral Dissertations,* University Microfilms, Inc., Ann Arbor, Michigan.
   - C. *Education Index.*
   - D. *Encyclopedia of Education,* Atkinson, *et al.,* Prentice-Hall, Inc., Englewood Cliffs, N.J., 1961.
   - E. *Encyclopedia of Educational Research,* The Macmillan Co., 60 Fifth Avenue, New York 11, N.Y.
   - F. *International Index to Periodicals.*
   - G. *The New York Times Index,* The New York Times Company, New York 36, N.Y.
   - H. *Readers' Guide to Periodical Literature.*
   - I. *Vertical File Index,* The H. W. Wilson Co., 950 University Ave., New York 52, N.Y. A subject and title index to selected pamphlet material.

5. Periodicals.
   - A. *Curriculum Bulletin,* published by School of Education, University of Oregon, Eugene, Oregon.

     Send for Bulletin #206, September, 1960, *Annotated Bibliography and Index of the Curriculum Bulletins.*
   - B. *Educational Leadership.*
   - C. *Elementary School Journal,* The University of Chicago Press, 5750 Ellis Ave., Chicago 37, Ill.
   - D. *Journal of Educational Research,* Box 737, Madison 3, Wisconsin.
   - E. *Journal of Secondary Education.*
   - F. *Review of Educational Research,* American Educational Research Association, N.E.A., Washington, D.C.
   - G. *School Review,* The University of Chicago Press, 5750 Ellis Ave., Chicago 37, Ill.
   - H. *Social Education.* "Charting Curriculum Change," C. H. Adair, Feb., 1960.

6. State departments of education. Send for bibliographies of curriculum research publications and courses of study.
   A. California State Department of Education, Bureau of Textbooks and Publications, Sacramento 14, California.
   B. State Department of Education, Hartford, Conn.
   C. Department of Public Instruction, Dover, Del.
   D. Department of Education, Tallahassee, Fla.
   E. State Department of Education, Augusta, Ga.
   F. Office of the State Department of Public Instruction, Springfield, Ill.
   G. State Department of Education, Trenton, N.J.
   H. New York State Education Department, Albany, N.Y.
   I. Department of Public Instruction, Raleigh, N.C.
      "Guides to Curriculum Development and Study," "Suggested Twelve-Year Program for North Carolina Public Schools."
   J. State Printing Office, Pierre, South Dakota.
      Write for bulletins on curriculum planning.
7. Selected study councils and college centers.
   A. Delaware School Study Council, University of Delaware, Newark, Del.
   B. Metropolitan School Study Council, Institute of Administrative Research, 525 W. 120th Street, New York 27, N.Y.
   C. Suburban School Study Councils, affiliated with University of Pennsylvania, Philadelphia 4, Penna., and Temple University, Philadelphia 22, Penna.
   D. New England School Development Council, Spaulding House, 20 Oxford St., Cambridge 38, Mass.
   E. Bureau of Publications, Teachers College, Columbia University, 525 W. 120th Street, New York 27, N.Y.
   F. Bureau of Educational Research and Service, The Ohio State University, Columbus, Ohio.
8. Local curriculum development and courses of study. Request these from comparable districts in local area and state. The following districts will send free lists of materials available.
   A. Baltimore Public Schools, Department of Education, Bureau of Publications, 3 East 25th Street, Baltimore 18, Maryland.
      Ask for *Price List of Publications and Curriculum Materials,* prepared by the Division of Secondary, Vocational and Adult Education.
   B. Los Angeles City Schools, Division of Instructional Services, Los Angeles, Calif.
   C. Bureau of Curriculum Research, Curriculum Center, 130 West 55th Street, New York 19, N.Y.
   D. Board of Education of the City of New York, Publications Division, Room 232, 110 Livingston Street, Brooklyn 1, N.Y.
   E. School District of Philadelphia, The Board of Public Education, Parkway at Twenty-first Street, Philadelphia 3, Penna.
   F. Denver Public Schools, Division of Instructional Services, Department of General Curriculum Services, 414 Fourteenth Street, Denver 2, Colorado.
      Ask for *Price List of Instructional Publications.*
   G. El Paso Public Schools, Box 1710, El Paso, Texas.
      Ask for *Price List of Courses of Study and General Publications.*

9. *Textbooks in Print,* published annually by R. R. Bowker Company, 62 West 45th St., New York, N.Y.
   An author and title index to elementary and junior and senior high school books classified by subject. Includes supplementary readers and professional texts. Indispensable for curriculum personnel.
10. Sources of free and inexpensive materials.
    A. Educators Progress Service, Randolph, Wisconsin.
       Write for list of publications. Included are guides to free materials, films, filmstrips. Rather expensive but excellent.
    B. Field Enterprises, Merchandise Mart, Chicago, Ill.
       Guide to free and inexpensive materials distributed by the publishers of World Book Encyclopedia.
    C. Division of Surveys and Field Services, George Peabody College for Teachers, Nashville 5, Tenn.
       Free and Inexpensive Learning Materials.

appendix two

Curriculum Resource Materials—Language Arts

1. *Research Helps in Teaching the Language Arts,* N.E.A. Publications.
2. *Grammar, A Tool for Better Composition,* Curriculum Bulletin No. 202, March 10, 1960, School of Education, University of Oregon, Eugene, Oregon.
3. *Grammar in the Grades?,* by Robert C. Pooley. Reprint from *N.E.A. Journal,* September, 1958, p. 422.
4. *Teaching English Grammar,* book by Robert C. Pooley, published by Appleton-Century-Crofts, Inc., New York, N.Y.
5. *Creative Writing,* by Paul McKee. *McKee Language Service Bulletin,* Houghton Mifflin Co., New York, N.Y.
6. Publications of the U.S. Office of Education.
   A. *Language Arts in the Junior High School: A Bibliography,* by Arno Jewett, Circular No. 429, Revised, March, 1958.
   B. *Teaching Guides and Courses of Study in High School Language Arts: An Annotated Bibliography,* by Arno Jewett. Circular No. 412, Revised April, 1958.
   C. *A Check List of Practices for Teaching High School English,* by Arno Jewett. Circular No. 405, Revised, May, 1958.
7. *References on the Teaching of English in Elementary and Secondary Schools,* Research Division, N.E.A. RL 60-16, March, 1960.
8. National Council of Teachers of English, 704 South Sixth Street, Champaign, Illinois. Write for Publications List.
   A. *The Basic Issues in the Teaching of English.*
9. State English Committee, Department of Public Instruction, Box 911, Harrisburg, Penna. Write for all committee reports and recommendations.
   A. *Suggested Program in Written Composition, Grades 10-12.*
   B. *English Practices in the Typical Pennsylvania High School.*
   C. *Employers' Reactions to English Competence in High School Graduates.*
   D. *English Instruction Opinion Poll of High School Graduates.*
   E. *The Speech Role in the English Curriculum,* by the Speaking Division, State English Committee.
10. *Teaching Trends—1960: Let's Teach All the Language Arts,* by Marion Monroe, Scott, Foresman & Company, Chicago.
11. *What Makes a Good English Program?,* by Nellie John, Paulene M. Yates, Edward N. DeLaney, and John J. DeBoer, Harper & Row, Services to Teachers, New York, N.Y.
12. *Language Service Bulletins,* by Paul McKee, Houghton Mifflin Company, New York.

A. *Developing the Pupil's Vocabulary.*
B. *Letter Writing.*
C. *Creative Writing.*
D. *Reports.*

Children's Literature

1. *High Interest, Low Vocabulary Booklist,* by Donald Durrell and Helen Sullivan, Educational Clinic, Boston University School of Education, 332 Bay State Road, Boston 15, Mass.
2. The Children's Book Caravan, 810 Ingleside Place, Evanston, Ill.
   An excellent list of current children's books prepared by Ruth Tooze.
3. Publications of the Department of School Services and Publications, Wesleyan University, Middletown, Conn.:
   A. *Why Have a Planned Literature Program?,* by Leland Jacobs, Curr. Letter No. 1.
   B. *What Is a Balanced Literature Program?,* by Leland Jacobs, Curr. Letter No. 2.
   C. *Enjoying Literature Together,* by LaVerne Strong, Curr. Letter No. 3,
   D. *How Well Do Elementary Schools Feel They Are Teaching Children's Literature?,* by Eleanor M. Johnson, Curr. Letter No. 4.
   E. *What Reading Abilities Are Needed to Appreciate Literature?,* by William S. Gray, Curr. Letter No. 5.
   F. *What Is a Planned Literature Reading Program?,* by Eleanor M. Johnson, Curr. Letter No. 6.
   G. *Personal Values in Literature,* by David H. Russell, Curr. Letter No. 7.
   H. *When Poetry Pleases,* by Leland Jacobs, Curr. Letter No. 8.
   I. *Children Need Literature,* by LaVerne Strong, Curr. Letter No. 9.
   J. *Let's Consider Independent Reading,* by Leland Jacobs, Curr. Letter No. 11.
   K. *Literature Comes Alive Through Creative Dramatics,* by Carrie Rasmussen, Curr. Letter No. 13.
   L. *Guided Literature Experience Stimulates Child Growth,* by LaVerne Strong, Curr. Letter No. 16.
   M. *Give Children Literature,* by Leland Jacobs, Curr. Letter No. 20.
   N. *Literature Stages a Comeback,* by Leland Jacobs, Curr. Letter No. 25.
4. *A Literature Reading Program for the Elementary School,* Bulletin No. 20, *Education Today,* Notebook Bulletin, Charles E. Merrill Books, Inc., 400 S. Front Street, Columbus 15, Ohio.
5. *Aids for Knowing Books for Children and Youth,* Circular 450, Revised, 1960, Office of Education, U.S. Department of Health, Education, and Welfare, Washington 25, D.C.
6. *Best Books for Children,* R. R. Bowker Co., 62 West 45th St., New York. Definitive list of 3,300 approved titles arranged by school grade and subject.
7. The Children's Book Council, 175 Fifth Avenue, New York, N.Y.:
   A. *The World of Children's Books.*
   B. *Aids to Choosing Books for Your Children.* (A brief book list used by librarians, teachers, and P.T.A. groups.)
8. The American Library Association, 50 East Huron Street, Chicago, Ill.:

A. *Basic Book Collection for Elementary Grades,* by Miriam Braley Snow, Chairman, 1951.
B. *The Booklist. A Guide to Current Books* (published semi-monthly, except monthly in August).
C. *Inexpensive Books for Boys and Girls.*

9. Association for Childhood Education International, 1200 Fifteenth St., N.W., Washington 5, D.C., 1953:
   A. *Bibliography of Books for Children* (published annually).
   B. *Today's World in Books for Boys and Girls* (revised annually).
10. American Council for Education, Washington, D.C.
    A. *Literature For Human Understanding.*
    B. *Reading Ladders For Human Relations.*
11. *Children's Catalog,* by Estelle Fidell and Dorothy Cook, The H. W. Wilson Co., 950 University Avenue, New York, N.Y.
12. *Library Journal,* starred books annually, Library Journal, 62 West 46th St., New York, N.Y.
13. *New York Times* and *Herald Tribune* Book Reviews. (Biannual) Spring and fall lists.
14. *Language Arts Leaflets,* by Mildred A. Dawson, Nos. 2, 10, 11, 13, 18. World Book Co., Yonkers-on-Hudson, New York, 1952.
15. *Exploring Literature with Children in the Elementary Grades,* by Jean Betzner, *Suggestions for Teaching,* No. 7, Teachers College, Bureau of Publications, Columbia University, New York, N.Y., 1943, pp. 65-74.
16. *Improving Reading in All Curriculum Areas,* Supplementary, "The Goals of the Literature Period and the Grade Sequence of Desirable Experiences," by Dora V. Smith, in *W. S. Gray Educational Monographs,* No. 76, University of Chicago Press, Nov. 1952.

Choral Speaking and Reading

1. *Children Enjoy Choral Reading,* by Carrie Rasmussen, Curr. Letter No. 14, Dept. of School Services and Publications, Wesleyan University, Middletown, Conn.
2. *Effective Choral Speaking and Reading,* by Philena Cox and Rosalind Hughes, Ginn and Co. Contributions in Reading, No. 9, Ginn and Co., Boston, Mass.

Handwriting

1. *Handwriting Today, a Guide for the Classroom Teacher,* New England School Development Council, Spaulding House, 20 Oxford Street, Cambridge 38, Mass.
2. Publications of the Zaner-Bloser Co., Columbus 8, Ohio.
   A. *Handwriting Measuring Scales for Each Grade.*
   B. *Handwriting Faults and How to Correct Them.*
   C. *Handwriting Is Up-to-Date,* by Frank N. Freeman.
3. The Peterson System of Directed Handwriting, Greensburg, Penna. Write for sample materials and information.
4. *What Research Says About Writing Tools for Children,* by Virgil E. Herrick, Reprint from *N.E.A. Journal,* February, 1961, p. 49.
5. N.E.A. Write for *Publications List.* Check Subject Index.

Reading

1. N.E.A. Write for *Publications List.* Check Subject Index. Also, from Research Division: References on *Reading Instruction.*
   A. *Individualized Reading,* by Dorothy White, Elementary Instructional Service, N.E.A.
2. Publications of the U.S. Office of Education:
   A. *Improving Reading in the Junior High School,* by Arno Jewett, Bulletin 1957, No. 10.
   B. *How Children Learn to Read,* by Helen K. Mackintosh, Bulletin 1952, No. 7.
3. Available from Ginn and Co., Boston—*Contributions in Reading:*
   A. No. 1—*The Basic Reading Program in the Modern School,* by David Russell.
   B. No. 2—*The Literary Aspects of a Basic Reading Series,* by Doris Gates.
   C. No. 4—*Some Applications of Meaning Theory to Reading Methods,* by B. R. Buckingham.
   D. No. 7—*Eight Controversial Issues in the Teaching of Reading,* by David Russell and Gretchen Wulfing.
   E. No. 10—*Independent Reading Activities,* by Constance M. McCullough. (Includes *A Primary-Grade Weekly Reading Program.*)
   F. No. 11—*Helping the Slow Learner,* by Gretchen Wulfing.
   G. No. 13—*A Reading Program for the Seventh and Eighth Grades,* by David H. Russell.
   H. No. 14—*Helping the Superior Reader,* by Gretchen Wulfing.
   I. No. 24—*Aids for Retarded Readers,* by Mary T. Hayes.
4. Available from Department of School Services and Publications, Wesleyan University, Middletown, Conn.:
   A. *Individualized Reading,* by Eleanor M. Johnson, Curr. Letter No. 35.
   B. *Reading in Depth: Interpretation,* by Eleanor M. Johnson, Curr. Letter No. 43.
   C. *News Reading and the Curriculum,* by Eleanor M. Johnson, Curr. Letter No. 44.
   D. *Ways to Enrich Vocabulary,* by Eleanor M. Johnson.
5. Available from Houghton Mifflin Company, New York:
   A. *Teaching Children to Read in the Primary Grades,* by Paul McKee.
   B. *Teaching Children to Read in the Intermediate Grades,* by Paul McKee.
6. *My Weekly Reader Aids for Teachers,* American Education Publications, 1250 Fairwood Ave., Columbus 16, Ohio.
   A. *How to Get Best Results in Reading.*
   B. *Eleven Steps to Reading Success.*
7. *The Reading Teacher,* published by the International Reading Association, five times a year. Timely reports of research in reading. Russell G. Stauffer, Editor, 5835 Kimbark Avenue, Chicago 37, Illinois.
8. *Learning to Read.* Dated 1945, but is exceptionally fine as a demonstration of integration of all areas of school activities with the language arts program. Board of Education, Madison, Wisconsin.
9. *First Steps in Word Recognition,* a guidebook for teaching initial steps in

word-attack skills, assembled by a committee of teachers of Queen Anne County, Centerville, Maryland, 1954-55.

10. *Techniques for Teaching Phonics and Other Word Skills.* A publication of "Bucks County Contributions to the Improvement of Instruction." Compiled by Morton Botel, Assistant Superintendent, Bucks County Schools, Penna.
11. Scott, Foresman & Company, Chicago, Ill.:
    1. *An Administrator's Handbook on Reading.*
    2. *Developing Children's Word-Perception Power, Grades One-Three.*
12. *Reading Troubleshooter's Checklist* (includes pupil analysis chart), Webster Publishing Company, St. Louis 26, Mo.
13. *Reading for Today's Children,* 34th Yearbook, Dept. of Elementary School Principals, N.E.A.
14. *Reading Aids Through the Grades,* Bureau of Publications, Teachers College, Columbia University, New York, N.Y.
15. "Improving the Reading of Academically Untalented Students," by Edwin Mingoia. *The English Journal,* Vol. XLIX, No. 1, Jan. 1960.
16. "Comparative Reading Helps," by James H. McGoldrick, *The English Journal,* Vol. I, Jan. 1961.
17. "A State Superintendent Comments on Some Problems in a State Reading Program," by Charles H. Boehm, *The Reading Teacher,* May 1961.
18. "Looking Ahead in Reading," by William S. Gray, *The Education Digest,* Vol. XXVI, No. 6, Feb. 1961, pp. 26-29.
19. "What Research Says About Phonics Instruction," by Nila B. Smith. *Journal of Educational Research,* Vol. 51, Sept. 1957.
20. "Do We Teach Reading in the Core Curriculum?" *The N.A.S.S.P. Bulletin,* Vol. 43, No. 244, pp. 98-102, Feb. 1959.
21. "Supplementary Books For the Primary Level," by Cunvor Thuresson, *Delaware School Journal,* Jan. 1957. Complete list available from The Reading Clinic, University of Delaware.
22. *Improving Reading in the Junior High School,* edited by Arno Jewett. Articles by reading authorities, Bulletin, Supt. of Documents, U.S. Government Printing Office, Washington 25, D.C.
23. "Readability: An Appraisal of Research and Application," by Jeanne S. Chall, *Bureau of Educational Research Monographs,* No. 54, Ohio State University, 1958.

Spelling

1. N.E.A. publications:
    A. "Spelling," May, 1959 issue of *National Elementary Principal.*
    B. *What Research Says to the Teacher—Teaching Spelling,* by Ernest Horn.
    C. *References on Spelling,* RL 60-35, Research Division.
2. Available from Charles E. Merrill Books, Education Center, Columbus 16, Ohio:
    A. *Pack of Teacher's Memos on Spelling.*
    B. "Research Points the Way to Better Spelling," *Education Today,* Notebook Bulletin No. 16.
3. *What About Spelling?* by Emmett A. Betts, Reprint from *Education,* January, 1956.

4. Simpler Spelling Association, Lake Placid Club, New York. Write for publications.
5. "No Two Are Alike," by Thorsten Carlson, *Language Arts Notes,* No. 9, Harcourt, Brace & World, Inc., New York.
6. *A New, Unified Approach to Spelling,* by Thomas J. Maloney, Curr. Letter No. 24, Dept. of School Services and Publications, Wesleyan University, Middletown, Conn.
7. Scott, Foresman *Service Bulletin,* Spring 1961, *The Supervisor's Notebook.* Vol. 23, No. 1. "A Spelling Program for First Graders." Scott, Foresman & Co., Chicago, Ill.

appendix three

Curriculum Resource Materials–Science

1. National Science Teachers Association, N.E.A. Write for publications list in all subject areas, such as physics, chemistry, biology.
   A. *Elementary School Science Bulletin.* Request back issues and ask to have your name placed on mailing list.
   B. *Planning for Excellence in High School Science.*
   C. *It's Time for Better Elementary School Science.*
2. U.S. Office of Education:
   A. *Analysis of Research in the Teaching of Science,* by Ellsworth Obourn and Charles Koelsche, OE-29000, Bulletin 1960, No. 2.
   B. *Teaching Elementary Science,* by Glenn Blough and Paul Blackwood, Bulletin 1948, No. 4.
   C. *Science Fairs and School Public Relations,* by Richard Harbeck, Reprint from *School Life,* February, 1960. OE-29009.
   D. *Elementary Science Series,* by Glenn Blough, Reprint from *School Life.*
   E. *Aids for Teaching Science, Selected Business-Industry Publications,* by Ellsworth Obourn and Charles Koelsche, OE-29004.
3. Department of School Services and Publications, Wesleyan University, Middletown, Conn.
   A. *An Up-to-Date Elementary Science Program,* by Glenn Blough, Curr. Letter No. 19.
   B. *Using Books in an Active Elementary Science Program,* Glenn Blough, Curr. Letter No. 12.
4. *The Place of Science and Mathematics in the Comprehensive Secondary School Program,* Reprint from the Sept. 1958 issue of *The Bulletin of the Nat'l Assn. of Secondary School Principals,* N.E.A.
5. *Growing Up With Science Books,* by Julius Schwartz and Herman Schneider, *Library Journal,* 62 West 45th Street, New York 36, N.Y.
6. *The AAAS Science Book List,* American Association for the Advancement of Science, AAAS Publications, 1515 Massachusetts Avenue, N.W., Washington 5, D.C.
7. *Guides to the Out-of-Doors* and other nature publications, National Audubon Society, 1130 Fifth Avenue, New York 28, N.Y.
8. *The Book Corner Catalogue,* The American Museum–Hayden Planetarium, 81st St. and Central Park West, New York, 24, N.Y.
9. *Science–Suggestions for Teaching,* Philadelphia Suburban School Study Council, Group C. Order from the Interstate Printers and Publishers, 19-27 N. Jackson St., Danville, Ill.

10. *Organizing the Science Program in the Elementary Schools,* by Levin Hanigan. Available from Ginn and Co., Boston, Mass.
11. *Science in Action and Elementary Science Helps.* Series of science resources available from Dept. of Public Instruction, Box 911, Harrisburg, Penna.
12. *Physics in Your High School, A Handbook for the Improvement of Physics Courses,* prepared by the American Institute of Physics. Published by McGraw-Hill Book Co., Inc., New York, N.Y.
13. *Matter, Energy and Change, Explorations in Chemistry for Elementary School Children,* published by Holt, Rinehart, & Winston, Inc., New York, N.Y.
14. *Teaching Guide for the Earth and Space Science Course,* Dept. of Public Instruction, Box 911, Harrisburg, Penna.
15. *Exploring Space—Project Mercury,* U.S. National Aeronautics and Space Administration, Washington 25, D.C.
16. *Space, Challenge and Promise,* Aerospace Industries Assn., 610 Shoreham Building, Washington, D.C.
17. National Aviation Education Council. Ask to be placed on the mailing list. The Council address: 1025 Connecticut Avenue, N.W., Washington 6, D.C.
    Skylights, monthly bulletin and aviation units for primary grades; aviation units for intermediate grades.
18. *Teacher's Resource Reference,* prepared by American Petroleum Institute, Delaware Oil Men's Association, 305 South State Street, Dover, Delaware.
19. *Guide to Education Aids,* available from *The Chemical Industry, 1960,* Manufacturing Chemists' Association, Inc., 1825 Connecticut Ave., N.W., Washington 9, D.C.
20. *The Cement Story and the Teacher's Manual,* Cement Editor, American Education Publications, 1250 Fairwood Avenue, Columbus 16, Ohio.
21. *Indian Point Atomic Energy Plant,* Consolidated Edison Co., 4 Irving Place, New York 3, N.Y.
22. Commonwealth Edison Co., 72 West Adams St., Chicago 90, Ill.:
    A. *Dresden Nuclear Power Station.*
    B. *Atoms to Kilowatts.*
23. *101 Atomic Terms and What They Mean,* Esso Research and Engineering Co., P.O. Box 45, Linden, N.J.
24. *The Atomic Revolution,* General Dynamics Corp., 445 Fifth Avenue, New York 22, N.Y.
25. *Your New Atomic Power Plant Is Under Construction,* Northern States Power Co., Minneapolis, Minn.
26. *The Atom In Our Hands,* Union Carbide Corp., 30 E. 42nd Street, New York 17, N.Y.
27. *Catalog,* Science Materials Center, A Division of the Library of Science, 202 E. 23rd Street, New York 3, N.Y.
28. *The National Elementary Principal,* Department of Elementary School Principals, N.E.A.
29. *Guides for Improving Science Programs, K-12,* Science Committee Report for the Group "A" Schools, Philadelphia Suburban School Study Council, Educational Service Bureau, University of Pennsylvania, Philadelphia 4, Penna.

30. *Looking Ahead in Science,* California State Department of Education, Sacramento, California, 1960.
31. *NASA Facts,* A series of charts about current space projects, N.A.S.A., Washington 25, D.C.

Current Science Curriculum Projects

1. Biological Sciences Curriculum Study, Attn. Dr. Arnold Grobman, University of Colorado, Boulder, Colorado. Name placed on mailing list at no charge.
2. Chemical Bond Approach Project, Attn. Dr. Lawrence Strong, Director, Earlham College, Richmond, Indiana.
3. Chemical Education Materials Study, Attn. Dr. J. Arthur Campbell, Study Director, Harvey Mudd College, Claremont, California.
4. Physical Sciences Study Committee, Educational Services, Inc., 164 Main Street, Watertown, Mass.
5. Dr. Robert Stevenson, Executive Secretary, American Geological Institute, American Chemical Society Building, Washington 6, D.C. Write for sourcebook in the geological sciences.
6. Science Manpower Project, Bureau of Publications, Teachers College, Columbia University, 525 W. 120th Street, New York 27, N.Y.

   Eleven monographs available on such topics as "Modern High School Physics," "Problem-Solving Methods in Science Teaching," "Modern Junior High School Science," "Modern Elementary School Science."
7. University of California Elementary School Science Program, Attn. Dr. Robert Karplus, Department of Physics, University of California, Berkeley, Calif.
8. University of Illinois Elementary School Science Project, 805 Pennsylvania Avenue, Urbana, Ill. Attn. Dr. J. Myron Atkin, Director.

appendix four

Format for Course of Study Outline

SUBJECT AREA:

COURSE OBJECTIVES

LEVEL:

Subject-matter units or topics with specific objectives	Concepts, generalizations, attitudes, and skills to be developed	Suggested teaching techniques and pupil experiences	Teacher-pupil resources and instructional materials

appendix five

How Good Is Your Supervisory Program?

An Instrument for Self-Analysis

by

Sam H. Moorer

Florida State Department of Education

A good supervisor is constantly seeking to narrow the gap between *what is* and *what might be* in the county supervisory program. This means that the supervisor often takes stock of *what is* and looks at the present program in the light of *what might be*. It is important to know where the program stands along the line of development from an *inferior program* to a *superior program*.

Progress along this line is possible only when *thinking* has *run ahead* of *realization*. You dream of a better program of supervision, and as time goes on you discover the means of bringing it about and become more proficient in the ways of working which will bring the program closer to realization of your dreams.

In case your dreams are to some extent vague and nebulous, this instrument is designed to give substance to them with respect to *what might be*. Study of the best writers and most successful practitioners in the field of supervision reveals certain principles and purposes upon which nearly all agree. These agreed-upon principles and purposes provide the clue to *what might be*. Here they are:

Reliance Upon Democratic Leadership	Development of Educational Leadership	Total Program of Education	Materials and Resources

Long-Range Plans	Research and Experimentation

Purposes of Education	Human Growth and Learning	Coordination of Effort	Cooperation with Other Agencies

Every supervisory program makes use of these principles to some extent. It is important to know how far the county program has advanced along the line of progress from an *inferior program* to a *superior program*. To help you find out, this instrument presents a sharp *contrast* between some of the more important elements of an *inferior program* and a *superior program* of county supervision. You can approximate the status of the present program on a *scale*. In most instances it is likely that the program of supervision in your county will fall somewhere *between* the two extreme points on this scale. That is the problem for *you* to decide.

Here is the scale:

1	2	3	4	5
Inferior Program	Moving Toward	Average Program	Moving Toward	Superior Program

The marking of the scale is simple. If you circle the number four (4) for *Materials and Resources*, for example, this means that in your best judgment the supervisory program in your county is above average and moving toward a superior program.

Each of the principles is placed on a separate page with the scale for marking at the bottom of the page.

Place Your Faith in the Step-by-Step Progress. Nobody expects you to achieve the finest possible supervisory program by next year. But the children of Florida and their parents have a right to expect *some* improvement. This instrument is designed to challenge the alert supervisor. If you can get the folks in the schools and communities in which you work pulling together; and if a program for the improvement of instruction can be worked out in terms of commonly accepted, long-range goals; and if it can be decided who is going to do what and how; things are bound to happen!

The Aims of Supervision

The ultimate purpose of a county program of supervision of instruction is to make the maximum contribution to the realization of the purposes of education in a democracy. The immediate purpose is to improve the conditions which surround the growth and learning of teachers and pupils.

Reliance Upon Democratic Leadership. The supervisory program should rely upon democratic leadership for the achievement of its purposes.

Inferior Program	*Superior Program*
1. The supervisor assumes that he or she knows what is best for teachers to do and proceeds to tell them what they should do and how they should do it.	1. The supervisor realizes that working together in pursuit of improvement is at the same time a challenging adventure and the best procedure.
2. Teachers who do not respond readily to new ideas are scolded, criticized, reported to the superintendent as recalcitrant and otherwise rejected.	2. Slowness to respond to new ideas which break sharply with old traditions is recognized as a trait common to most people. The supervisor realizes that only through providing stimulating learning experience for teachers can progress be made.
3. Relationships with teachers are impersonal and authoritative. No attempt is made to develop good human relationships. Communication with teachers is usually in the form of orders, directives, and regulations issued from the central office.	3. Relationships with teachers are cordial. There is high quality of human relationships between supervisors and teachers. Communication with teachers is on a personal basis. The supervisor spends much of the time working with teachers individually and in groups.
4. The supervisor relies mainly upon criticisms of shortcomings of teachers to secure results.	4. The supervisor seeks out the strong points of teachers and builds upon these.
5. The supervisor rejects contributions made by teachers which do not measure up to the highest professional standards.	5. The supervisor realizes that every teacher is capable of making some unique contribution to the improvement of education. Each contribution, no matter how small or insignificant, is graciously sought and accepted as an evidence of growth.
6. The supervisor assumes that the ways of democracy can be learned through imposition and coercion and that democratic practices can be *required.*	6. The supervisor knows that growth in understanding and practice of democratic ideals cannot flourish in an authoritarian atmosphere.

1	2	3	4	5
Inferior Program	Moving Toward	Average Program	Moving Toward	Superior Program

Development of Educational Leadership. The supervisory program should develop educational leadership in schools and communities.

Inferior Program	*Superior Program*
1. It is assumed that teachers, pupils, and parents are not capable of contributing to the development of plans for the improvement of education.	1. The supervisor knows that a sound program of democratic education cannot be developed without participation of all groups concerned.
2. The supervisor does not give teachers, pupils, and parents an opportunity to grow by living through experiences in taking responsibility for doing those things in which their help could make a definite contribution to improvement.	2. The program provides experiences for teachers in accepting responsibilities and in making decisions in matters which are of concern to them because it is recognized that understanding and support will be gained and growth in doing these things better in the future can be expected to occur.
3. Leadership on the part of pupils, teachers, and parents in educational matters is looked upon as a threat to the authority of the supervisory staff.	3. Growing leadership on the part of pupils, teachers, and parents is recognized as the only way to achieve genuine and permanent progress.
4. The supervisor has a few trusted cronies among the teaching staff who can be depended upon to assist in carrying out plans which the supervisor has made.	4. The supervisor seeks diligently to discover and develop leadership on the part of the largest number of individuals in the school and community. The supervisor knows that the more people who feel a personal responsibility for the program, the more successful it is likely to be.

1	2	3	4	5
Inferior Program	Moving Toward	Average Program	Moving Toward	Superior Program

Total Program of Education. The supervisory program should be concerned with developing a total program of education at all grade levels and in all areas of human experience.

Inferior Program

1. The supervisory staff is highly specialized. Instruction services are sharply divided into separate units which operate independently. Special subject-matter supervision is stressed, to the exclusion of general supervision.
2. Curriculum programs for elementary grades are developed with no regard to programs for secondary grades, and vice versa. Programs for certain subjects are developed with no relationship to programs for other subjects. The program is fragmentary and highly compartmentalized. Some subjects or grade levels are emphasized at the expense of others.
3. The supervisor in counties where there is only one general supervisor hesitates to work at a grade level where he or she has had no experience. Also, there is hesitation to work with teachers of subjects in which the supervisor has had no experience.
4. The program of supervision makes no provision for working toward improving the quality of living in the community. The school is assumed to be independent and apart from the daily life of the people. Lay citizens are not encouraged to share in school planning.

Superior Program

1. General supervision, with provision for expert consultative service in special subjects, is the prevailing pattern. There is provision for coordinating and integrating special supervisory services so that all phases of the program are directed toward commonly accepted goals.
2. Curriculum programs reflect a high degree of articulation and coordination between subject areas and grade levels. In building a unified program, all areas of human experience have been analyzed for their potential contributions to the growth of young people in desirable directions.
3. The supervisor does not claim to be a specialist in every subject and grade level, but *is* a specialist in working with teachers on such things as the requirements of successful teaching and the purposes of education, which are substantially the same at all levels.
4. The program of supervision reflects the understanding that the community educates as well as miseducates the young, and that one of the important clues to improvement of the quality of living and learning in the school lies in the improvement of living and learning in the community.

1	2	3	4	5
Inferior Program	Moving Toward	Average Program	Moving Toward	Superior Program

Materials and Resources. The supervisory program should make use of appropriate materials and resources available for operating its program.

Inferior Program	*Superior Program*
1. Concern for materials of instruction is limited to providing a textbook for each child in each subject.	1. Provision is made for securing a wide variety of both textbook and supplementary materials.
2. Concern for materials of instruction is limited to printed materials only.	2. Provision is made for an adequate supply of maps, charts, globes, films and filmstrips, recordings, and the like.
3. Available consultants from the state department of education and from the state universities and other state agencies are not utilized.	3. Available consultants and resource people from state agencies and institutions are frequently used. Plans are made in advance for securing the maximum contribution from these people.
4. Available resource people from local agencies and the community at large are neither known nor utilized.	4. An inventory of human resources in the community has been made. Teachers know who is available and use them frequently.
5. There are no professional materials for teachers available on a county-wide basis.	5. There is a county materials bureau with an adequate supply of appropriate materials for the use of teachers. These materials are readily available and widely used.
6. There is no medium for sharing ideas and experiences on a county-wide basis.	6. Provision is made for sharing ideas and experiences on a county-wide basis through newsletters, teachers' meetings, personal conferences, and the like.
7. Necessary but expensive materials and equipment are not available to smaller or rural schools.	7. Some types of materials and equipment which cannot be purchased for all schools are placed in the county materials bureau and made available on a rotating basis to all schools.
8. Teachers are not kept informed about free and inexpensive materials.	8. Teachers are kept informed about available free and inexpensive materials.
9. Little use is made of first-hand observation in the community.	9. Facilities and information relative to field trips are readily available.

1	2	3	4	5
Inferior Program	Moving Toward	Average Program	Moving Toward	Superior Program

Long-Range Plans. The supervisory program should provide for cooperative development of both immediate and long-range plans which are continuously adapted to the needs and conditions in the county.

Inferior Program

1. Activity proceeds according to the exigencies of the moment, or in response to immediate pressures. There are no cooperatively developed, comprehensive, long-range plans which serve to give direction to the program. The program is on its way, but no one knows where it is going.
2. Whatever plans exist are static and routine in nature. Plans are not subject to revision although conditions may have changed to such an extent that they are no longer valid.
3. All county plans are made by the administrative and/or supervisory staff and handed down to teachers. Teachers do not understand these plans or see the relationship of present activities to an over-all long-range program of improvement.
4. Activity proceeds for its own sake. Much "busy-work" goes on which is fleeting and fragmentary and in which there is no continuity. Passing fads and fancies are taken up with no appraisal of their real significance to the county program.
5. Whatever plans exist are so vague and indefinite or so out of tune with the experience and ability of the teachers, the social outlook of the community, and the financial status of the county school system that there could be little likelihood of their realization.

Superior Program

1. There are carefully developed, comprehensive long-range plans. Plans for immediate action are always made in terms of long-range goals. Specific next steps are set up for short periods of time, and achievement is evaluated in terms of accomplishment of these.
2. Plans are flexible and subject to adjustment in light of changing needs and conditions.
3. Teachers and parents know what the supervisory plans for the county are and understand and support them because they have had a part in making them.
4. There is a balance between activity and reflection upon activity. The criteria for determining the relevance of specific activities are found in long-range plans for improvement of instruction in the county.
5. Plans are concrete and specific. They are consistent with the capacities and thinking of the teaching personnel and the lay citizens. Plans for immediate action are those which are judged to have the best chance of succeeding.

1	2	3	4	5
Inferior Program	Moving Toward	Average Program	Moving Toward	Superior Program

Research and Experimentation. The supervisory program should base planning as far as possible upon realities of the situation which are discovered through the use of simple research techniques and careful experimentation.

Inferior Program	*Superior Program*
1. The necessity for securing factual information as a basis for planning is ignored. Planning is done largely on the basis of unsubstantiated opinion and subjective judgment, even in instances where accurate, objective information could be secured.	1. Factual information needed in planning is secured whenever possible. Readily available data as to such things as holding power of the schools, age-grade distribution of pupils, and census data about the county are always kept up to date and widely disseminated to teachers and lay citizens.
2. New programs are hurriedly devised or borrowed from somewhere else *in toto* and imposed on a wide scale without preliminary experimentation to determine suitability for local schools. There is no attempt made to develop means of appraising the success of new programs at frequent intervals.	2. New programs are always developed on a tentative basis and given a trial run on a small scale before being widely adopted. Teachers are encouraged and assisted in devising experimental programs and in sharing their findings. Whenever a new program is tried out, some method of determining the degree of success has been worked out to go along with it.
3. The findings of research on many of the common problems of teaching are largely unknown to the supervisory staff. There is no means of disseminating and interpreting to teachers what is already known.	3. The supervisory staff is informed as to the findings of educational research which are pertinent to problems being worked on in the county. These findings are made available to teachers in easily understood and usable form.
4. The supervisory staff is not acquainted with elementary theory and techniques of educational testing and with standard research and statistical procedures.	4. At least one member of the supervisory staff or someone in the county school system knows enough about testing and evaluation techniques and about standard research and statistical procedures to help teachers devise simple methods of appraising the outcomes of learning.

1	2	3	4	5
Inferior Program	Moving Toward	Average Program	Moving Toward	Superior Program

Purposes of Education. The supervisory program should contribute to the development of understandings relative to the purposes of education in light of the nature and needs of our society.

Inferior Program	*Superior Program*
1. The functions of education as one of the basic institutions of society for its own perpetuation and improvement are not clearly perceived. Information and skills are taught as ends in themselves without reference to what they have to contribute toward the growth of the individual and the improvement of society. The supervisor is chiefly concerned with how well the teachers cover certain bodies of subject matter.	1. There is county-wide study going on at all times relative to the purposes of education. Such study is on a voluntary basis and findings of competent authorities as to the purposes of education are widely disseminated among teachers and parents. Teachers are encouraged to select knowledge to be taught in terms of the needs and capacities of children and the needs of society.
2. There is no provision for systematic study of the needs and resources of the local community. Information as to the social and economic conditions of the county which have a direct bearing on what the school should do is largely unknown.	2. Study guides, state bulletins, and supervisory assistance are available for making studies of the community and developing an educational program which better serves its needs.
3. The supervisory staff is not equipped or disposed to assist teachers, pupils, and parents in reaching common agreement as to what the school should do and how to tell to what extent it has been done.	3. The program makes provision for continuous work toward widening the area of agreement among teachers, pupils, and parents as to the purposes of education. The aim is always a broadened vision of what education might be.
4. Parents are not consulted as to what they think the school should do for pupils. Where parents have limited conceptions as to the purposes of education, no attempt is made to broaden their thinking.	4. Parents are consulted to find out what they think the school should do. Through study and discussion groups, parents are helped to understand our society better and needs which must be met if its problems are to be solved.

1	2	3	4	5
Inferior Program	Moving Toward	Average Program	Moving Toward	Superior Program

Human Growth and Learning. The supervisory program should contribute to the development of understandings relative to the essential factors of human growth and development, particularly with reference to the nature of the learning process and its implications for teaching.

Inferior Program	*Superior Program*
1. The supervisory staff does not recognize that parents and teachers are frequently opposed to newer teaching techniques because they do not understand how children grow and how they learn.	1. The supervisory staff recognizes that one of the obstacles to wider acceptance and use of modern teaching practices is largely due to the lack of understanding on the part of parents and teachers of how growth and learning take place.
2. The supervisory staff does not recognize that supervision is a form of teaching and that activities which are designed to bring about changes in people are learning situations. Supervisory activities frequently violate the principles of good teaching, thus revealing an inadequate conception of the nature of learning by supervisors.	2. The supervisory staff recognizes that activities designed to improve instruction are frequently learning situations and, as such, must be consistent with the principles of good teaching. Educational experiences are planned which demonstrate the characteristics of a good learning experience.
3. Curriculum programs and materials developed in the county ignore the growth characteristics of children at various age levels.	3. Curriculum programs and materials developed for use in the county are constructed in terms of their consistency with the known facts of child growth and development and the nature of the learning process.
4. Professional materials relating to learning and growth are not available to teachers for study. There are no study groups working in this area at the county or individual school level. State bulletins which have sections devoted to growth and learning are not used.	4. Professional materials in the areas of child growth and development and learning are readily available. Teachers are encouraged to join voluntary study groups investigating child growth and implications for teaching. State bulletins and other professional materials for study are available and extensively used.
5. No member of the county supervisory staff or the individual school staffs is prepared or seeking to become qualified to initiate and lead groups in child study. Available consultants in this field are not utilized.	5. At least one person in the county is prepared to organize and conduct child study groups. Out-of-county consultants in this field who are available are utilized.

1	2	3	4	5
Inferior Program	Moving Toward	Average Program	Moving Toward	Superior Program

Coordination of Effort. The supervisory program should contribute to the coordination and integration of efforts of all agencies and institutions in the community which are interested in the improvement of education.

Inferior Program

1. There is no conscious effort made to coordinate and integrate the efforts and services of the various community agencies interested in the welfare and education of young people. There is frequent conflict in youth activities of these groups, and young people often find several organizations competing for their time and energy.
2. There are no clearly defined procedures and policies whereby the wishes and demands of various groups interested in certain learnings being provided in schools may receive consideration. The schools frequently find themselves at the mercy of pressure groups which do not represent the consensus of the community. There are no policies regarding the consideration of requests for the cooperation of the schools in enterprises sponsored by certain groups.
3. Community agencies are permitted to come into the schools and carry on educational activities which bear no relationship to, or duplicate, services already provided in the schools.

Superior Program

1. Through community planning, the efforts and services of such institutions and agencies as P.T.A., service clubs, Boy and Girl Scouts, churches, welfare agencies, health department, and the like, are coordinated and integrated so as to utilize effectively the contributions of all.
2. There are carefully worked out policies and procedures for considering the wishes and demands of groups interested in getting certain things taught in the schools, or in getting the schools to take part in enterprises sponsored by certain groups. The policies and procedures used by the schools make specific provision for discrimination between pressure groups and community consensus.
3. Learning activities carried on in the school by other agencies are not permitted unless they are carefully integrated into the school curriculum.

1	2	3	4	5
Inferior Program	Moving Toward	Average Program	Moving Toward	Superior Program

Cooperation with Other Agencies. The supervisory program should cooperate with local, state, national, and international agencies in the improvement of education.

Inferior Program	*Superior Program*
1. There is a low degree of cooperation with other agencies which are interested in the improvement of education. The supervisors seldom attend meetings of these groups and do not participate in the development of programs formulated by these groups. While willing to enjoy the benefits secured by these groups, no help is offered.	1. There is a high degree of cooperation with all agencies interested in improving education. Supervisors belong to and encourage teachers to join groups such as F.E.A., N.E.A., A.C.E., etc. Provision is made for supervisors and representatives of the teaching staff to attend meetings of these groups. Those who attend take an active part in furthering the work of these groups.
2. There is a low degree of cooperation with the state department of education. Supervisors attend state-wide and regional meetings only when required to do so. Invitations to participate in the development of state-wide plans and programs are ignored.	2. There is a high degree of cooperation with the state department of education. Provision is made for the supervisory staff and teacher representatives to attend state-wide and regional meetings called by the state superintendent. There is active participation in developing state-wide plans and programs of improving the state system of education.
3. Requests for information needed by research workers in the state department of education and in institutions of higher learning in the planning of improved programs are ignored.	3. Provision is made to secure prompt return of information requested by representatives of reputable agencies and institutions seeking data to be used in improving education.
4. The supervisory staff makes no attempt to keep informed as to the aims and programs of other agencies interested in improving education. No attempt is made to explain and interpret the work of these groups to teachers and lay citizens.	4. The supervisory staff is informed as to the work of other agencies interested in education. Information is shared with teachers and lay citizens.

1	2	3	4	5
Inferior Program	Moving Toward	Average Program	Moving Toward	Superior Program

Index

A

B

C

D

T